# AN INTRODUCTION TO STRATEGIC STUDIES

# An Introduction to Strategic Studies

## Military Technology and International Relations

Barry Buzan

*Senior Lecturer*
*Department of International Studies*
*University of Warwick*

St. Martin's Press    New York

in association with the
INTERNATIONAL INSTITUTE FOR STRATEGIC STUDIES

© International Institute for Strategic Studies, 1987

All rights reserved. For information, write:
Scholarly & Reference Division,
St. Martin's Press, Inc.,
175 Fifth Avenue, New York, NY 10010

First published in the United States of America in 1987

Printed in Great Britain

ISBN 0–312–01177–6
ISBN 0–312–01178–4 (pbk.)

Library of Congress Cataloging-in-Publication Data
Buzan, Barry.
An introduction to strategic studies.
Bibliography: p.
Includes index.
1. Military policy.    2. International relations.
I. Title.    II. Title: Strategic studies.
UA11.B84    1987      355'.0335      87–13116
ISBN 0–312–01177–6
ISBN 0–312–01178–4 (pbk.)

To Deborah,
who wisely doesn't let the grass grow under her feet, and
whose partnership happily prevents me from letting it grow
too much under mine

# Contents

# List of Tables

# List of Abbreviations

| | |
|---|---|
| ABM | anti-ballistic missile |
| AD | assured destruction |
| ASAT | anti-satellite |
| ASW | anti-submarine warfare/weapons |
| BMD | ballistic missile defence |
| CBM | confidence-building measures |
| CBW | chemical and biological warfare/weapons |
| CTB | comprehensive test ban |
| C3I | command, control, communications and intelligence |
| ECM | electronic countermeasures |
| ED | extended deterrence |
| GCD | general and complete disarmament |
| GLCM | ground-launched cruise missile |
| GNP | gross national product |
| IAEA | International Atomic Energy Agency |
| ICBM | intercontinental ballistic missile |
| IISS | International Institute for Strategic Studies |
| INF | intermediate-range nuclear forces |
| LNO | limited nuclear options |
| LNW | limited nuclear war |
| LoW | launch-on-warning |
| LRTNW | long-range theatre nuclear weapons |
| MAD | mutually assured destruction |
| MIRV | multiple, independently manoeuvrable, re-entry vehicle |
| MIT | Massachusetts Institute of Technology |
| NATO | North Atlantic Treaty Organization |
| NPT | Non-proliferation Treaty |
| NTM | national technical means |
| PGM | precision-guided munitions |
| PNE | peaceful nuclear explosion |
| Pu239 | plutonium 239 |
| R&D | research and development |
| RUSI | Royal United Services Institute |
| SALT | Strategic Arms Limitation Talks |
| SD | strategic defence |
| SDI | Strategic Defence Initiative |

| | |
|---|---|
| SDV | strategic delivery vehicle |
| SIPRI | Stockholm International Peace Research Institute |
| SLBM | submarine-launched ballistic missile |
| SSBN | ballistic missile-carrying nuclear submarine |
| START | Strategic Arms Reduction Talks |
| TNW | tactical or theatre nuclear weapons |
| U235 | uranium 235 |
| U238 | uranium 238 |

# Foreword

This book is addressed to everyone who wants to understand the contemporary strategic debate in some depth. Many of these people will be students taking first courses in Strategic Studies. Some will be students in the related subjects of International Relations and Peace and Conflict Research. Some, I hope, will be individuals whose interest is driven not so much by the need to pass an exam as by concern about the implications of the strategic debate for the future of humankind.

The book has a long history. I intended to write something like it in the late 1970s, but the work I began then led me instead to write the volume on the concept of security that was published in 1983. Robert O'Neill proposed this project to me in December 1982, and I am grateful to him for encouraging the direction of my writing. In many senses this book is an outgrowth of the earlier one, though it is much more specific in focus. The earlier book tried to explore a subject about which too little had been written. This one tries to make sense of a subject where some of the confusion arises because so much has been written. It will only have succeeded if it charts a clear path through the jungle of the literature as well as over the landscape of the subject.

The book posed two intellectual problems: how to cope with the enormous body of literature, and how to define Strategic Studies. Given the size of the literature, and the speed with which it grows, it was clear to me that I could not possibly read everything. In addition, there was the problem posed by the newly-emergent literatures on strategic defence and non-provocative defence. Both of these subjects occupied important sections in my intellectual scheme, and yet neither literature was fully-enough developed so that I could confidently characterise its major features. Most of what I eventually read is in the list of references. I adopted a strategy of diminishing returns, which is to say that I read in an area until I felt that I was no longer learning anything more of basic importance. This doubtless caused me to miss some worthwhile works, and perhaps some important insights. I apologise to their authors, and plead only that one has at some point to repay one's sponsors, and to unburden one's mind, by writing oneself. If some authors like

Colin Gray and Robert Jervis seem to have been given generous treatment, that is because they write copiously and well, and represent major schools of thought clearly.

The problem of how to define Strategic Studies turned out to be much more difficult than I anticipated. One cannot write a textbook without a clear idea of the boundaries of the subject, but the more I thought about it the more it became apparent that Strategic Studies does not have clear boundaries. Since I felt strongly that the purpose of an introduction should be to offer a coherent interpretation of the field, the option of simply presenting a menu of chapters reflecting the average contents of first courses in Strategic Studies did not appeal to me. My eventual solution is explained in Chapter 1. It will probably not convince everyone, but it does allow the book a greater thematic coherence than would otherwise be possible. I do not think that there is any formulation of the subject that would escape criticism. My hope is that the approach I have taken will put the subject into a clear and interesting perspective, and provide a basic referent that others can use to sharpen their own understanding of the field. One penalty of this approach is that the book is structured around a cumulative argument, and is therefore best read in sequence. The individual Parts and Chapters are not as self-contained as would ideally be the case for a textbook, and I have tried to compensate for this by cross-referencing.

I am grateful to the many people who have given me their time and mental energy to help this work along. The fact that they did so is a tribute to the collective realities of the academic enterprise despite its often egocentric appearance. Jonathan Alford, Pamela Divinsky, Mariangela Franchetti, Richard Little, Robert O'Neill, Gerald Segal, Robert Skidelsky, and Steve Smith laboured through the whole manuscript, and by so doing saved me from some errors and much obscurantism. Lawrence Freedman and Kenneth Waltz did the same on earlier parts, and a passing remark of Ken Booth's helped me to find a way around what at the time appeared to be an impasse. All of these people deserve a share of the credit for such merit as the book possesses, and I am happy to field the brickbats for whatever errors and infelicities of judgement remain. My wife Deborah cheered me up through the deepest of the difficulties, and came to my rescue when the collapse of my old word processor required a painful midstream switch of format. My thanks also to the University of Warwick, which allowed me two terms of study leave without which I could never have found the level of concentration necessary to pull together a first draft, and to the IISS. I am particularly grateful to the late Col. Jonathan Alford, the deputy director of the IISS, who dealt willingly with both the substantive and the administrative aspects of the project right up until his unexpected death. His contribution to this book is but one of the many ways in which he contributed to the development of Strategic Studies. The field will be the poorer for his untimely demise.

BARRY BUZAN

# 1 Introduction: Strategic Studies and International Relations

> If every prospective writer on international affairs in the last twenty years had taken a compulsory course in elementary strategy, reams of nonsense would have remained unwritten.
>
> (Carr, 1946 (1981), p. 111)

Since E. H. Carr made his remark a whole field of literature has grown up under the name 'Strategic Studies'. Paradoxically, this development has in some ways complicated rather than eased the problem raised by Carr. The literature of Strategic Studies is now so vast and so intricate that those wanting to understand it cannot easily find a place to start. Nor, having made a start somewhere, can they know with much assurance how what they know relates to the rest of the field.

The need for an introduction to Strategic Studies stems most obviously from the size of the strategic literature. More than three decades of writing have accumulated since the first competitive deployments of nuclear weapons caused Strategic Studies to emerge as a distinct field during the 1950s. In addition, pre-nuclear strategic thinking has a literature dating back 2500 years to the writings of Sun Tzu. During the last 30 years the expansion of strategic literature has been driven by fast-moving developments in technology, conflict and politics. These range from new weapons, like cruise missiles, to new wars, like that in the Gulf, to changes in political alignments, like the Sino-Soviet split. Such changes have to be understood not only in themselves, but also in terms of their impact on prevailing strategic theories and policies. One purpose of an introduction is therefore to provide readers with a sufficient sense of the shape and direction of Strategic Studies literature so that they can locate what they read within an over-all conception of the field.

An introduction is also needed because both the literature and the practitioners of Strategic Studies have become specialized. Most strategists have responded to the pressure of change, and to the

1

demand for policy analysis and prescription, by narrowing the focus of their attention within the field. Only by doing so can anyone actually follow important areas in sufficient depth to maintain a professional level of expertise. At the professional level, keeping up with a subject like Gulf politics, or strategic arms control negotiations, or missile technology, is a full-time job.

The imperative to specialize means that Strategic Studies has produced few generalists. Its literature mostly reflects an intense, short-term policy orientation that is closely tied to the agenda of government decision-making on defence and military issues. Such a literature dates quickly. Although it does have underlying continuities, these are often buried under the detail of an ever-shifting technological and political context. It suits experts, because it enables them to structure their own writing easily, and to select their own reading from a menu so rich that no one can now possibly get through it all. It is, however, a barrier to those seeking entry to the subject. It confronts them with an unassembled jigsaw puzzle of parts with little guide as to how they all fit together. A random sampling of parts can mislead more than it informs. The structure of strategic literature does not clearly reveal the essentials of the subject, and therefore does not serve the needs of the many non-experts who rightly feel that they want to understand what is going on. Even for experts, excessive surrender to the unavoidable specializing demands of the subject does not, in the long run, serve the goal of better understanding. A second purpose of this book is therefore to offer an interpretation of the field. Such an interpretation must explain the basic ideas of Strategic Studies and provide a framework that links these ideas into a coherent subject. Neither of these objectives can be achieved without a perspective that places the field within the wider context of International Relations.

## 1.1   STRATEGIC STUDIES AND INTERNATIONAL RELATIONS

The task of defining Strategic Studies is not straightforward. The field contains a diverse set of topics, and is embedded within the broader field of International Relations. Although Strategic Studies has a distinct focus of its own, there is no hard boundary that separates it from International Relations. The two fields blend into each other at many points.

The embedded character of Strategic Studies within International Relations is similar to that of a major organ within a living body. One can study the heart and circulatory system as a distinct subject, and there are advantages of specialization to be gained from doing so. But many other parts of the body impinge on the heart and circulatory system in important ways. The lungs feed gases into and out of the bloodstream, the liver and the kidneys act as filters for it, and the glands and the bone marrow feed a variety of substances into it. Just as one cannot understand the whole organism without understanding the heart and circulatory system, neither can one understand the purpose and function of the heart and circulatory system without seeing them in the context of the complete body. Strategic Studies is similarly a vital component of the larger whole of International Relations. It has elements that make it distinct, but it is connected in myriad ways that severely limit the extent to which the two can be disconnected without risking potentially fatal misunderstanding. International Relations without Strategic Studies would seriously misrepresent the major realities in play between states. Strategic Studies detached from International Relations would be in constant danger of seeing only the conflictual element in relations between states and taking it as the whole reality.

The distinctive identity of Strategic Studies stems from its focus on military strategy. Strategy can be broadly defined as 'the art or science of shaping means so as to promote ends in any field of conflict' (Bull, 1968, p. 593). For Strategic Studies, the means to be shaped are military ones, the field of conflict is the international system, and the ends are the political objectives of actors large enough to register as significant in the international context. Since states command the overwhelming bulk of military power, Strategic Studies is mostly about the use of force within and between states. Some substate entities like separatist or national liberation movements, or terrorist revolutionary groups, are substantial enough to register in this 'game' of nations, but the main actors are states. The pre-eminence of states is underlined by the fact that most of the substate entities deploying force do so in order either to capture an existing state, like the African National Congress, or to create a new one, like the Palestine Liberation Organization.

Strategy in this more specific sense has been defined as 'the art of distributing and applying military means to fulfil ends of policy' (Liddell Hart, 1968, p. 335), 'exploiting military force so as to attain given objects of policy' (Bull, 1968, p. 593), 'the relationship between military power and political purpose' (Gray, 1982b, p. 1), and 'the art of the dialectic of two opposing wills using force to resolve their dispute' (Beaufre, 1965, p. 22). Halle offers one of the few attempts to define the whole field of Strategic Studies: 'the branch of political studies concerned with the political implications of the war-making capacity available to nations' (Halle, 1984, p. 4).

From these definitions it is clear that the essence of strategy is that it is about 'force, or the threat of force' (Gray, 1982a, p. 3). Strategic Studies is usually understood amongst its practitioners to be about the use of force in political relations within and between states. Since 'use' means threat as well as actual deployment in battle, Strategic Studies is also very much about the instruments of force, and the way in which those instruments affect relations among the states that possess them. Indeed, as we shall see, the advent of nuclear weapons has greatly raised the relative importance of threats to use force, while at the same time increasing the restraints on the actual use of military power in combat. Because of this development, the study of strategy since 1945 has developed a strong emphasis on the instruments of force themselves, on the use of threats, and on the problem of how to prevent the use of nuclear weapons. The study of strategy in terms of warfighting aimed at decisive military victories has lost its centrality because of the overawing hazard of nuclear cataclysm, though it is still highly relevant to the extensive array of military relations that are not subject to nuclear paralysis.

At first glance, the idea of strategy and the use of force seems to provide a clear basis for distinguishing Strategic Studies from International Relations. International Relations covers a broad spectrum which includes political, economic, social, legal and cultural interactions as well as military ones. One can thus see Strategic Studies in the same light as International Law, simply as a sub-field specializing in one aspect of a larger whole. Unfortunately, this enticingly simple view does not stand up to a searching examination. The problem is that many crucial elements of strategy just cannot be disentangled from the political and economic parts of the international system. One might think, for example, that the subject of war belonged clearly to Strategic Studies. While it is true that states may threaten each other with war on the purely military grounds that each is a potential attacker of the other, the threat and use of force usually bespeak grounds for rivalry rooted in considerations of power, status, ideology and wealth. Most of the major theories of war are based on ideas about the political and economic structure of the international system (Buzan, 1984a, 1986; Gilpin, 1981; Waltz, 1959). It is therefore impossible to study the causes of and cures for war without ranging deeply into the broader subject matter of International Relations. Those in Peace and Conflict Research would also resist vigorously a definition that allocated war exclusively to strategists.

Other well-established subjects such as alliance and crisis management also straddle any attempt to draw a crude boundary between Strategic Studies and International Relations on the basis of strategy and the use of force. In one sense both subjects seem to be part of Strategic Studies. Alliances are a central mechanism in military relations, and crisis is often a critical stage in the process by which states move towards, or away from, the use of force. But both just as clearly belong in the domain of political relations between states, and therefore to International Relations. Alliances reflect common political interests, and crises are a form of political process that may reflect political interests as much as, or more than, military ones. The difficulty of deciding what falls into one field and what into the other is even more problematic at the level of day-to-day events and policies, where their entanglement is thickest. Who can say where the line between Strategic Studies and International Relations runs in relation to diverse events like the Iran–Iraq War, the history of American relations with Cuba, Atlantic relations, or the impact of French nuclear testing in the South Pacific?

The complex way in which Strategic Studies is embedded within International Relations makes it difficult to define the contents for the introduction to Strategic Studies that this book is supposed to provide. Any attempt to be comprehensive necessitates introducing not only Strategic Studies, but also a large part of International Relations, including the whole of its political side. To accomplish that task at a depth sufficient to give a full grasp of the ideas and the literature would produce a work of unpublishable length. The problem with any narrower agenda is that it poses difficult choices of selection, and risks constricting the subject unduly. The book takes the selective path on the grounds that only by doing so can it treat the essentials of the subject in adequate depth. It must therefore begin with an explanation of what it includes, what it leaves out, and why. To do that it must establish a general principle of inclusion and exclusion that distinguishes the core matter of Strategic Studies from the extensive contextual surround of International Relations. In order to identify such a principle, it is necessary to look at the basic features of the international system from which both subjects derive.

The subject matter of Strategic Studies arises from two fundamental variables affecting the international system: its political structure, and the nature of the prevailing technologies available to the political actors within it. The key feature of the political structure over the last several centuries is that the system is composed of independent political entities. These entities are mostly states. They all possess the capability to use force against each other to some degree, and their interests conflict with sufficient frequency and intensity that the threat of force is an unavoidable and constant feature of their existence. In formal terms, this political structure is an *anarchy*: the system has no overarching political controller – no world government – to restrain the use of force and to impose universal law and order. The global anarchy is fundamentally different from anarchy in a group of individuals whose relations are totally without government. In an international anarchic structure most people live under governments. The structure is anarchic only in the sense that political power and authority are vested in the parts of the system – the states – rather than in the whole. States therefore relate to each other according to the dictates of their own values and the limits of their own power. Relations in such a system take the form of a balance of power. Order in a balance of power depends on the extent of disagreement amongst the major powers, the willingness of the largest powers to underwrite it, and on the willingness of other states to agree on rules and norms.

The structure of anarchy sets the political context in which strategy becomes relevant to the affairs of states. Anarchy is a self-help system in which political entities are responsible for their own survival. Relations amongst independent actors always contain the possibility of conflict over political, economic, and social issues, and sometimes these conflicts will result in the use of force. Strategy is an almost unavoidable accompaniment of political life within the international anarchy. The structure of anarchy has proved highly durable, and so long as it continues to be so, strategy will continue to feature in the affairs and relations of states.

The second variable from which the subject matter of Strategic Studies arises is the nature of the prevailing technologies available to political actors. Anarchy creates the over-all need for strategy, and sets the conditions that determine the ends for which force is used. Technology is a major factor in determining the scope of military options, the character of military threats, and the consequences of resorting to the use of force. Technology, in other words, is a major variable affecting the instruments of force available to political actors. The nature of those instruments sets a basic condition of strategy, and one that is subject to continuous pressure of technological change.

The problem of distinguishing between Strategic Studies and International Relations becomes clearer when viewed in the light of these two basic variables. The structure of anarchy defines the basic political conditions of both fields. As a subject in its own right, however, political structure clearly stretches well beyond any reasonable definition of Strategic Studies. It is not the business of strategists to address the basic political organization of the international system. Neither is it their business to investigate the many fundamental issues of political economy that arise from the question of structure. The subject of political structure belongs to International Relations even though it sets one of the core conditions for strategic thinking (Waltz, 1979).

The variable of military technology, by contrast, clearly belongs to Strategic Studies. If strategists can claim any unique expertise, it is on matters relating to the instruments of force, and their significance for relations among states. This formulation makes Strategic Studies a sub-field of International Relations. Political structure is what links the two, and professional expertise about the effect of the instruments of force on political relations within the international system is what justifies the specialized sub-field. Any other approach would risk making International Relations subordinate to strategy, and so biasing the whole study of the international system towards relations of conflict and away from relations of harmony and indifference.

## 1.2 THE AGENDA OF STRATEGIC STUDIES AND THE ORGANIZATION OF THE BOOK

The objective of the book is to explain the basic concepts of Strategic Studies and to link them together into a coherent framework. Approaching the subject in terms of concepts not only facilitates the distinction between Strategic Studies and International Relations, but also highlights the most durable elements of the field. The concepts of a subject are its intellectual foundations. They set the boundaries of discussion, define the terms of argument, and reveal the depth of understanding that a field has achieved. Although the surface subject matter of Strategic Studies changes quickly as new technologies and new conflicts come and go, its concepts are relatively stable. Ideas like disarmament and arms racing are very longstanding, and even more recent additions to the strategic vocabulary such as deterrence and arms control have been central to strategic discourse for several decades. The day-to-day debates of strategy are often quite narrow and short term, as one would expect of a subject closely tied to developments in the realm of policy. As a consequence, they seldom raise the deeper questions of the subject, and seldom generate discussion of it as a whole. My hope is that the conceptual approach in this book will provide readers with the basic tools necessary for dealing with the turbulent whirl of facts and arguments that constitute the contemporary strategic debate.

If one accepts that the essence of Strategic Studies is expertise about the effects of the instruments of force on international relations, then it becomes possible to define an agenda for this book. One can distinguish those concepts most central to Strategic Studies in the nuclear age because they derive primarily from the variable of military technology. Those lying more within the realm of International Relations derive primarily from the variable of political structure. By this principle of differentiation, the main concepts of Strategic Studies are arms racing, nuclear proliferation, defence, deterrence, arms control, and disarmament. All are part of the common currency of Strategic Studies, and all are directly concerned with the instruments of force. These six concepts can be formed into a coherent set lying at the heart of Strategic Studies, and they will be the principal focus of this book. Discussion of them leads to many subsidiary ideas that play an important role in strategic debate. These include parity, extended deterrence, minimum deterrence, conventional deterrence, mutually assured destruction, and others, all of which will be developed in their appropriate context.

This selection leaves aside a wealth of concepts that are relevant to Strategic Studies including power, security, war, peace, alliance, terrorism and crisis. All of these have deep roots in political structure. Although they are relevant to Strategic Studies, they fall substantially outside the boundaries of its distinctive core. All of these boundary concepts will be mentioned, and some will play a major role in the discussion of other concepts. Deterrence, for example, cannot be discussed without reference to limited war and crisis instability, and arms control cannot be discussed without talking about crisis management. None of these concepts, however, will be examined at length in its own right. This restrictive approach to Strategic Studies requires that political structure be treated as the relatively constant background factor against which the theme of military technology plays. Since the raw fact of anarchy is in many ways a constant within the international system (Buzan, 1984b; Waltz, 1959, 1979), this approach to the subject does not represent a major distortion.

The method of the book will be to explore the technology-based concepts up to the points at which they lead either into the durable realities of anarchic structure in general, or into the more particular territory of the boundary concepts. This approach is designed to highlight the linkages between the two fields, and to stress the fact that neither can be fully understood without reference to the other. The presence of the boundary concepts, and their role in the discussion, stands as a useful reminder that serious distortions of understanding result if the practitioners of Strategic Studies and International Relations allow their pursuit of specialization to result in too much isolation from each other. Their proper relationship is interdependence based on a division of labour.

The book has four main parts. Since military technology plays such a central role in strategic thinking, Part I lays the necessary foundations with an extensive discussion of it. This discussion is built around two themes: the revolution in technology that has accompanied the industrial revolution; and the process by which the military and political impact of that revolution has spread, and is still spreading, around the planet. Nuclear proliferation and the arms trade receive particular attention as part of the process of that spread. In addition, the close relationship between civil and military technology is emphasized as a point with crucial implications for many other aspects of strategic thinking.

The argument is that the technological aspect of the global strategic environment is part way through a centuries-long process of transformation. The twin elements of that transformation are technological advance, and the diffusion of advanced technology. Before the process took off during the nineteenth century, the standard of military technology in most parts of the globe was similar, and the pace of change was slow. The industrial revolution accelerated the pace of technological innovation, and created marked disparities in the quality and quantity of military technology held by different countries. We are still living with these inequalities, which will only be removed either when the whole planet achieves a similar level of industrial sophistication, or when the structure of anarchy gives way to a more unified global political system. In the meantime, the two elements of advance and diffusion interact powerfully. The play between them, and the particular stage of development they have reached, are major factors affecting the core concepts of Strategic Studies. A full understanding of the roots, and the nature, of military technology is therefore a prerequisite for an appreciation of the field.

Under conditions of international anarchy each political actor faces a central security worry, not only about the quantity and quality of military technology in the hands of other actors, but also about the pace and direction of change in these variables. This concern leads directly to Part II, on the arms dynamic, and Part III on deterrence, and carries the discussion from the factual and descriptive realm into the conceptual and analytical one. The discussion of the arms dynamic is placed first, partly because arms racing, which is central to it, has a longer history than deterrence as a major term in strategic debate, but mostly because the important question of how the two relate is easier to approach through the arms dynamic. The arms dynamic is perhaps the major phenomenon arising in the international system as a direct consequence of the instruments of force. The main attempts to explain it are examined at length. The phenomenon of arms racing is incompletely understood, the use of the term is undisciplined and often polemical, and the literature is disjointed and incomplete. I therefore undertake a substantial revision of the concept aimed at setting it more clearly into the context of an overarching arms dynamic, and filling in some of the gaps in the literature. Only by doing so can the necessary foundations for the discussion in Parts III and IV be constructed.

Part III takes up the linked ideas of defence and deterrence. Deterrence provides the most well-developed body of theory that distinguishes Strategic Studies from International Relations. Like arms racing, defence and deterrence are rooted in the variable of military technology. The discussion opens with a clarification of the relationship between defence and deterrence, and then shifts into an in-depth look at deterrence. This begins with a history of deterrence that stresses the peculiar political and technological conditions that dominated its development. It continues with an assessment of the pure logic of the concept, asking whether deterrence is easy or difficult to achieve, and using that question to simplify what otherwise seems to be an inordinately complicated literature. Part III concludes with a survey of the main debates about deterrence. This covers the relationship between defence and deterrence (asking whether they are complementary or mutually exclusive), the argument about whether rationality is a reasonable assumption in deterrence theory, the ethical case for and against deterrence, and the question of how deterrence relates to the arms dynamic.

Part IV examines the main concepts that have arisen in response to military technology seen not primarily as a problem in the hands of others, as in Parts II and III, but more as a problem in itself. The view that military means are a problem in their own right stems from the increasing destructiveness of war that has accompanied the advance and diffusion of modern military technology. This fear of war relates back to arms racing and deterrence, both of which can be seen as contributing to it. Arms racing and deterrence thereby take on a paradoxical role. They are solutions if the problem is military means in the hands of others, but causes of insecurity if the problem is military means in themselves. The old concept of disarmament, the newer one of arms control, and the recently revived one of non-provocative defence, are all tested against the full measure of the problem they seek to redress. Each is examined in terms of its political, economic, and military logic, and the strengths and weaknesses of its prescription are assessed.

The concluding chapter considers the merits of regulation versus *laissez-faire* approaches to international military relations. Since *laissez-faire* seems to be the most likely future, the question is asked whether the future must follow the pattern of the past. The main issue here is whether, and in what way, developments in military technology have transformed international relations.

Even within the restrictive definition of the subject used here, there are several topics that this book might have covered, but does not. It hardly touches at all on national security policy and policy-making in different countries, nor does it attempt any survey of contemporary regional or global security problems. These two large subjects are among the most accessible in the field, and are being constantly updated in hosts of books and articles. To treat either of them in any comprehensive way would require a whole book in itself, and such books fall quickly out of date. For those who prefer a mix of policy and concepts, two books are already available

(Baylis *et al.*, 1975; Russett, 1983b). In leaving out national, regional and global security problems, I also leave out concepts like national, regional, international, collective and common security. This omission is made on grounds of space rather than preference. These concepts are based more within International Relations than Strategic Studies, and I have already dealt with them at length elsewhere (Buzan, 1983, 1984b; Buzan, Rizvi *et al.*, 1986, chs 1 and 9).

The book does give some historical account of how contemporary strategic thinking has evolved, but the historical approach is not the main one used. The intention is only to set the historical context, not to develop the history itself in detail. Those seeking a detailed portrait can look at the valuable standard work along these lines that already exists (Freedman, 1981). Neither does it make much attempt to cover the military operations branch of strategy – the actual art of using armed force in combat – in any systematic way. This job has been done by both classical and modern writers like Clausewitz, Liddell Hart, and Beaufre. The conduct of military operations is, anyway, relatively peripheral to the contemporary strategic debate. Most of the concepts of Strategic Studies address operational questions in the more political sense of how the instruments of force can be used to prevent war, rather than in the strictly military sense of how they can be used to fight it. The main thrust of the field occupies the territory between the broad approach of International Relations and the specific skills of the military professional. As Michael Howard has argued, however, the principle that operational logic is a vital part of strategy cannot be ignored without introducing serious weaknesses into strategic analysis (Howard, 1973, 1979). The significance of this principle for the strategic debate is addressed in the discussion of defence and deterrence.

The last thing that the book does not attempt is an exhaustive description and critique of Strategic Studies as a field. Analysis of Strategic Studies has become a minor industry in itself, and there is a good collection of works that combine histories and descriptions of the field with critical and justificatory commentaries on both its normative and practical aspects. The history, sociology, epistemology, and professional politics of Strategic Studies have already been explored in sufficient detail by people better qualified to do so than me (for example, Baylis *et al.*, 1975, chs 1–3; Booth, 1979; Burns,

1965; Bull, 1968; Freedman, 1981, 1984a; George and Smoke, 1974, esp. chs 1–3, 21; Gray, 1971b, 1977, 1982a, 1982b; Green, 1968; Herken, 1984; Howard, 1970, ch. 10, 1976; Rapoport, 1964a, 1964b; Ropp, 1981).

# Part I

# Military Technology and Strategy

# 2 The Revolution in Military Technology

Technology defines much of the contemporary strategic agenda, and generates much of the language in which strategy is discussed. Broader, more political, concepts like war, crisis, alliance, terrorism, power and security are all heavily conditioned by the character of prevailing technology. Compare, for example, the military security problem of Britain in the years before air power and the years since, or that of the United States in the decades before the deployment of intercontinental ballistic missiles (ICBMs) and in those since. Directly stategic concepts like defence, deterrence, mutually assured destruction (MAD), arms racing, arms control, and disarmament, largely derive from technology. The great array of acronyms and abbreviations for which strategic discourse is notorious – ABM, ASAT, ASW, CBW, GLCM, MIRV, TNW, and many more – are almost all directly descriptive of military technology. But technology was not always as central as it is now. This chapter will look first at the revolution in military technology that has been going on since the middle of the nineteenth century, then at the foundations of that revolution, and finally at its consequences.

## 2.1 THE HISTORY OF THE REVOLUTION

Technology has been an important factor in military strategy throughout recorded history. Several good studies analyse and describe both its development and its role (Brodie and Brodie, 1973; Diagram Group, 1980; Howard, 1976b; McNeill, 1982; Pearton, 1982; Tsipis, 1985; Wintringham and Blashford-Snell, 1973). A host of classical cases illustrate the significance of military technology in strategic affairs. The ancient Egyptians, who used weapons made of bronze, were defeated by enemies equipped with harder iron swords. The ancient Greeks were able to defeat larger numbers of Persians, partly because their generalized use of body armour for troops allowed them to develop close-formation fighting tactics. The development of the longbow, the crossbow, and the pike, ended the

17

supremacy of the mounted and armoured knight in medieval Europe. During the fourteenth century the coming of primitive cannon made the existing construction of thin-walled fortifications highly vulnerable. By the late 1850s developments in shipbuilding, steam-engines, and gun design were making it suicidal to go to war in the wooden sailing ships that had formed the backbone of naval power for the previous three centuries.

The historical record clearly demonstrates the long-standing importance of technology to military strategy. But the significance of modern military technology is defined more by recent changes than by any long-standing patterns of continuity. The historical norm has reflected a pace of technological innovation so slow that the continuity of weapons systems has been more conspicuous than their transformation. The military technology of the Roman legions changed little in the six centuries between the conquest of Greece and the fall of Rome. The galleys used by the Ottomans and the Christians during their Mediterranean wars as late as the sixteenth century were quite similar to those used by the Greeks against Xerxes in 480 BC. The ships of the line that fought at Trafalgar in 1805, and even as late as the Crimean War (1854–6), were easily recognizable as the same class of ship pioneered by Henry VIII in the first half of the sixteenth century. In other words, revolutionary changes like the shift from oars to sail at sea in the sixteenth century, and the development of giant siege cannon in the late fourteenth century, were infrequent before the nineteenth century. Evolutionary changes, like the 300-year development of the modern repeating rifle out of the sixteenth century harquebus, proceeded so slowly that they seldom created upheavals in the conditions of strategy. Napoleon's astonishing victories at the end of the eighteenth century were based almost wholly on innovative use of existing types of weapons, and scarcely at all on innovations in the weapons themselves.

By the middle of the nineteenth century, however, a fundamental transformation in military technology was underway. The industrial revolution, with its ever expanding use of energy and machinery in the process of production had by that time developed such momentum that major changes in technology began to occur frequently. From around the middle of the nineteenth century, long periods of technological continuity virtually disappeared, and a new norm of continuous change asserted itself. That norm still prevails, and it shows little sign of weakening. It is therefore possible to identify the mid-nineteenth century as a major historical boundary in the relationship between technology and strategy. On both sides of it technology is important. On the older side the main theme is continuity measured in centuries, and the minor theme is change. On the more recent side, change is so dominant that the continuity of major weapons systems like battleships, tanks and long-range bombers can only be measured in decades. Even then, the degree of change within the type is so marked that earlier models (like the bombers of the 1920s) can hardly bear comparison in terms of capability and cost with later ones (like the B-1, 'Stealth', or *Backfire*).

The new norm of technological change meant that the conditions of military strategy were doomed to permanent upheaval. The revolution in technology was quantitative in two senses: first, the number and frequency of changes were large, and secondly, the ability to mass-produce huge numbers of new items increased dramatically. It was qualitative in the sense that each new innovation either improved an old capability substantially, like the machine-gun, or opened up a capability never before possessed, like the submarine, the aeroplane, and the reconnaissance satellite. Given the rapid pace of change, these qualitative improvements quickly added up to an enormous expansion of technological capabilities for both military and civil purposes. Changes occurred on a broad front and affected every aspect of society. They were both manifestations and movers of profound changes in human knowledge and social organization. The changes were not solely, or even mainly, motivated by the desire to improve military instruments, but such improvement was one of their major effects. As a consequence, no new war would ever be fought under the same conditions as a previous one, and therefore little could be accumulated in terms of reliable strategic wisdom. Under the new norm, technological change began to lead a permanent revision of military strategy.

The scale and scope of this technological revolution make it too vast to describe here in detail. Its principal military effects can be indicated in terms of five capabilities: firepower, protection, mobility, communications, and intelligence.

### 2.1.1   Firepower

The technological revolution made an early and dramatic impact on firepower. This has remained perhaps its principal effect down to the present day, where nuclear weapons dominate the strategy of the great powers. Earlier innovations often made only marginal differences in capability: there was not all that much to choose from, for example, between the firepower performance of a medieval crossbow or longbow and that of a seventeenth-century smoothbore musket. Firepower began to increase in the 1840s, with the widespread replacement of muzzle-loading muskets by much faster-firing breech-loading rifles. The arrival of qualitatively superior weapons meant that firepower could be increased more effectively by improving weapons than by the traditional method of increasing the number of soldiers in the field. Ten soldiers each able to fire 30 rounds per minute were in terms of their weight of fire three times more powerful than 20 soldiers each able to fire 5 rounds per minute. Higher rates of fire, together with improved accuracy, steadily multiplied the killing power of the individual soldier.

Advancing knowledge in chemistry, metallurgy, and engineering thenceforth opened the floodgates to enormous increases in firepower. Higher rates of fire were accompanied by longer ranges, greater accuracy, better reliability, and more powerful destructive effects on the target. Machine-guns first appeared in combat use in the American Civil War, and by 1883 were capable of firing up to 650 rounds per minute. The contrast between that number and the three or four shots per minute of which the most skilled musketeer was capable, indicates the magnitude and pace of change at this time. Artillery also improved apace. Better steel allowed bigger and more powerful cannon. Better engineering allowed breech loading, which in turn allowed rifled barrels. Such artillery had longer range, faster rates of fire, and better accuracy than the old smoothbore muzzle loaders. The new guns quickly grew to many times the size of even the largest naval guns of the pre-industrial era. Heavy naval cannon during the Napoleonic Wars fired solid shot weighing 32 pounds, but during the mid-nineteenth century, explosive shells replaced solid shot, and by 1914 there were guns capable of firing shells more than one ton in weight. The battlefield consequences of increasing firepower were suggested by the 600 000 dead of the American Civil War. This lesson did not register on either élite or public awareness in the main world power centre of Europe until the awful carnage of the First World War.

The increase in firepower has continued down to the present, though some technologies have peaked, either because further expansion of capability is hard to achieve or because it has no compelling use. Rates of fire have nearly reached their mechanical limits, and given available capabilities are a less attractive priority than greater reliability and accuracy. Nuclear weapons can be made with an explosive potential far larger than is called for by any military mission: there are no targets that cannot be destroyed more efficiently by several one-megaton warheads than by a single 60-megaton device. Indeed, as one writer has noted of the nuclear revolution:

> For thousands of years before [1945], firepower had been so scarce a resource that the supreme test of generalship lay in conserving it for application at the crucial time and place. Suddenly, it promised to become so abundant that it would be madness ever to release more than the tiniest fraction of the total quantity available.
>
> (Brown, 1977, p. 153)

This surplus capacity of destructive power is the unique historical condition that has shaped contemporary strategic thinking, and it will be a recurrent theme throughout the book.

Raw firepower has also been enhanced by increases in the range and accuracy of delivery systems. Heavy bombers and intercontinental missiles have achieved the maximum strike range that can be of use on this planet, and accuracy is perhaps the most dynamic remaining area of innovation in firepower. Precision-guided munitions are steadily approaching the goal of 'single shot equals kill', even at ranges of several thousand kilometers. As they do so, they reduce the need for both volume of fire and weight of destructive capability delivered to the target.

### 2.1.2 Protection

The revolution in firepower was for a time accompanied by a revolution in the capability of self-protection. The knowledge of higher quality steels that made possible improvements in cannon, also made possible improvements in armour plate. In the early phases of the technological revolution armour occasionally outperformed firepower, the most famous instance being the stalemate between the warships *Monitor* and *Merrimac* during the American Civil War. But although armour still provides useful protection, in an absolute sense the victory of firepower has been complete. Nothing can be armoured so effectively that it cannot be destroyed, a fact that underlay the unease of the early 1980s about the vulnerability of ICBMs based in fixed silos. Self-protection is now best pursued by concealment. This can be achieved either by disrupting the opponent's means of detection with electronic countermeasures (ECM), or by locating one's targets in ways that make detection difficult, such as by making them mobile, or putting them into submarines.

Ironically, the revolution in firepower has progressed so far that it is beginning to provide the most effective countermeasures against itself. Small, fast, accurate, powerful missiles have become the scourge of larger weapon platforms like tanks, aircraft, and surface warships. The most sophisticated of these precision-guided munitions (PGM) can even be used against other missiles in anti-missile mode. Enthusiasts for President Reagan's Strategic Defence Initiative (SDI) are putting vast resources into developing forms of defensive firepower that will block attack by hitherto unstoppable ballistic missiles. But until such technologies restore the effectiveness of defence, which may be a long time, if ever, protection will have to rely on the psychological barrier of deterrence. The protection of deterrence rests on a balance of firepower in which each side can inflict huge damage on the fixed assets of the other, and neither can physically prevent such damage from being inflicted on itself. Under such conditions, the incentives to use force are constrained by the consequence of one's own vulnerability to the firepower of the other.

### 2.1.3  Mobility

A revolution in mobility also began in the middle of the nineteenth century. At sea, this took the form of a rapid replacement of wooden, sail-powered ships by iron, steam-powered ones. In 1850 the old ships-of-the-line were still completely dominant, but by the early 1870s an extraordinary period of innovation had produced the first all-steam-powered modern battleship, *HMS Devastation*. Iron ships could be built much larger than wooden ones, and by the time of the First World War battleships weighed more than six times as much as the largest wooden warships ever built. Given continuous improvements in firepower and armour, each new model of these ships was more powerful than its immediate predecessors. Perhaps the most famous instance of this process took place in 1906, with the launching of the all-big-gun battleship *HMS Dreadnought*. This ship contained many technological innovations including steam turbine engines and telephones, and was based on the design innovation of carrying ten identical heavy guns. Previous types of battleship had carried four heavy guns and a mixture of medium guns. A Dreadnought had such an advantage in the weight of its long-range firepower that it was reckoned to be equal to at least three of the older types.

On land, the revolution in strategic mobility started with railways, which spread rapidly throughout the latter half of the nineteenth century. Railways enabled enormous numbers of men to be moved and supplied with hitherto undreamed of speed. Like firepower, the technology of mobility multiplied the effectiveness of military forces possessing it in relation to those without it. Not only could they mobilize faster than opponents, they could be shifted *en masse* from one scene of battle to another. The effect of railways on the speed with which armies could be deployed was so crucial that railway capabilities became the centrepiece of war planning in Europe before the First World War (Pearton, 1982, pp. 64–76, 117–39). The whole German plan was based on using superior mobilization speeds to crush France in the few weeks available before the slow-moving Russians could bring their forces into play. In the event, this technological condition underpinned a rigid and unstable balance of power which itself contributed to the outbreak of war in 1914.

With the manufacture of reliable internal combustion engines at the end of the nineteenth century, the revolution in mobility broadened in scope. Road vehicles added greatly to the flexibility of the mass transportation already created by railways. Developments of them soon began to give armies, not only the independence of movement typical of today's motorized divisions, but also highly mobile firepower in the form of tanks. The internal combustion engine also made possible powered flying machines and efficient submarines. These technologies enabled military activity to move on a large scale into two dimensions that could previously only be reached by the use of hazardous and unreliable devices. Submarines quickly developed into a major new element of naval power. Given the increasing vulnerability of surface ships to PGMs, they may one day be its only reliable constituent.

Aircraft started out in reconnaissance during the First World War. But they quickly graduated to ground attack and aerial combat, where they easily outperformed the lumbering and vulnerable *Zeppelins*. Major strides in aircraft technology between the wars transformed the air arm into the most potent weapon of war. Bombing aircraft spelled the end of the battleship as the backbone of naval power, and control of the air became a critical element in any use of naval forces. Air power enabled states to inflict massive damage on each other at long ranges without first defeating each other's armies. Aircraft further multiplied the mobility of troops, and the combination of land mobility and air power made possible the *Blitzkrieg* (lightning war) tactics employed so effectively by the German armed forces during the early years of the Second World War. The technology of aircraft is now relatively mature. The useful limits of speed, altitude, endurance, and carrying capacity were all reached more than a decade ago, and improvement since then has come mainly in terms of efficiency, agility, versatility, weapons systems, and electronics. Aircraft remain the most effective way of performing many missions, but missiles have usurped some of their functions, and pose a threat to their ability to survive in combat.

In the last few decades, the revolution in mobility has begun to move into what may be the last and biggest dimension available: space. So far, the presence of human beings in space has been on a small scale and in very temporary conditions. But a permanent presence is not far off, and as many a science-fiction writer has suggested, the potential for expansion of the technological revolution in space is unlimited (Langford, 1979). To date, however, space has been of relevance mainly to the revolutions in communication and intelligence.

### 2.1.4 Communications

The revolution in communications began in the mid-nineteenth century with the invention of the telegraph. Like the railways, the telegraph spread rapidly, adding instant long-distance communication to the revolution in mobility. The development of radio-communications ('wireless telegraphy') at the end of the nineteenth century added flexibility to the rigid telegraph system. With radio, mobile units on land and ships at sea could be kept in constant touch with central control. This revolution has travelled into space with satellites, which enable huge increases in the range and flow of communications to be achieved easily. Its effect has been to enhance central command and control of military forces on a scale unimaginable even in the early nineteenth century, when the speed of a horse or a clipper ship measured the number of days or weeks it would take to transmit a complex message between two distant points.

## 2.1.5 Intelligence

The revolution in intelligence is closely linked to improved communications. The same links that enabled the centre to exercise command and control over widely-scattered forces also served to feed information about local conditions into the central command. Without such information, command authorities would not have an adequate basis on which to make decisions about strategy. In addition, the electronics technology that spawned radio communication also gave rise to detection devices like radio location, radar and sonar, and later to information-processing computers of enormous power. The Battle of Britain was an early example in which the use of radar as a force multiplier helped numerically smaller forces to defeat larger ones. Superior knowledge of the location of enemy forces enables smaller numbers to concentrate against individual sections of a larger opposing force, and so defeat it piecemeal. Detection devices not only increased the flow of information into the command and decision-making process, but also played a large role in the improvement of accuracy that has been a major part of the firepower revolution over the last several decades.

The revolution in intelligence technology is now dominated by space-based systems and by computers. The former allow the countries possessing them to observe each other in astonishing detail (Jasani and Barnaby, 1984) while the latter make it possible to handle the vast amount of incoming data that result. The superpowers monitor each other constantly right across the radio and light spectrum. They can detect missile launches at the point of ignition, and satellite cameras have become so powerful that they can take pictures of the earth's surface in which human faces are recognizable (Tsipis, 1985, p. 245). Such capabilities can provide powerful reassurance against the sort of surprise attacks that Hitler was able to launch against the Soviet Union, and Japan against the United States, as recently as 1941. Satellites have also created a revolution in navigation by enabling ships to determine their location to within a few metres. By using such precision, ballistic missile submarines can target their missiles with much greater accuracy than was previously possible.

Only the deep oceans have successfully resisted effective penetration by detection technology. Water absorbs electromagnetic radiation and plays innumerable tricks with the one energy that moves easily through it: sound.

## 2.2  THE CIVIL FOUNDATIONS OF THE REVOLUTION

It is easy to think of this revolution in military technology as an independent process, somehow separable from human activity in non-military spheres. That cast of mind is encouraged by the ill-disciplined use of terms like 'the arms race' to describe the process of continuous improvements in weaponry, and 'militarism' to infer the dominating influence of military interests on the rest of society. There is, indeed, an important element of truth in the idea that a definable military sector exists in society, as will be seen in Chapter 7. A full understanding of military technology must nevertheless acknowledge the extensive and fundamental links that connect it to technology in the civil sector. Despite its distinctive elements, the revolution in military technology needs to be seen, not as a thing apart, but as an integrated element of a broader revolution in science, technology, and the human condition as a whole.

Quite what is the driving force behind this revolution is difficult to say with any certainty. Some people see technological advance as an expression of human intelligence; some see it as a historical manifestation of Western civilization; some see it as a product of the competitive, materialist, and profit-orientated ethic of capitalism; and some see it as a result of the revolution in thinking unleashed by the discovery of the scientific method. Whatever the answer, the point is that the process of technological advance now has a momentum that is deeply rooted in human society. Just as it cannot be implanted in third-world societies without transforming their indigenous cultures, so it cannot be stopped where it already exists without destroying much of the social structure that generated it, and that now depends on its continuance. The technological revolution is not only a phenomenon of material objects, but also one of social organization. The take-off in rates of technological innovation both reflected and promoted the development of high levels of social organization. Highly organized societies were able to extract much more productive energy of all sorts from their populations than had hitherto been possible. This organizational factor contributed as much to the power of the state possessing it as did the hardware of the technological revolution.

For the foreseeable future, we are therefore locked into a process of continuous, and probably quite rapid, technological change. Since it began, this process has had a profound impact on all aspects of society, including the military, and there is little reason to expect that this pattern will not continue. The close linkage between civil and military technology can be seen most clearly in the early stages of the technological revolution during the nineteenth century, but the basic fact of linkage is just as strong now as then (Shapley, 1978, pp. 1102–5; Vayrynen, 1983a, pp. 150–2).

The closeness of civil and military technologies during the nineteenth century is evident in terms of both the common body of knowledge underlying them, and the numerous overlaps between civil and military applications of technology. The existence of a single body of knowledge underlying the technological revolution as a whole is evident from any general study of the phenomenon (Landes, 1969). Both Brodie and Brodie (1973, esp. chs 5–9) and Pearton (1982) explore in some detail the specific linkages between military technological developments and the over-all advance of scientific and technological knowledge. During the nineteenth century, the knowledge of metallurgy, engineering technique, and design, that generated the revolution in firepower, was the same knowledge that produced ever more efficient steam-engines for mining, shipping, railways and industry in the civil sector. Similarly, the knowledge of chemistry that produced more effective explosives was intimately related to the knowledge that underlay the burgeoning industry in chemicals for civil applications ranging from paint to pharmaceuticals. In these two cases, as well as many others, the knowledge and skills that produced the revolutions in military technology were almost indistinguishable from those that served the development of civil technology.

The essential wholeness of the industrial revolution is even more obvious in terms of overlapping applications of technology. The railways and the telegraphs that so transformed the conditions of warfare in the late nineteenth century were technologies that would have been developed even if they had had no military use. In several areas, developments in civil technology preceded, and laid the foundations for, later military applications. Such a sequence was true of iron-built ships, where the civil sector was years in advance of the military. Vessels like Brunel's *Great Britain* (1845) led the way in integrating iron construction and steam propulsion, a combination that was not fully adopted by the navy until late in the 1850s. The civil sector also led in the development of aircraft and motor vehicles. Only the pressure of the First World War aroused military interest in these devices, both of which had been manufactured in the civil sector for more than a decade. The aeroplanes that had been successfully developed since the Wright brothers' triumph in 1903, and the motor vehicles that had been developed for commercial and private use, were only adapted and seriously developed for military use after 1914.

Similarity of function between the military and civil sectors means that many civil technologies will always have military applications in mobility, communications and intelligence. Transport aircraft, trucks, computers, and telecommunications equipment are clear examples. Many other elements of military technology are superficially quite distinct from the civil sector, especially those associated with firepower. Few civil applications can be found for machine-guns, large cannon, small missiles, and nuclear warheads. Even here, however, the difference between the military and civil sectors is more one of degree than of kind. A civil economy capable of manufacturing advanced steam-engines could build machine-guns quite easily. One capable of making large passenger aircraft could also make bombers. One capable of exploring space will be able to make military missiles. And one capable of making nuclear power plants to generate electricity has nearly all the knowledge, material and skill necessary to build nuclear explosives. Even the most distinctively military technologies are just variations on the main themes of whatever knowledge and skill is available to society as a whole.

On this basis, it can be argued that any civil industrial society contains a latent military potential. This potential lies in its stock of knowledge, equipment, material, technique and capital. Depending on the character and extent of that stock, the society will have the capacity to turn itself almost immediately to some kinds of arms production, and with various measures of delay to others. Military potential cannot be removed from industrial society even if it is not actually expressed in the manufacture of weapons. Some civil equipment can be turned directly to military use, like transport aircraft and poisonous chemicals. Manufacturing facilities for a wide range of civil goods involving engineering, chemicals, aerospace and electronics, can quite quickly be converted to military production.

As will be seen in Chapter 4, perhaps the clearest example of this latent potential in today's world is the civil nuclear power industry. Most of the concern about the proliferation of nuclear weapons over the last two decades has focused on the spread of civil nuclear technology. Long-standing efforts to separate the civil from the military applications of nuclear technology have not solved the problem convincingly. The fundamental similarity is inescapable, and leads to persistent worries that countries mastering civil technology give themselves an option to produce nuclear weapons within a short time of their decision to do so. Several countries, notably India, Pakistan, Argentina, Brazil, Iraq, Israel and South Africa seem clearly to be pursuing civil nuclear technology with a military option in mind.

## 2.3 THE GENERAL CONSEQUENCES OF THE REVOLUTION

For the foreseeable future the norm of change established in the mid-nineteenth century will remain dominant. The technological revolution, in other words, is not a transitory event between two conditions, but a permanent condition in itself (Bull, 1961, pp. 195–9). It is irreversably linked to a general advance of human knowledge which shows more signs of accelerating than of slowing down. It is merely one part of a much broader revolution in the material condition of human society. That broader revolution has both challenged and reinforced the state system in a variety of dimensions, of which the military is one. Just as the growth of military power has seemed to undermine the state as a meaningful unit of defence (Herz, 1957), so the expansion of a world industrial economy has outgrown it as an economic unit, and the spread of ideas has eroded it as an autonomous political and cultural unit. At the same time as technology appears to transcend the state, it also bolsters it by providing an immense increase in the size and variety of resources available to support the purposes of government.

The military consequences of this broad revolution are enormous. They have transformed the character of military relations between states in ways that will be explored in detail in Parts II and III. As has been seen, the generation of new technological capabilities is substantially, though not totally, independent of specific military demand for them. Technological options emerge from the general advance of human knowledge, and because they are in many ways independent of specific military demand, they put constant pressure on the formulation of military strategy. The coming of steam propulsion, for example, made irrelevant much of the tactical and strategic wisdom accumulated during the age of sail. As the debate about an as yet non-existent SDI option illustates, the pressure from technological options has now become so great that it shapes much of the strategic debate.

The most obvious general consequence of the technological revolution for strategy has been the increase in the difficulty of assessing military strength. The evolution of complex technologies has added large numbers of variables into the equation, many of which are qualitative, and almost all of which are subject to frequent change. One way to look at this problem is in terms of the much debated offensive and defensive utility of weapons (Jervis, 1978; Quester, 1977). An environment of continuous technological change generates a vigorous dialectic between offensive and defensive capability. Sometimes the one will be dominant, as defence was during the First World War, and sometimes the other, as offence was during the Second World War. As Jervis argues, the question of which is dominant is central not only to the military side of individual national security policy, but also to the whole character of military relations between states. When the defensive is dominant, and known to be so, then military relations should be easier to manage than when the offensive is dominant, and known to be so. This issue will be explored further in the discussion of non-provocative defence in Chapter 17.

Unfortunately, war is the only foolproof test of whether the offensive or the defensive is dominant, and because the character of military power can change substantially between wars there may be considerable peacetime uncertainty or misjudgement on the question. Misjudgement was very much the case in 1914, when general expectation favoured the offensive. The immensity of this error seems puzzling from a contemporary perspective, in which awareness of technological impacts has been sharpened by long experience. It can perhaps be explained by the fact that the societies of the day had lived with the technological revolution for a relatively short time, and therefore lacked much historical perspective on it. Specifically, they lacked much experience of all-out war between industrial societies. Their expectations of war therefore underestimated its destructiveness, and turned out to be wildly out of line with reality. The shock of this misperception contributed to an over-reaction during the 1930s, when expectations of war in Britain and France were exaggerated in the opposite direction. A premature fear of Armageddon underlay the excessive reluctance of these two democracies to resort to war.

Since 1945, nuclear weapons are widely held to have ushered in several decades where offensive capability seems so firmly ascendant that expectations of war are almost certainly an accurate reflection of what its reality would be. In this environment, the difficulties of living with an offensive-dominant military capability have been strongly influenced by the additional technological factor of the surplus capacity of destructive power provided by large stocks of nuclear weapons. Whether that influence has been malign or benevolent is a hotly contested question. Either way, as will be seen in Part III, this combination has made deterrence the central concept of contemporary strategic thinking. Nuclear weapons have even raised the question, explored in Chapter 1, of whether or not the revolution in military technology has transformed the basic nature of international relations (Gilpin, 1972). Have nuclear weapons paralysed the use of war amongst the great powers as a major instrument of change and adjustment within the international anarchy?

## 2.4 THE CONSEQUENCES OF THE REVOLUTION FOR STRATEGIC THINKING

The history of strategic thinking can usefully be set against the backdrop of the revolution in military technology. Ken Booth has already done much of this job in his succinct account of the evolution of traditional strategic thinking into the modern field of Strategic Studies (Baylis *et al.*, 1975, ch. 2). Before the nuclear age, strategic thinking was about how to fight and win wars. Strategists from classical times, like Sun Tzu and Thucydides, through the major military writers of the nineteenth century, Jomini, Clausewitz, and Mahan, to the military theorists of mechanized warfare in the 1920s and 1930s like Fuller, Liddell Hart, Douhet, Trenchard and Mitchell, all concerned themselves with the art of fighting. This tradition continues into the nuclear age among professional military strategists almost everywhere. It is also very much alive in the works of theorists of revolutionary war like Mao Zedong and Che Guevara.

One can see the roots of modern Strategic Studies most clearly in the trends that shaped strategic thinking from the nineteenth century to the Second World War. The two most important of these trends were the increasing scale and speed of war in relation to the size of the societies generating it, and the decreasing degree of similarity between each new war and the ones that preceded it. The factors underlying these changes were the rising wealth and organizational power of states, and the apparently bottomless cornucopia of technological innovation opened up by the industrial revolution.

Clausewitz, who was the most durably influential of the nineteenth century strategists, wrote in response to the transformations in scale and technique of warfare revealed by the Napoleonic Wars. His work just preceded the take-off of technological change which began towards the middle of the nineteenth century, but it captured the new political element in war that had been unleashed by the French Revolution. Revolutionary France had discovered the military power of mass mobilization, and the ideological and nationalist tools by which that power could be controlled. This discovery transformed the conditions of power, and enabled one country to dominate or occupy most of Europe for more than two decades. It forced other countries to find their own ways of tapping the same source of power, and in the process transformed warfare from being mostly an élite affair of states, to being mostly a mass affair of nations.

The social transformation of warfare began in revolutionary France and America, and its spread and development were major features in the changing character of war right through into the nuclear age. The continued relevance of Clausewitz rests to a considerable extent on his being the first to capture the political essence of the transformation that had begun in his time. The political thread in his thinking provides a strong connection to more modern revolutionary strategists from Lenin onwards, whose concerns, though different from those of Clausewitz, also focus on the political elements of military strategy. This social and political dimension of strategy could be developed here as a complementary theme to the technological dimension under investigation. Given space, interesting questions could be asked, for example, about the interaction of democracy, mass conscription, and military strategy. Does democracy lower the social acceptability of casualties, and so create incentives to replace labour with capital (that is, technology) in the armed forces? Does the natural preference for the use of capital over labour in capitalist societies reinforce this democratic pressure? Do capitalist democracies therefore pursue technological advance for reasons additional to the general attraction of possessing more potent weapons?

Most other nineteenth-century military strategists were concerned with the continuous transformation in the conditions of war resulting from new technologies. The interaction of these technologies with the greatly enhanced mobilization potential of the nation-state rapidly outdated centuries of military wisdom, and pushed technological factors into the forefront of military planning and calculation. The full cumulative impact on warfare of the steady increase in technological and mobilization capabilities was unfortunately not revealed by the small number of mostly bilateral wars fought in Europe during the latter half of the nineteenth century. By the turn of the century, only a few people had correctly foreseen what the technological revolution was doing to military capability. The most notable of these thinkers were Ivan Bloch and Norman Angell. Bloch calculated in detail the effects of increased firepower, and argued that an all-out war could not be won, and might well destroy the societies undertaking it (Pearton, 1982, pp. 137–9). Angell argued an early version of the contemporary interdependence thesis, that under modern conditions, war no longer served the economic interests of society. For industrial societies, war destroyed more wealth than it created because it disrupted the global trade on which wealth had come to depend. No longer could states gain in wealth by seizing territory and resources from each other as they had done during the mercantilist period in the seventeenth and eighteenth centuries (Howard, 1981, pp. 70–1).

Despite the existence of this wisdom, the main strategic effect of increasing military capabilities prior to 1914 was to encourage doctrines of the offensive (van Evera, 1984). In reality, however, the pace and character of change in the conditions of war had so outrun the development of strategic thinking that war bore almost no resemblance to what had been expected. When the full revelation came in the four years after 1914, it was in the form of big surprises not only in the military domain, but also in the social and political domain on which the war-making capacities of states rested. As Bloch had predicted, the defence was almost everywhere dominant, making war a contest in resources and endurance. Instead of the rapid and decisive war of offense and manoeuvre planned by the European military staffs, what occurred in most major theatres of war was an indecisive, drawn-out stalemate that consumed human and material resources on a gigantic scale.

The war required national mobilization in such depth as to

transform the social and political structures of most of the states engaged in it. The Russian Revolution was only the most spectacular of these transformations. Even in relatively advanced and stable polities like Britain, the war resulted in a broadening of the franchise big enough to have a marked effect on the social base of electoral politics. The war's huge costs required the invention of reasons for it – 'the war to end war' – that bore no relation either to its actual causes or to its eventual outcome. One historian has described the impact of the war in terms of a historic divide between the character of the nineteenth and twentieth centuries:

> The Great War of 1914–18 lies like a band of scorched earth dividing that time from ours. In wiping out so many lives which would have been operative on the years that followed, in destroying beliefs, changings ideas, and leaving incurable wounds of disillusion, it created a physical as well as a psychological gulf between two epochs.
>
> (Tuchman, 1967, p. xv)

The vast extent of the war's physical and social costs confirmed Angell's view that war had become economically counterproductive. It raised serious doubts in some countries as to whether war could any longer serve as an instrument of state policy within Europe for any objective short of national survival. In Britain and France there were real fears among both leaders and public that another general war in Europe would promote revolutions on a wide scale, and might actually destroy the physical base of European civilization. These apocalyptic visions were strikingly similar to those of the nuclear age. They raised fundamental questions about the huge disproportion between means and ends which modern conditions imposed on all-out war. These questions are precisely those that preoccupy modern Strategic Studies, though it took another war and another leap in the technology of destruction before strategic analysts confronted them directly.

The military strategists of the interwar years did not stop thinking about war: they were military professionals and could not easily do so without abandoning their whole training and tradition. Instead, the most creative amongst them sought ways to restore the efficiency of military means, which meant in effect restoring the dominance of the offensive (Baylis *et al.*, 1975, pp. 30–1). Only if victory could be achieved quickly would war no longer generate a huge disproportion between means and ends. Their principal hope for restoring the power of the offensive lay in the emerging new technologies of armoured vehicles and aircraft. To some extent, the restoration of mobility achieved in the Second World War vindicated their vision. However, because the new technology and tactics also enhanced the power of the defence, they did not produce quick victory. Consequently they did nothing to reduce the duration and scale of the fighting, the necessity for total national mobilization, or the immensity of the resources consumed. The list of those killed in the Second World War was five times as long as that for the First.

The Second World War broke the world power of the Western European states. Even without the advent of nuclear weapons, it drove home the lesson of the First World War that the major European states could no longer wage war amongst themselves without bringing about the political and physical impoverishment of their societies, and perhaps without destroying them completely. By 1945 it was clear that all-out war had become an irrational instrument in relations among major powers. Almost no conceivable national objective short of last ditch survival justified the costs of undertaking it. This lesson was as manifestly true for revolutionary workers' states like the Soviet Union as it was for conservative, bourgeois, capitalist states like Britain and France. Amongst the world's leading powers, only the United States had escaped the harsh lesson that the cost of victory in all-out modern war was running close second to the cost of defeat.

If this lesson needed any reinforcement, it was provided by the opening of the nuclear age with the dropping of atomic bombs on Japan in the closing stages of the war. The orders of magnitude leap in destructive power represented by atomic bombs made unarguable the lesson already obvious to those parts of the world where whole cities, and almost whole countries, had been devastated by conventional military means. But perhaps more important for the development of Strategic Studies was the fact that the atomic bomb had been dropped by the one great power not to have experienced the devastations of modern war on its own heartland. Bernard Brodie captured the new strategic situation created by the military technology of the nuclear age with his much-quoted statement of 1946 that: 'Thus far the chief purpose of our military establishment has been to win wars. From now on its chief purpose must be to avert them. It can have almost no other useful purpose' (Brodie, 1946, p. 76).

# 3 The Global Spread of Military Technology

The process of qualitative advance in military technology is accompanied by the spread of both technology, and knowledge about technology, ever more broadly throughout the international system. This chapter examines the relationship between the qualitative advance of technology on the one hand, and its spread on the other, and the process by which the spread of military capability has occurred. The theme from Chapter 2 of the close relationship between civil and military technology continues to be central here, and it ties into the argument that the process of spread is uneven and incomplete. Particularly important is the fact that the military products of the technological revolution have been much more widely diffused by the arms trade than has capability to produce them.

## 3.1 THE INTERACTION BETWEEN SPREAD AND QUALITATIVE ADVANCE

The unequal distribution of military capability was a normal feature of the international system before, as well as after, the technological revolution. That technological capabilities were a part of this unequal distribution is a fact illustrated by the European successes in empire-building against more numerous, but more primitively equipped, peoples during the sixteenth, seventeenth and eighteenth centuries, most notably in North and South America. In addition to technology, differences in factors like population, resources, political and economic organization and geography also ensured that the military power of states would be distributed across a wide spectrum. Once the technological revolution took hold, however, it greatly amplified the relative importance of technology in the distribution of military power, and consequently enlarged the range of difference between states. For a time in its early stages, it meant that the few states in possession of the technological revolution gained an enormous advantage over the rest. As Hilaire Belloc wrote of the late nineteenth-century colonial wars:

> Whatever happens
> we have got
> the Maxim gun,
> and they have not.
>
> (quoted in Sampson, 1977, p. 50)

As the influence and the products of the technological revolution spread, the absolute distinction between 'haves' and 'have nots' became less important. The 'have nots' might still be unable to produce modern weapons themselves, but the increasing trade in modern infantry weapons meant that there would be no major recurrence of situations in which the wielders of modern arms would face opponents armed only with bows, clubs and spears. The diffusion of the technological revolution and its products thus tended to restore the weight of traditional factors like population and wealth. Despite the levelling effect of the spread of military technology, a major element of qualitative distinction remains because the process of diffusion occurs in parallel with continued qualitative advance. The trade in arms works to redress the imbalance between 'haves' and 'have nots', but qualitative advance continues to open up new distance between those states at the forefront of the ongoing revolution and the rest. For the small group of states able to ride the crest of technological innovation, a qualitative edge remains a decisive ingredient of military strength. The importance of maintaining such an edge has been a major theme in American military strategy since 1945.

The relationship between spread and qualitative advance is, however, more complicated than the simple one of leaders and followers: each process actively promotes the other. The process of spread stimulates that of advance, because only by staying ahead in quality can some countries maintain their power position and/or their security. The leading powers in the system *have* to keep close to the front edge of technological advance unless they want to fall back into the second rank of power. Aspirants to first rank power status must acquire the capability to compete at the leading edge of technological innovation. The twentieth-century rise of Japan and Russia/the Soviet Union to first rank status can be seen in these terms, as can the post-1945 consolidation of the Soviet Union's status as a superpower.

Because the leading edge of technological advance sets the standard for the international system, its continuous forward movement exerts pressure on the whole process of spread. As the leading edge creates ever higher standards of military capability, followers have either to upgrade the quality of their weapons or else decline in capability relative to those who do. States at the leading edge have political and economic reasons for pumping qualitative advances back into the pipeline through the mechanism of arms aid and sales. Competition between them can become so intense that they may even find it difficult to reserve all of the latest innovations for their own armed forces. By diffusing the products of qualitative advance, the leading-edge states inexorably raise the standard of military power in the lower ranks. This adds to their incentives to find further lines of technological advance with which to maintain their military advantage.

Where rivalries exist between states, the level of technology between them becomes crucial. At the leading edge, rivals have to guard against their opponents making some decisive technological breakthrough, and consequently they are always under pressure to maintain high levels of innovation. Much of the controversy about SDI is based precisely on the fear that unequal capability in strategic defence would create a major imbalance in military potency between the two superpowers. In the lower ranks, the relative level of technology is no less important. The states on both sides of the Arab–Israel and the India–Pakistan rivalries have been extremely sensitive to the quality of their opponent's weapons. Both Israel and Pakistan have consistently sought to offset their inferior size by acquiring superior weapons.

In one sense, the qualitative pressure created by the arms trade is no different from the general upward qualitative pressure that trade creates in the civil sectors of technology. In a trading environment, any state that fails to keep pace with international standards will be unable to sell its goods abroad, and only able to sell them at home if it restricts imports of cheaper and/or better quality goods. But although the process may be similar, the consequences are different. Technological weakness in the civil sector results at worst in lower standards of living. Technological weakness in the military sector can result in the overthrow or destruction of the state itself. For this reason, there is a compulsion to acquire modern military technology that is not matched in the civil sector.

So while the arms trade helps to even out the military differences between states, it does so only at the cost of setting a high, and continuously rising, global standard of military technology. The standard is high because it is set by the quality of the leading edge, and it is upwardly mobile because it is driven along at the pace of qualitative advance in the top-rank military producers. Since the pace of advance is itself pushed by military rivalry among the top-rank powers, the technological consequences of superpower rivalry are quite quickly imposed on the rest of the international system. States that can afford to buy modern weapons will do so either to match, or gain an edge on, their rivals. States that cannot afford modern weapons, but see their security needs as requiring them, may have to make political arrangements with a supplier state in which allegiance, bases, or economic assets are traded for arms aid. The relationship between Somalia and the Soviet Union during the 1970s can be seen in this light, as can the more longstanding one between the United States and Pakistan. Others will make do with the offerings on the second-hand market, keeping pace with the forward qualitative movement of the leading edge, but only at some distance behind it.

## 3.2   THE MECHANISMS OF SPREAD

Advanced military technology has spread throughout the international system in three ways: by the physical and political expansion of those states possessing it; by the transfer of weapons from those capable of manufacturing them to those not; and by the spread of manufacturing capability to ever more centres of control. In historical terms, these three mechanisms of diffusion have operated simultaneously, but not evenly. The mechanism of direct physical expansion was prominent during the colonial period, and has declined in importance since 1945. It is now relevant principally in the form of the overseas bases of a few great powers. Conversely, the spread of independent centres of manufacture has been increasing in importance, especially in the period since the Second World War. The mechanism of the arms trade has been steadier than either of the other two, remaining central to the diffusion of military technology throughout the period from the late nineteenth century to the present day.

Before giving a historical account of the process of spread as a whole, it is useful first to examine the reasons for the durable centrality of the arms trade. The key to understanding the apparent permanence of the arms trade is the powerful constellation of vested interests that support it: 'supply push' from producers, and 'demand pull' from consumers.

Supplier interests can be both political and economic. Possession of an arms industry serves two political interests of the state additional to the basic security value of self-reliance: the pursuit of power, and the pursuit of influence. Any state seeking to attain a prominent position in the international power hierarchy needs its own arms industry, both as a source of status and as a manifestation of capability. If great power status is, at the end of the day, measured by the independent ability to wage war, then a substantial measure of domestic arms production is an essential requirement. Once attained, an arms industry can add to the tools of influence at the government's disposal. As most clearly illustrated by the superpowers, arms supply is one of the classical ways in which great powers compete for the allegiance of lesser powers. States in control of their own arms industry can supply arms to others for political purposes like supporting allies, or winning friends, or opposing the influence of rivals. The character and the importance of political motives in the arms trade, and the difficulty of achieving them, has been exhaustively researched by several authors (McKinlay and Mughan, 1984; Pierre, 1982, part 1; Stanley and Pearton, 1972, ch. 4).

Political motives for states to acquire arms production capabilities cannot be disentangled from economic ones. In a trading environment the market sets standards of both quality and price that determine whether the pursuit of self-reliance by any state is a viable or desirable policy. The basic economic motives for arms production are to save the cost of importing weapons, and to improve the balance of payments by exporting them (Brzoska and Ohlson, 1986, pp. 279–80; Evans, 1986). Once an arms industry exists, however, it can generate other economic interests, some of which intersect significantly with domestic politics. The arms industry generates vested interests in employment and in preserving high technology capabilities. Both of these interests can lead to pressure to export in order to sustain the companies concerned.

A more potent pressure to export is the fact that only states with very large domestic requirements for arms have any hope of achieving economies of scale in their own production. Longer production runs lower the unit cost of the items produced. If the number of sophisticated items like tanks and aircraft required for domestic consumption is small, then home production will result in high unit costs unless exports can be found to lengthen the production run. Long production runs are especially necessary to amortise investment in high technology items where research and development (R&D) accounts for a high proportion of total cost. States with domestic requirements large enough to support economies of scale are very few in number. Consequently, nearly all arms producers have strong incentives to export in order to achieve reasonable costs for that part of their production that they wish to buy for their own use. Second rank powers like Britain and France are the most vulnerable to this squeeze, which is why they have been aggressive in seeking export markets. France, in particular, has established a reputation for having few political scruples about the buyers of its weapons. The need to guarantee economically attractive production runs for expensive modern weapon systems also explains why the Western European arms producers have increasingly resorted to multinational arms production projects like the *Jaguar*, the *Tornado*, and the new European fighter.

Even the superpowers have not been immune from the need to achieve economies of scale, despite their starting advantage of large domestic arms requirements. The process of qualitative advance means that the unit cost of sophisticated modern weapons is always higher than the cost of the previous generation. Both this cost, which tends to outrun the general rate of inflation, and the fact that the newer weapons are more capable than the older ones they replace, create pressure to acquire smaller numbers. Shrinking domestic demand in terms of numbers of weapons in turn raises the incentives to lengthen production runs by finding export markets.

The desire of producers to transfer arms is complemented by the stout defence of the right to receive arms mounted by those countries unable to manufacture some or all of their own weapons. Though they might support the denial of the right to buy as a policy against a special case like South Africa, they will oppose as an assault on their sovereignty, dignity, independence and equality any general attempt to restrict the supply of arms. The principle that non-producers have the right to buy technologies that they cannot make themselves is as strong a feature of the trade in conventional weapons as it is of the trade in civil nuclear technology. Without such a right, non-producers would become second-class states, unable to match the military forces of producers, and relegated to a politically unacceptable category of those judged incapable of being allowed to manage their own affairs.

There is thus a potent community of interest between suppliers and recipients in maintaining the arms trade. Because that community is backed by strong incentives on the part of suppliers to sell, and strong motives on the part of recipients to maintain their access to the market, it will almost certainly ensure that the trade remains a durable feature of international relations. The various proposals to regulate or restrict the arms trade (Blomley, 1984; Brzoska and Ohlson, 1986, pp. 289–90; Pierre, 1982, part 4; Stanley and Pearton, 1972, part 4) seem unlikely to make much headway against the interests in favour of maintaining it.

## 3.3 THE HISTORICAL PROCESS OF THE SPREAD

During the nineteenth century, only a handful of states managed to acquire the capability for sustained industrial development that was the key to manufacturing modern weapons. Britain was the leader in the early stages, but Germany, France, the United States and some smaller European countries quickly caught up. Russia and Japan constituted the tail end of this first wave of industrialization. Among the members of this group, trade and investment provided a major mechanism for the transfer of technology. Technological leaders were generally more than willing to sell their products, and investment from Europe underpinned the industrialization of countries like the United States and Russia. The later entrants to the group were able to use this transfer of finance and technology to bring their own process of industrialization up to the point at which it became self-sustaining. All of these countries fairly quickly attained sufficient command of basic industry to develop and manufacture weapons up to the leading technological standard of the day. As they did so, their dependence on arms purchases declined, and they often entered the market as sellers.

The leaders of the first wave, particularly Britain and Germany, did good business selling such military fruits of industrialization as artillery, machine-guns, and Dreadnoughts to countries unable to manufacture them. Late industrializers, such as Japan, purchased major weapon systems like battleships until they developed the capacity to manufacture their own. Many countries, like Brazil and the Ottoman Empire, were not at this time serious entrants in the industrialization process. Others, like Belgium and the Netherlands, were industrializing, but did not command the scale of the industry or markets necessary to make domestic production of the whole range of modern arms an economic proposition. Both types of country were forced to depend on the arms trade in order to keep pace with progress in military technology. Under these conditions of unequally distributed capability to manufacture modern weapons, notorious arms salesmen like Basil Zaharoff set the model for 'the merchants of death' by selling modern weapons to both sides of rivalries between non-producers: submarines to Greece and the Ottoman Empire, Dreadnoughts to Argentina, Chile and Brazil (Sampson, 1977, ch. 2).

The industrialized group contained most of the states that were already established as imperial powers – Britain, France and Russia – and some – Germany, Belgium, Japan and the United States – that became imperial powers during the last rounds of empire-building. In their imperial roles, these powers spread elements of the technological revolution all through the areas of the world over which they exercised control, including most of Africa and large parts of Asia. They created local economies geared to their own resource needs. They built transportation networks of ports and railways, both to serve those economies, and to strengthen their military control. They deployed the military fruits of industrialization to seize and maintain occupation of vast colonial areas. In these areas there was little in the way of transfer of technology comparable to that among the first wave of industrializing countries. Since the local peoples were not independent, neither was there any arms trade on a scale comparable to that between the industrialized powers and the independént countries in the Balkans, the Far East, and Latin America. Then as now, political and economic motives ensured that arms always found their way to areas of high demand. Within their own empires, each colonial power as a rule made available only selected products of industrialization, and not the process of industrialization itself. Most of the industrial products that were transferred to colonial areas remained under the control of the colonizing power, especially those associated with military capability.

The diffusion of military capability remained very much in this quite concentrated pattern until the Second World War, especially in terms of the capability for producing advanced weapons. Europe and America continued to be the focus of qualitative innovation in technology, and Japan and the Soviet Union caught up in terms of independent production capability. Technology was taken to the areas under colonial control, but seldom implanted there. Independent non-arms producers like the Latin American countries mostly made little progress towards industrialization and so remained dependent on the arms trade.

After the Second World War, and in no small measure as a result of it, the spread of military capability picked up speed across the world. This acceleration was closely linked to the vast process of decolonization, and involved both political and technological factors. When Portugal surrendered the last of its empire in the mid-1970s, the process of decolonization was virtually complete. In three decades, the number of states in the international system tripled as more than half of mankind moved from foreign rule to self-government.

The struggle for independence, and its achievement, increased the spread of military capability in two ways. First, it increased the level of political organization among the local populations, making them harder to dominate and easier to mobilize for armed resistance. Although only a few colonial powers were actually thrown out of their empires, most found rule increasingly difficult, expensive, and hard to reconcile with their domestic political values. More than anything else, guerrilla warfare came to symbolize the potency of political mobilization as a weapon for peoples unable to match the weapons of their opponents. The spread of a will for independence among colonized peoples thus became a central element in the spread of military capability. Because of it, no power, however great its military superiority, can now contemplate large-scale imperial ventures with anything like the ease that prevailed up to the Second World War.

Secondly, independence added enormously to the number of non-producing countries needing to get their military equipment via the arms trade. Instead of being denied modern arms, the ex-colonial peoples became legitimate customers for the producers. Their need arose not only from the symbolic domestic order requirements of self-rule, but also from the complex pattern of relations with neighbours that replaced the simpler, and often more coherent, patterns of colonial rule. Where India and Pakistan and the smaller states of South Asia now worry about each other, Britain formerly worried about the security of the subcontinent as a whole. Decolonization thus facilitated the spread of military capability both by creating many new independent centres of political power, and by unleashing a host of local disputes and rivalries.

Because most of the new states had little or no industrial base, decolonization initially just increased the number of non-arms-producers in the system. The military imbalance between the producers and the newly-independent non-producers was rectified to the extent that arms were now available rather than denied, but it was maintained inasmuch as the non-producers remained dependent on a small number of suppliers for their weapons. Yet decolonization also carried with it a strong imperative towards industrial development. Because of this imperative, non-producers in both the newly-independent areas of Africa and Asia, and the older ex-colonial area of Latin America, were no longer satisifed to remain economically and industrially dependent. Many of them actively set about acquiring industrial economies of their own. In several of the developing countries – India and China, and later Argentina, Brazil, Iran and South Africa – acquiring the capability for at least some military production was a priority.

Some of these development projects have made scant progress. Others, most spectacularly in Iran, have destroyed the political structures that promoted them. But some have succeeded, albeit in varying degrees. By the 1970s this success resulted in a broadening group of countries able to supply some of their own military needs. In a few of these, most notably Brazil, India, Israel, South Africa and China, the quality and quantity of production were high enough to enable them to compete in some sectors of the arms trade, and thereby multiply the sources of armaments within the international system (Brzoska and Ohlson, 1986; Evans, 1986; Neuman and Harkavy, 1980, ch. 17; Pierre, 1982, pp. 123–7; SIPRI, 1971, ch. 22).

The mechanism by which arms production capabilities have spread to these countries are similar to those that created the first group of producers. Straight transfers of arms do not assist development of production capability unless a sufficient industrial base already exists to enable local copies to be made. As argued in the previous chapter, civil industrial capability carries military potential, and so some of the new production capability simply reflects spin-offs from a broader process of economic development. In many cases, however, the development of arms production has also been stimulated by the direct transfer of manufacturing capability from producer to non-producer countries, though even here the success of the transplant depends on the existence of a civil industrial base

(Brzoska and Ohlson, 1986, esp. ch. 10; Evans, 1986, p. 101; Klare, 1983). The Soviet Union played this role for China during the 1950s, several Western suppliers were doing the same for Iran up to 1979, and both East and West have done so for India.

Such transfers reflect both economic and political competition among the supplier states. After the Second World War, the arms trade was initially dominated by the United States and Britain. The small number of suppliers created a seller's market. As other industrial states such as France, the Soviet Union, Germany, Czechoslovakia, Belgium and Italy recovered from the war, the number of arms suppliers increased, a trend recently reinforced by the development of arms industries in some Third World states. As the number of suppliers increases, competition among them for the export market becomes more intense, with the result that buyers have more leverage. In the buyer's market that the increase in the number of suppliers has now created, many states have used that leverage to get production facilities and knowledge as part of their major arms purchases.

India, for example, has negotiated many such deals with the Soviet Union, Britain and France. From being almost a pure purchaser during the 1950s, India has steadily built up an indigenous arms production capability of considerable sophistication. Licencing production arrangements seldom transfer technology quickly, and do not represent a short path from dependence to independence. Typically, they start with assembly of imported components, which leaves the importers only marginally more independent, and possibly less well off financially, than if they imported complete weapons. Despite the well-established view that licencing does not lead to independent production (Brzoska and Ohlson, 1986, pp. 283–5), India has demonstrated that over the years such arrangements can promote the development of local component suppliers as well as capability for maintenance and design. India has built up a solid independent capability in the less technologically advanced areas of military production, and a firm base on which to rest advantageous licenced production arrangements for more sophisticated weapons. Its exceptional success in this development has been in large part due to its possession of a broadly-based industrial economy in which to integrate its arms industry. Without devoting the much larger resources necessary to bring its own R&D up to the pace and standard of the leading edge of qualitative advance, however, even a country like India will not be able to achieve more than semi-independence in arms supply. Although it will be able to produce a variety of less-sophisticated weapons independently, it will remain partly dependent on more advanced suppliers if it wishes to deploy weapons close to the highest standard of technology available (Brzoska and Ohlson, 1986, ch. 7; Mansingh, 1984, ch. 4; Marwah, 1980, ch. 4; SIPRI, 1971, ch. 16 and pp. 742–58; Thomas, 1978; Viksnins, 1979).

## 3.4 THE CURRENT POSITION AND THE OUTLOOK

The result of the spread of military technology to date has been to create a hierarchy of states defined in terms of their capabilities for military production (Neuman, 1984). At the top are those capable of producing the whole spectrum of modern weapons. These need to import little or no military technology from abroad, and can act as suppliers to states further down the hierarchy. Membership in this top class is defined not only by possession of a complete arms manufacturing industry, but also by the fielding of a sufficient R&D capability to keep the products of that industry at the leading edge of technological quality. Britain, Germany, the United States and France were members of this class before 1914. Japan and the Soviet Union joined it during the interwar years, but by the 1960s only the United States and the Soviet Union could claim full first-rank status.

At the bottom of the hierarchy are those states with little or no capability for independent military production. This group expanded as a result of the influx of the Afro-Asian states into the international system. Many of these new states lacked either or both of the industrial capability and the economies of scale necessary to produce modern weapons. Some, like Nigeria, Indonesia and Egypt, might hope one day to supply a good proportion of their own arms needs. Small, underdeveloped states such as Sierra Leone, Guyana and Laos are unlikely ever to develop a significant level of arms production. To the extent that they seek modern weapons to preserve or symbolize their independence, the larger underdeveloped states are temporarily, and the small ones permanently, dependent on the arms trade.

The middle range of the hierarchy is occupied by several strata of what can be called 'part-producers'. Part-producers have a significant enough arms production capability to distinguish them from non-producers, but they do not match the scope and/or the quality of the full-producers. In the lowest strata are countries like Mexico, that have barely struggled up from the ranks of non-producers, and will only be able to produce undemanding items like small arms and coastal patrol vessels. Next up are countries such as Pakistan and Spain that have the beginnings of more sophisticated production capabilities. Higher still are those like Israel, Sweden, South Africa and Argentina that can produce a fair range of military goods, some capable of competing in the international market. This stratum blends into a more ambitious one, including India and Brazil, where foundations for a broadly-based arms industry are being developed. China stands on the boundary between the top group of full-spectrum producers and the middle ranks of part-producers. It has achieved virtually a full-range of production, and a high level of independence, but does not have the industrial or R&D sophistication to produce weapons of leading-edge quality.

Almost all of the part-producers remain dependent on members of the top group for important elements of their arms production capability (Brzoska and Ohlson, 1986; Newman, 1984; Tuomi and Vayrynen, 1982). This dependence is especially marked in high technology areas like precision engineering, special materials, and advanced electronics. The part-producer countries can only achieve independence in arms by one of two routes. They can match the R&D pace of the leading-edge powers, as the Soviet Union did after the Second World War, or they can pursue independence at a level of technology lower than that set by the leading edge, as China did after its break with the Soviet Union. Matching the leading-edge powers requires a size of economy and a level of industrialization possessed by very few states. Given the huge resources devoted to R&D by the superpowers, the leading edge of technology moves rapidly away from aspirant arms producers. The impact of R&D on technological advance in weapons has thus become the key to maintaining a qualitative hierarchy of arms producers. The respective drawbacks of the paths to independence (high cost and inferior armaments) are sufficiently compelling to ensure that most middle-rank states will stay in a position of semi-dependence for a long time. So long as top-quality producers are compelled by economic and political rivalry to pass on the higher levels of military technology, either through production licences or finished products, a degree of dependence does not pose unacceptable vulnerabilities on the security policies of recipient states. In this sense, the existence of a buyer's market is an economically attractive and politically acceptable substitute for domestic manufacture of arms for many states. Because of the arms trade, non-producers like Libya, Ethiopia and Papua New Guinea, and part-producers like India, Australia, Argentina and Israel, can maintain modern military forces proportional to the size of their economies in a way that would be impossible if they had to rely solely on their own manufacturing capability.

The middle range also contains lapsed first-rank powers. Some of these, like France, Britain, Germany and Italy are capable of independent competition with the first-rank powers in some, but not all, areas of advanced military technology. These countries undertake sufficient R&D to keep up with the leading edge in some areas, and not to fall too far behind it in any. They compete with the first-rank powers in the arms trade, but they may be dependent on them not only for whole types of weapons that they do not produce themselves, but also for sophisticated components for weapons that they do produce. Britain, for example, depends on the United States for the submarine-launched missiles that carry its nuclear deterrent, but competes with it in the international market for tanks, tactical missiles and fighter-bombers. France, which produces a nearly complete range of high-technology military equipment, relies on the United States for such items as in-flight refuelling and early-warning aircraft. Other lapsed first-rank powers, most notably Japan, choose not to turn their formidable industrial capability to the large-scale production of weapons. Germany formerly took this position, but since the 1970s has expanded its role as both producer and supplier (Lucas, 1985).

Most of the part-producer countries are both buyers and sellers in the arms trade. Some, like China and India – and for quite different reasons Israel and South Africa – pursue quite broad independent production capability in order to reduce reliance on arms imports, and therefore minimise their political vulnerability to supplier pressure. Others, like Sweden, Switzerland and Austria, strive as part of their policy of neutrality to maintain the maximum self-reliance that is compatible with their economic base. These countries value independence but have small home markets, and so face strong pressure to export in order to maintain the breadth and reduce the costs of their domestic production base. Yet others, like Belgium, Italy and Canada, cultivate specialized niches of arms production. This strategy enables them to participate in the arms trade at a level appropriate to their economies, and so help offset the costs of imports. It does, however, leave them dependent on imports for the principal weapons systems of their armed forces.

The expanding ranks of part-producers make increasingly difficult any attempt to sustain the simple distinction from the pre-Second World War era between producer/suppliers and non-producer/recipients of arms. Even the superpowers, who come closest to the pure producer/supplier model, choose to import some arms from other producers. The part-producers, like Britain, Israel and Germany, are often simultaneously producers, suppliers and recipients. Only the still numerous group of non-producers occupy an unmixed role.

The spread of military technology to date has thus been very uneven. The military products of the technological revolution are, with some important exceptions like nuclear weapons, easily available and widely distributed. But the ability to produce advanced weapons is much more restricted, even though it has spread significantly since the Second World War. For the most part, the diffusion of arms production capability follows closely the general spread of industrialization, which is itself very uneven. This linkage supports the general argument about the close relationship between military and civil technology made in Chapter 2. Some exceptions to the rule occur when political considerations override economic ones. Because of their role in the last war, Japan, and to a lesser extent Germany and Italy, are less prominent as arms producers than might be expected from their industrial capabilities. Conversely, China, South Africa and Israel, because of the intense military and political pressure to which they have been subjected, are more prominent as arms producers than their industrial base would warrant.

The trend of a slow but steady diffusion of capability for military production seems firmly established for the future. Its product will be an increasingly complex hierarchy in which more and more states occupy mixed positions between the top-rank producers and the non-producers. Sources of supply for armaments, especially of the less sophisticated sort, seem bound to increase. The arms trade will continue to reflect the current mix of trade in both weapons and production capability, and the middle ranks will expand in number and grow in sophistication. The hierarchy of arms producers will nevertheless be maintained by the process of technological advance. Only a few states will be able to stay in the top-ranks of R&D. All the lesser producers will face a continuous challenge to the military utility and market value of their products from an ever-rising standard of technological sophistication.

The outlook for the top rank is harder to foresee with any certainty. The two current members will almost certainly retain their position. The question is whether any new powers will rise to join them. Given its industrial size and sophistication, Japan is in a position to add itself fairly quickly to the top-rank of producers should it choose to do so. Any such choice would, however, require a major reversal of Japan's anti-military policies of the last four decades. China, because of its weak industrial base, is not a candidate for top rank until some time well into the next century, although its size, location, pace of development and strong political will may give it apparent first-rank status before then.

Whether the slow and fractious movement of the Western European states towards a more integrated arms industry and foreign policy will succeed is another major question for the future shape of the top rank of producers (Bull, 1983; Lellouche, 1981; Taylor 1984; Wallace, 1984). Mounting pressure to achieve economies of scale explains both the move towards joint production projects, and the persistence of talk about a more integrated European arms industry to compete with the Americans within NATO. Neither this pressure, nor perceptions of common European security interests, has yet triumphed over the still strong traditional values of national self-reliance in arms production in the major European states, or over their rival interests as arms exporters.

## 3.5 THE ARMS TRADE LITERATURE AND ITS CONTROVERSIES

Although the spread of military technology is a broadly-based phenomenon, the major literature on it is rather narrowly cast in terms of the arms trade. The term 'arms trade' refers not just to international sales of weapons, but also to transfers of weapons on a political basis, and to the international workings of the arms industry. Several survey works exist which give good overviews of the history and the workings of the arms trade, and which look at the interests, motives, and policies of both suppliers and recipients (Cannizzo, 1980; Neuman and Harkavy, 1980; Pierre, 1982; Sampson, 1977; Stanley and Pearton, 1972). Comprehensive and up-to-date information on the trade is hard to come by. Even routine arms purchases are often considered sensitive by governments, and there is a whole world of covert transfers many of which never surface into the public domain. Two independent annual publications provide valuable registers of known deals (*Military Balance*; SIPRI Yearbook).

There is also a host of works that focus on the particular problems of the arms trade with the Third World (Benoit, 1973; Gilks and Segal, 1985; Hutchings, 1978; Leiss, Kemp *et al.*, 1970; Kemp, 1970a; McKinlay and Mughan, 1984; Oberg, 1975; Pauker *et al.*, 1973; SIPRI, 1971). This subject has almost become a distinct sub-field. It connects to the literatures on military government (Kennedy, 1974; McKinlay and Cohan, 1975; Sarkesian, 1978; Wolpin, 1972, 1978), intervention (Ayoob, 1980; Girling, 1980; Stauffer, 1974), and development (Albrecht *et al.*, 1975; Luckham, 1977a, 1977b; Whynes, 1979, ch. 8). Through, and frequently within, these literatures, concern with the arms trade to the Third World ties into the critical, and often radical, body of thought that sees the arms trade as a major disease of the international system.

Without the arms trade, however, there would be, as in the late nineteenth century, a tremendous disparity in military power between those states able to produce modern weapons, and those not. The existence of the trade enables non-producers to narrow, if not to close the gap between their own military standing and that of producer states. Despite the strong support for it from both suppliers and recipients, the arms trade arouses intense controversy. This controversy in part reflects that which generally attaches to the role of the instruments of violence in society. In part, however, it reflects the problematic mix of commercial interests with large-scale means of destruction captured by the phrase 'the merchants of death'.

In the early decades of the technological revolution – up to the First World War – the arms trade was dominated by mostly private companies like Krupp and Vickers that were the leading producers and innovators of weapons. The rather freewheeling activities of these companies and their salesmen up to 1914 created the 'merchants of death' image that caused a reaction against the arms trade during the interwar years (Noel-Baker, 1936). The free mixture of market-place morality with armaments created a commercial vested interest in the promotion of military rivalries that was later judged unacceptable on both moral and political grounds.

The solution adopted in those countries where the manufacturing companies remained in the private sector, was to bring the trade under government control, or at least supervision, by a system of export licencing (Stanley and Pearton, 1972, ch. 3). In this way, the foreign policy interests of the state would filter out the undesirable political effects of an arms trade conducted for purely commercial motives. But at this time the rising capital demands of the arms industry, and the increasing importance of high technology for military security, were anyway leading to a situation of increasing state involvement in the arms industry as monopoly or dominant buyer. The rising resource requirements for the development and production of modern weapons was also concentrating arms production into an ever smaller number of large companies. By the end of the Second World War there was thus close government involvement with the arms industry even where the industry was not formally nationalized (Pearton, 1982, pp. 177–258; Stanley and Pearton, 1972, ch. 1).

When states took control over the arms trade, they inherited responsibility for all of the pressures in the trade that had led to the 'merchants of death' image. State control did not eliminate these pressures. Instead, it ensured that they would be filtered through the political process for determining the national interest, rather than through the narrower and less politically responsible interests of individual companies. The result has been an awkward mix of economic and political interests. Although governments are more inclined than companies to consider the political consequences of their actions, they are by no means immune from the economic temptations of the arms trade in terms of employment, export earnings, and maintaining their own arms industry at a tolerable cost.

The arms trade thus still attracts criticism no less intense, and perhaps more wide-ranging, than that during the interwar period. The imposition of state control on the arms trade has not removed the suspicion that it stimulates military competition, though it has changed the form of the problem. Rather than buyers being manipulated into arms purchases by unscrupulous economic interests, concern now is more that recipients get caught up in arms races fed by political competition among supplier states, particularly the superpowers. The classic example here is the Middle East, where an intense local rivalry between Israel and the Arab states has become militarized to a very high level, partly as a result of competitive support for clients by the United States and the Soviet Union.

In a broader sense, criticism of the arms trade reflects not just concern about the stimulation of specific military rivalries, but about the way in which the whole planet has been drawn into the rivalry between the superpowers. States with virtually no industrial base, like Libya, Saudi Arabia, and Syria, are none the less lavishly equipped with the most modern weapons. They find themselves in a security environment that is not only defined by the technological standards of the leading powers, but also where those powers actively promote the diffusion of military technology through the arms trade. Looked at from this perspective, the arms trade cannot be seen simply as serving the right to equality of non-producers. It also forces them to participate in a military system that is often beyond their economic means, damaging to their political structures, and disproportionate to the security needs arising from their local environment. Participation is forced because of the security competition that is inherent in the international anarchy: states that do not keep up with the prevailing military standards make themselves vulnerable to those that do. Some critics use the term 'the world military order' to describe this situation (Kaldor, 1982, ch. 5; Kaldor and Eide, 1979).

Entanglement in the world military order is seen as adding to the already difficult economic and political problems of Third World countries. On the economic side, expenditures on modern arms clash with both the immediate welfare needs of poor populations, and with the investment needs of underdeveloped economies (Benoit, 1973; Report of the Secretary General, 1977). Establishing and maintaining a modernized military sector draws not only capital, but also skilled labour, out of struggling economies where both are in short supply (Kemp, 1970b; Neuman and Harkavy, 1980, ch. 15; SIPRI, 1971, pp. 805–9). The need to finance arms purchases can distort the whole economy away from development priorities towards exports geared to earning hard currency, especially since weapons have to be replaced periodically if the country is to maintain its military standing (Luckham, 1977a, 1977b).

On the political side, it may contribute to domination of national politics by the military in many Third World countries, and to interference by supplier states in the politics of clients. In states where government does not have well-developed social foundations, modernized armed forces can easily become the most powerful organization in the country. From such a position, the armed forces face constant temptation to intervene in politics, either to pursue their own interests, or to replace inefficient, weak or corrupt civilian governments. By encouraging development of the armed forces in weak states, the world military order may encourage the tendency towards military rule. The arms trade also provides suppliers with a channel into the armed forces of clients which may be politically significant if the armed forces are active in politics. Because modern weapons require training contacts between suppliers and recipients, many officers will have spent extensive periods in the supplier country, which therefore has a chance to shape both their attitudes and their personal contacts (Neuman and Harkavy, 1980, chs 14, 16).

It can also be argued that the world military order does not serve the military interests of Third World countries (Kaldor and Eide, 1979, pp. 7–12). It imposes on them an integrated package of military technology, doctrine and organization which was evolved to meet the needs of quite alien societies, and which may be in many respects wholly unsuited to the actual military needs of countries in the Third World. Weapons and doctrines designed to fight European-style wars are difficult to maintain in the low technology environment of many Third World countries. They heighten tensions by posing threats to neighbours, and they may be of little use against the domestic level threats that are frequently the main security problem facing governments in the Third World.

The arms trade is therefore a subject that attracts great controversy. Looked at in the broad context of the spread of military technology, it appears to be an inevitable process, and one that has the merit of moderating the huge power imbalance that would otherwise exist between producers and non-producers of weapons. Looked at in detail, it raises serious questions about the negative economic, political and military consequences for Third World countries. The negative aspects of the arms trade will always arouse controversy for both moral and political reasons. So long as there are underdeveloped states there seems likely to be a plentiful supply of cases like Iran, Uganda and Argentina to illustrate them.

Although the negative case raises many telling and important points, most of its propositions are difficult to prove in any systematic way. Conditions in developing countries cover a wide range, and it is not clear that military spending necessarily and everywhere impedes economic development (Benoit, 1973). Neither is it clear that military governments perform much differently from civil ones (Sarkesian, 1978; McKinlay and Cohan, 1975), or that the arms trade puts the military into a stronger or more disruptive position in weak states than it would be anyway. It is also not always clear that because modern weapons are sometimes ill-suited to Third World needs, they are always so. Regardless of whether or not one approves of their purposes, countries such as India, Vietnam, Egypt, Morocco and Ethiopia have made effective use of modern weapons.

# 4 The Special Case of Nuclear Proliferation

As noted in Chapter 2, nuclear proliferation is a prominent contemporary case of the diffusion of military capability. It is a special case, partly because the great destructive power of nuclear weapons puts them in a different class from other military technology, and partly because the study of nuclear proliferation has developed as a subject in its own right.

In this discussion, there is a standard distinction between *horizontal* and *vertical* proliferation. Horizontal proliferation is defined as the spread of nuclear weapons to states not previously possessing them. Vertical proliferation is defined as the increase in stockpiles of nuclear weapons by states already holding them, or the positioning of nuclear weapons in additional locations outside the territory of the nuclear power itself. Such external positioning can be in overseas bases, like the American ones in Western Europe and East Asia, or in naval vessels or aircraft that patrol outside the state's national territory. In this chapter the main focus will be on horizontal proliferation. This choice needs to be justified, because in terms of both numbers of nuclear weapons and their geographical dispersal around the planet, vertical proliferation is more significant than horizontal. There are two reasons for concentrating on horizontal proliferation: first, because the political significance of a spread of control is higher than that of a spread of numbers; and secondly, because the spread of control is widely thought to have critical negative implications for deterrence and strategic stability.

## 4.1 THE PROCESS OF PROLIFERATION

In most basic respects, the proliferation of nuclear weapons shows the same pattern of slow and uneven spread as that of military technology in general. It also shows the same linkage between civil and military technology. But in one respect, nuclear proliferation follows a distinctive pattern. The leading-edge powers have shown a much greater reluctance to allow the spread of nuclear weapons than has been the case with any previous military technology. So far as is known, there has never been any direct trade in nuclear weapons. The closest approaches to such trade have been the co-operation between the United States and Britain, and between the Soviet Union and China. The Anglo-American co-operation started during the Second World War, and flourished only after both states had independently achieved nuclear status. The brief co-operation between the Soviet Union and China during the 1950s ended when the two countries fell out politically (Baylis, 1981; Freedman, 1980b; Garthoff, 1966, chs 5, 6, 8; Simpson, 1983). More noteworthy than these two exceptions is the fact that the superpowers have devoted considerable effort, some of it co-operative, to instituting and maintaining a nuclear non-proliferation regime.

Whatever their motives, there can be no doubt that the superpowers have been anxious to retain for themselves the qualitative edge of nuclear weapons. There is doubtless a significant measure of truth in the cynical view that the superpowers oppose nuclear proliferation because they see the spread of such powerful weapons as a threat both to their own security and to their dominant position in the international system. There is at least equal truth in the view that opposition to proliferation is motivated by fear that the spread of nuclear weapons to more states will make the international system more difficult to manage, and therefore more dangerous to live in for all of its inhabitants. The worry is that more fingers on more nuclear triggers will increase the probability of nuclear weapons being used either by accident or by calculation. This fear reflects a fundamental doubt about the efficacy of deterrence in a multipolar nuclear environment. It raises basic questions about the relationship between nuclear weapons and deterrence that are taken up in Part III. Why should nuclear weapons enhance deterrence among small numbers of states and complicate it among larger numbers? Or is the problem not the numbers of states with nuclear weapons but their political character: are some states, especially those with unstable or idiosyncratic governments, less susceptible to deterrence logic than the existing nuclear powers?

The magnitude of the issues raised by nuclear proliferation means that the issue has spawned an extensive literature of its own. In part this literature relates to questions of deterrence (Dunn, 1982, ch. 4; Rosecrance, 1972; Waltz, 1981; Weltman, 1980). In part it relates to questions of arms control, especially in terms of the Non-proliferation

Treaty (NPT) of 1968, the International Atomic Energy Authority (IAEA), and the various other national and international instruments devised to support the non-proliferation regime, (Goldschmidt, 1977; Gummett, 1981; Quester, 1970; Schiff, 1984; SIPRI, 1974; Wilmshurst, 1982). In part it relates to technological issues, especially those involving the links between civil and military applications of nuclear power (Camilleri, 1977; Dorian and Spector, 1981; Greenwood, 1976; Lovins, 1980; Wohlstetter, 1977). And in part it concerns political and technological developments in those countries seen to have interests in acquiring either nuclear weapons, or a short-term option on the capability to manufacture them (Harkavy, 1981; Kapur, 1980b; Marwah and Schulz, 1975; Poneman, 1981; Quester, 1973; Yager, 1980).

This literature is rather isolated from thinking about the spread of military capability in general. Because it has developed almost as a subject in its own right, it has helped to mask awareness of the broader process of which it is a part. From reading the literature, it is easy to get the impression that nuclear proliferation is a unique problem of the post-1945 era, rather than a contemporary manifestation of a long-standing and deeply-rooted process of diffusion of military technology. It is, however, precisely the character of that broader process that makes the specific problem of nuclear proliferation so intractable.

Because there has been no direct trade in nuclear weapons, diffusion of them has taken place as a result of states acquiring the necessary knowledge, technology, and material to undertake independent manufacture. This absence of direct trade in weapons between producers and non-producers highlights the strong linkage between the civil and military sides of nuclear technology. In the nuclear field, the civil-military linkage lies primarily in the availability of fissile material, usually uranium 235 (U235) or plutonium 239 (Pu239). Neither of these materials is easy to manufacture. U235 has to be separated from the much more common uranium isotope U238, a process called 'enrichment', which cannot be achieved chemically, and which so far requires extremely costly and sophisticated technology. Pu239 does not exist naturally, but is a product of the irradiation of U238 inside a nuclear reactor. It can be chemically extracted from the fission products that are the leftovers of the fission process within a nuclear reactor. This extraction is not as demanding a task as enrichment, but it does require possession of a reactor, control over a supply of uranium, and the ability to build and run a chemical separation plant capable of handling materials that are radioactive, poisonous, corrosive, and inflammable (SIPRI, 1974; Wohlstetter, 1977).

U235 and Pu239 can serve either as reactor fuels or as fissile material for nuclear weapons. The basic design principles of nuclear weapons long ago passed into public knowledge as a result of the quite phenomenal advances in the understanding of physics made since the Second World War. Getting possession of weapons-grade fissile material is thus the principal obstacle to building one's own nuclear weapons. Most, though not all, nuclear reactors use partly-enriched uranium. The technology of enrichment is therefore part of the technology of civil nuclear power even though the level of enrichment required for weapons is much higher than that generally used for reactors. The main exception to this rule is naval propulsion reactors which need to be small, and therefore use weapons-grade enriched uranium. All reactors that burn natural or low-enriched uranium produce substantial quantities of plutonium as a byproduct. Because U238 is over 100 times more plentiful than U235, it is possible to design reactors, called 'fast breeders' that produce more fuel than they consume by converting non-fissile U238 into fissile Pu239. These reactors pose more severe technological problems than ones using uranium, and are not yet in widespread use. The prospect of them nevertheless makes recovery of Pu239 attractive, especially since the alternative is to treat it as permanent waste, which poses difficult long-term problems of disposal. The technology of reprocessing is thus also firmly embedded in the development of civil nuclear power (Patterson, 1976).

This close connection between the civil and military elements of nuclear technology has made trade in civil nuclear technology a possible mechanism for the proliferation of nuclear weapons. Without trade, many of those countries that now possess all or part of the equipment for generating nuclear power would not be in the nuclear game at all. Nuclear technology is still not too far from the leading edge of current capabilities in an advanced industrial society. Purely indigenous development of it requires an industrial base of a size and sophistication possessed by relatively few countries. Because trade in civil nuclear technology has generally been seen as legitimate, it has served to spread widely the knowledge, skills, technologies, and materials that provide the necessary foundation for a military nuclear option. Although direct trade in nuclear weapons has not occurred, the trade in civil nuclear technology has successfully transplanted varying degrees of production capability in many countries.

The detailed story of civil nuclear power is beyond the scope of this book, and is easily available elsewhere (Bupp, 1981; Burn, 1978; Patterson, 1976). The trade in civil nuclear technology boomed after 1973, when the oil crisis made nuclear energy seem both economically and politically attractive. Civil energy requirements provided a powerful independent justification for trade in nuclear technology, and like the arms industry, they generated a buyer's market. Major suppliers like the United States, France and West Germany, and minor ones like Canada and Switzerland, competed fiercely to meet demand from a wide variety of countries hit hard by the rise in oil prices. Because supply was in excess of demand, again like the arms industry, transfer of production capability often became a way of winning contracts. The most spectacular example of this tendency was the 1975 deal in which West Germany agreed to equip Brazil with a complete nuclear industry, including technology for enrichment and reprocessing (Gall, 1976). The case of Pakistan illustrates an equally interesting aspect of the civil-military link through trade. Denied the right to purchase a reprocessing plant directly from France, Pakistan organized the covert piecemeal purchase of component parts for an enrichment facility. The ruse worked well enough before it was discovered to give Pakistan the makings of a limited enrichment capability (Kapur, 1980; Khalizad, 1979; Sen Gupta, 1983).

The burgeoning of the trade in civil nuclear power technology transformed the whole problem of nuclear proliferation. Prior to the 1970s, the problem had seen primarily in terms of decisions to acquire nuclear weapons by countries such as West Germany, Japan and Sweden, which already possessed an advanced industrial economy. Such countries were capable of making their decision on the basis of their own resources. The dominant model of proliferation at this time reflected the existing history, which showed a record of states proceeding directly to military applications of nuclear energy. In all of the early nuclear powers – the United States, the Soviet Union, Britain, France, and China – military developments preceded civil ones. But after 1973, the problem came to be seen more in terms of less developed countries using civil nuclear technologies as the basis for a military option. The defining example for this model was India, which possessed the most long-standing, advanced, and best domestically-rooted civil nuclear programme outside the industrialized states. The testing of a nuclear device by India in 1974 showed how easy it was for a civil nuclear programme to act as the foundation for a military option. The fact that the Indian government labelled the device a 'peaceful nuclear explosion' (PNE) only underlined the connection between civil and military nuclear technology that was at the heart of the proliferation problem (Marwah, 1977; Rao and Imai, 1974).

The civil route to military nuclear status quite changed the character of nuclear proliferation. Formal arrival at military nuclear status became less important than it had been for the first five nuclear powers. Instead, attention focused on shrinking the *lead time*: the length of time between the decision to acquire nuclear weapons, and the ability actually to test or deploy them. The way to achieve such shrinkage was to acquire those elements of civil nuclear technology – particularly enrichment or reprocessing – that could provide fissile material for military applications. By doing so, a state could achieve the status of a 'threshold' nuclear power: not publicly possessing nuclear weapons, but clearly in a position to do so quickly. Threshold status was attractive to several states. It enabled them to get some of the benefits of nuclear weapon status without either violating non-proliferation norms or paying the cost of deployment. India, Israel and South Africa have all adopted threshold policies, and Israel is commonly assumed to have stockpiled nuclear weapons without either testing them or admitting to their existence. Pakistan appears to be heading for a threshold option, and so, in a rather quieter way, do Brazil and Argentina (Betts, 1979; Freedman, 1975; Harkavy, 1981; Husain, 1982; Marwah, 1981; Yager, 1980).

## 4.2  CONTROLLING PROLIFERATION

The linkage between civil and military technology in the nuclear field considerably complicates the attempt to control the spread of nuclear weapons. Because civil nuclear technology has an independent legitimacy, it is neither practicable nor politically acceptable to try to confine all nuclear technology to the relatively small group of states capable of producing it. Indeed, so strong has been both 'supply push' and 'demand pull' in favour of the right to trade in civil nuclear power technology, that the major international elements of the non-proliferation regime explicitly enshrine it. The NPT is based on a tradeoff by which those states that renounce nuclear weapons do so in return for the right of access to civil nuclear technology. The IAEA is obliged by its charter to promote the use of civil nuclear technology, as well as ensuring that civil technology is not used for military purposes. During the mid-1970s, the supplier states agreed amongst themselves to restrict exports of the sensitive technologies (enrichment and reprocessing) (*Strategic Survey*, 1975, 1976, 1977), but there has certainly been no general attempt to stop the diffusion of civil nuclear power.

The problem of non-proliferation is thus determined by conditions in which the restrictions on trade in nuclear weapons are substantially undermined by a regime which promotes the spread of civil nuclear technology. So long as civil nuclear power remains attractive in its own right, it will be politically impossible to undo this situation. There is some possibility that the attraction of civil nuclear power will succumb to the problems within the industry. Concern about the high costs, environmental problems, and political opposition that attended the construction and operation of the reactors of the mid-1970s boom were powerfully reinforced by the massive escape of radiation from Chernobyl in 1986. But short of the unlikely collapse of the civil nuclear power industry, non-proliferation can only be pursued by measures designed to block or deter the use of civil technology for military purposes.

Such measures lie at the heart of the IAEA safeguard system, which is the mainstay of nearly all non-proliferation agreements (IAEA, 1978; Imber, 1980, 1982). The safeguard system provides an accounting check on fissile materials for civil use. Its purpose is to create a climate of reassurance among states with civil nuclear facilities that fissile materials are not being diverted for military use. The IAEA system works well in a limited way. Nevertheless, several threshold states have facilities outside its jurisdiction, and it does nothing to prevent the continued diffusion of militarily significant civil nuclear capability. Safeguards deter large-scale clandestine abuses of civil nuclear facilities for military purposes. But the system carries no sanctions, and offers no physical restraint to a state that is unembarrassed about turning its civil nuclear capabilities into military assets. Such states are restrained only by the fear of what international reaction might be to such a move. Options range from pre-emptive attacks like those made by Israel against Iraq, even though the Iraqi facilities were under safeguards (Feldman, 1982;

Herzig, 1983), to the threats of withdrawal of aid that the United States has made against Pakistan if it conducts a nuclear test.

Although nuclear proliferation clearly deserves its status as a special case of the spread of military technology, it has produced results not markedly different from that of military technology in general. In nuclear technology, a hierarchy of full-producers, part-producers, and non-producers exists which is similar in form to that for conventional armaments, and which appears to share the same future of a trend towards expansion of the middle ranks. The process of diffusion of nuclear weapons has been slower than expected by some observers (Beaton, 1966), and certainly slower than the spread of conventional arms. A small number of states may have had their nuclear ambitions hampered by restrictions on direct trade in weapons, and by the superpower-led campaign against horizontal proliferation: Libya, for example, is reputed to have tried to buy nuclear weapons from China. The imposed restraints of the non-proliferation regime must, however, be seen against the background of other compelling reasons for states to doubt whether nuclear weapons would improve their national security. As illustrated by the experience of Britain and France, the cost of nuclear weapons and their delivery systems threatens the balance of other items in the military budget. Acquiring nuclear weapons may open up counterproductive military competitions, as it seems to have done between the superpowers. Going nuclear raises the risks if war does occur, and at least in its early stages, might invite preventive attacks like that of Israel on Iraq.

But although the horizontal spread of nuclear weapons has so far been quite limited, the diffusion of the technology necessary for their production has kept pace with that in the conventional weapons sector. It can thus be said that the nuclear weapons potential of the international system has increased markedly. As ever more states arrive at threshold status, the potential for rapid horizontal proliferation increases. This situation contrasts with that of previous decades when technological constraints would have made any rush to acquire nuclear weapons quite slow to bear fruit. In theory, greater nuclear weapons potential worsens the so-called '$n$th country problem', which is the fear that some single country will, by acquiring nuclear weapons, trigger a cascade of acquisition by previously non-nuclear weapon states. The '$n$' here refers to the unknown number that this country would occupy in the historical sequence of states that have become nuclear powers.

The theory of the 'nth country' is, however, much clearer than the practice, and the future of nuclear weapons proliferation is impossible to predict with any certainty. The firmest trend has been vertical proliferation by the existing nuclear powers. There is as much possibility that the superpowers will continue to expand their already vast nuclear stockpiles as that they will agree to reduce them. There is a near certainty that France and China will increase their nuclear arsenals. Whether Britain does or not is still a matter of intense political controversy.

The impact of vertical proliferation on horizontal is mixed, and therefore uncertain. On the one hand, vertical proliferation legitimizes nuclear weapons, and increases the incentives for rising powers to seek nuclear status. The demonstration effect of superpower deterrence cannot help but encourage nuclear aspirations among lesser powers. Nuclear deterrence among the great powers is therefore fundamentally at odds with the attempt to promote non-proliferation among the lesser powers that are outside the system of superpower nuclear guarantees. But on the other hand, vertical proliferation adds to what are already compelling reasons for many states to be hesitant about joining the ranks of the nuclear powers. It raises the costs of becoming a first-class nuclear power beyond the reach of all but a very few states, and faces possible aspirants like India with an endless and expensive treadmill of technological competition at the leading edge (Sen Gupta, 1983, ch. 1). If the superpowers reduced their own nuclear arsenals in line with article 6 of the NPT, they would reverse the demonstration effect only at the risk of making entry to the club cheaper and easier (Bull, 1980, pp. 19–21).

Whether the spreading capability for making nuclear weapons will actually be translated into military hardware remains an open question. Nuclear technology illustrates perfectly the close links between civil and military technology, and therefore the general problem of military potential latent in any industrial society. These links give depth to the impact of military technology on international relations in general, and in the case of nuclear weapons, underlie several key elements in the debates about deterrence.

# Part II

# Strategic Rivalry and Military Technology: the Arms Dynamic

# 5 Arms Racing and the Arms Dynamic

## 5.1 CONTROVERSIES ABOUT THE TERM 'ARMS RACING'

Perhaps the most obvious impact of military technology on international relations is the problem widely, but often inaccurately, referred to as 'arms racing'. The term arms racing suggests a self-stimulating military rivalry between states in which their efforts to defend themselves militarily cause them to enhance the threats they pose to each other. In other words, given the political condition of anarchy, states are vulnerable to a type of competition with each other in which military technology is a major independent variable. As was argued in Part I, military technology has its own historical dynamic of qualitative advance and geopolitical spread. The idea of arms racing thus suggests that the dynamic of military technology is in major part responsible for one of the central problems in relations between states.

There have been several attempts to define arms racing. Steiner, for example, defines it as 'repeated, competitive, and reciprocal adjustments of their war-making capacities' between 'two nations or two sets of nations' (Steiner, 1973, p. 5). Huntington defines it as 'a progressive, competitive peacetime increase in armaments by two states or coalitions of states resulting from conflicting purpose or mutual fears' (Huntington, 1958, p. 41). Bull defines it as 'intense competition between opposed powers or groups of powers, each trying to achieve an advantage in military power by increasing the quantity or improving the quality of its armaments or armed forces' (Bull, 1961, p. 5). In what is the most subtle and well-thought-through attempt, Gray defines it as 'two or more parties perceiving themselves to be in an adversary relationship, who are increasing or improving their armaments at a *rapid* rate and structuring their respective military postures with a *general* attention to the past, current, and anticipated military and political behaviour of the other parties' (Gray, 1971a, p. 40). All of these definitions suggest that arms racing is an abnormally intense condition in relations between

69

states reflecting either or both of active political rivalry, and mutual fear of the other's military potential. The problem with the concept is how to distinguish this abnormal condition from the norm of self-defence behaviour under conditions of anarchy.

Although arms racing is a central concept in strategic thinking, ambiguity about the boundary between normal and abnormal conditions makes it one of the least well understood, and most widely misused, ideas in the field. Not surprisingly, opinion about it is highly divided. Some scholars find the term so vague and problematic that they advocate avoiding it as far as possible (Bellany, 1975, p. 129), a position apparently also taken by the authors of a widely used textbook in which arms racing gets no chapter of its own, and does not even rate a mention in the index (Baylis *et al.*, 1975). The inclination to reject the term stems partly from the lack of any agreed understanding about what it means, and partly from the effective politicization of its negative image by those campaigning against militarism. The ambiguity of the term makes it applicable, at a stretch, to the whole process by which states maintain military capability. Its negative connotations therefore make it politically useful as a broad brush with which to denigrate the entire process of national defence. Political usage of the term encourages broad interpretation, and so makes it difficult to use with any precision even when a concise definition is offered.

At the other extreme stands a large body of opinion, both academic and lay, that sees arms racing not only as a major problem of international relations, but also as a fundamental dilemma of the whole attempt to seek national security through military means (Noel-Baker, 1958; Prins, 1984; Thompson and Smith, 1980). Many, though not all, who take this view would identify themselves with the field of Peace Research or with peace movements. Arms races have preceded the last two World Wars, and there are widespread fears that the contemporary race seen to be going on between the superpowers is the build-up to a Third World War. Arms racing is seen as a dangerous phenomenon in which the effects of individual state policies for military security are cumulatively self-defeating for the security interests of all states. From this perspective, arms racing is not only a phenomenon in need of study, and a problem in need of remedy, but also a basis for taking a critical view of the whole strategic approach to international relations.

In between these two extremes, and to some extent blending into them, lies a substantial academic literature on arms racing. Part of this literature takes the form of attempts to construct mathematical models of arms racing (Busch, 1970; Luterbacher, 1975; McGuire, 1965; Richardson, 1960; Saaty, 1968). Another part consists of broad discussions of the phenomenon, like the one that follows here, which attempt to explain the mechanisms, motives and definitions that underlie the concept (Baugh, 1984, ch. 3; Brown, 1973; Gray, 1971a, 1974, 1976; Huntington, 1958; Joynt, 1964; Russett, 1983b, chs 3–5). The rest consists of case studies, most commonly of the arms race between the United States and the Soviet Union (Holist, 1977; Kurth, 1973; Nacht, 1975; Thee, 1986; Wohlstetter, 1974), but also of historical (Steiner, 1973) and regional ones (Rattinger, 1976).

Regardless of whether one embraces the concept or rejects it, arms racing lies at the heart of what Strategic Studies is about: the way the instruments of force affect relations among the states that possess them. This centrality is evinced by the fact that arms racing connects to so many of the main subjects within Strategic Studies. Arms racing is inseparable from the broader subject of military technology that occupies so much of contemporary strategic literature. The notion of qualitative advance in military technology is basic to any understanding of modern arms racing. The diffusion of military technology is also an important determinant of the conditions within which arms races occur. Arms racing connects to war through the widespread, though strongly challenged, hypothesis that the two phenomena are causally related (Diehl, 1983; Howard, 1985, pp. 2–3; Intrilligator and Brito, 1984; Lambelet, 1975; Wallace, 1979, 1980, 1982). It connects to deterrence because the maintenance of a deterrence relationship does not seem to be possible without a form of institutionalized arms race (Gillespie *et al.*, 1979; Hoag, 1962; Kugler *et al.*, 1980; McGuire, 1968; Mandelbaum, 1981, ch. 5; Thee, 1986, ch. 4). Much of the discussion about disarmament is based on a problem defined in terms of arms racing, and arms racing plays a major role as the referent problem for thinking about both arms control and non-provocative forms of defence (Allison and Morris, 1975; Galtung, 1984b). Like the arms trade, arms racing links to subjects outside Strategic Studies such as economic development. Inasmuch as arms racing is about the political, and not just the military, relations between states, it also has important lines of contact with work in the broader field of International Relations (Waltz, 1979, ch. 8).

In the next four chapters the view is taken that it is worth trying

to make sense of arms racing as a concept. To abandon it because of
its complexities and ambiguities would be to lose one of the central
contributions that Strategic Studies can make to the broader
understanding of conflict in the international system. It would also
be to lose the ability to participate in the public debate. Whatever
its problems, the idea of arms racing identifies an important element
in relations between states that is distinct from other political and
economic sources of conflict and co-operation. If the term has
become too ambiguous, then it should be clarified. If it has been
hijacked by partisans within the political debate about war and
peace, then it should be reclaimed for the purposes of analysis.


## 5.2   THE ARMS DYNAMIC: AN ALTERNATIVE
FRAMEWORK FOR ANALYSIS

The charge against arms racing that it is too ambiguous to be a
useful concept has a lot of weight. One of the striking things about
the literature on the topic is that much of the subject matter does
not fit comfortably within the metaphor of a race (Buzan, 1983,
pp. 194ff.). The idea of a *race* suggests two or more states
strenuously engaged in a competition to accumulate military strength
against each other. It also suggests that winning is the object of the
exercise in terms of one party achieving a decisive change in the
balance of military power. Much of the literature, however, is about
the general process by which states create armed forces and keep
their equipment up to date. The competition involved in this process
may not be strenuous, and the objective may not be decisive victory
(Buzan, 1983, pp. 194–6). While these two subjects are clearly
related, they are not the same. Arms racing implies a notably
intense process of military competition that contrasts with whatever
passes for normality in military relations between states not at war
with each other. If the term arms racing is broadened to include all
peacetime military relations, then it loses its ability to label
abnormally intense military competition. If it is confined to the
narrower meaning, then we need both another term to identify
normal military relations among states, and definitional criteria to
clarify the boundary between normal relations and arms racing.

The temptation to use the broadest meaning is strong for the
political reasons suggested above. The broad meaning also avoids
the difficult analytical problem of distinguishing between normal

relations and abnormal ones. The one sound reason for adopting the broader meaning is that it draws attention to armaments as an independent global phenomenon, a perspective whose validity was explored in Part I. In other words, if we assume as normal an international system in which independent states possess armed forces with which to pursue political goals, then we can also say that armaments will have their own pattern of development within that system. That pattern has a distinctive effect on relations between states: it interacts with, but is separate from, the other elements that shape international relations.

In order to capture the full range of what needs to be discussed here, some new terms need to be adopted and used systematically. There is an especially strong need to find a term for the normal condition of military relations in an anarchic system, because it is the absence of such a term that has facilitated the over-extended use of arm racing. If we find a term for the normal condition of military relations, then we also need a term to describe the whole phenomenon including both normal behaviour and arms racing. In what follows, the term *arms dynamic*, which has some currency in the literature (Thee, 1986, ch. 5), is used to refer to the whole set of pressures that make states both acquire armed forces and change the quantity and quality of the armed forces they already possess. The term is used not only to refer to a general global process, but also to enquire into the circumstances of particular states or sets of states. One can refer, therefore to the arms dynamic between the superpowers, or one can ask how the arms dynamic affects a single state like Sweden. The terms *arms racing* is reserved for the most extreme manifestations of the arms dynamic, when the pressures are such as to lead states into major competitive expansions of military capability. The term *maintenance of the military status quo* is used to express the normal operation of the arms dynamic. Maintenance of the military status quo and arms racing can be used to describe either the activity of a single state, or the character of a relationship between two or more states.

Arms racing and maintenance of the military status quo relate to each other as extremes of a spectrum. Maintenance of the military status quo can escalate into arms racing, and arms racing can subside into maintenance of the military status quo. Between the two lies a gray area in which the direction of change may be a more appropriate guide to events than any attempt to locate a given case on one side or the other of some strict but arbitrary dividing line.

Occasionally, one can find instances where one state increases its military strength without attracting a response, such as when the United States began to build up its navy during the late nineteenth century (Huntington, 1958, pp. 41–2). Such cases of *arms build-up* depend on unusual geographical or political conditions, and are therefore rare. If sustained, they eventually lead to arms racing. If they taper off, they lead to maintenance of the military status quo.

Because arms racing and maintenance of the military status quo are manifestations of the same over-all arms dynamic, they share many characteristics, and differ more in degree than in kind. On the basis of these definitions, what is needed in order to clarify the subject is not just a model of arms racing, but a model of the arms dynamic as a whole. Such a model would have the advantage of retaining the important distinctive meaning of arms racing, while at the same time opening up the vital issue of armaments as an independent global phenomenon. It would avoid the vagueness and the political entanglements of too broad a usage of arms racing.

Most of the attempts to understand arms racing have been made in terms of models of the processes that induce states to increase their military strength, but these models can be applied to the arms dynamic as a whole. Two models dominate the literature. The first is the classical *action-reaction model*, which looks for the driving force of the arms dynamic in the competitive relations between states. The second can be called the *domestic structure model*. This seeks to locate the driving force of the arms dynamic in the internal economic, organizational and political workings of states. A third model, the *technological imperative*, will be added to these. It interprets the arms dynamic in terms of the general process of qualitative advance in technology explored in Part I. The term 'technological imperative' has been used by others, but usually in a narrower sense, more in line with what will be counted here as domestic structure (Thee, 1986, pp. 16–20). These three models are additive rather than mutually exclusive, though the process of establishing the domestic structure model in the face of action-reaction orthodoxy produced some attacks and defences that come close to casting the two in a mutually exclusive light (Allison and Morris, 1975; Nincic, 1982, chs 2–3).

These models are the subject of the next three chapters. They represent a step towards explanatory theories about the arms dynamic. The historical evidence does not suggest that any one of them is more correct than the others, or that they can be arranged in a permanent hierarchy of explanatory power. The relevant debate is thus not so much about which one is better in some absolute sense. It is about the weight that each should be given in explaining any specific case.

# 6 The Action-Reaction Model

The action-reaction model is the classical view of arms racing, and provides the basis for the metaphor of a race. Most attempts to define arms racing are rooted in it. The basic proposition of the action-reaction model is that states strengthen their armaments because of the threats they perceive from other states. The theory implicit in the model explains the arms dynamic as driven primarily by factors external to the state. An action by any state to increase its military strength will raise the level of threat seen by other states and cause them to react by increasing their own strength (Rathjens, 1973). In theory this process also works in reverse. If states are driven to arm by external threats, then domestic economic pressures to apply resources to other items on the political agenda should lead them to disarm in proportion to reductions in military capability by others. Whether in fact the logic of action-reaction works with equal facility in both directions has important implications for the logic of disarmament discussed in Chapter 15.

The action-reaction model posits something like an international market in military strength. States will arm themselves either to seek security against the threats posed by others, or to increase their power to achieve political objectives against the interests of others. Balances will be struck at higher or lower levels of armament depending on how willing states are to drive up the price of achieving military security. Counterpressure to open-ended arms competition is created both by the responses of other states to attempts by one to increase its military power, and by domestic resource constraints.

The definitive illustration for the action-reaction model is the much studied naval arms race between Britain and Germany before the First World War (Berghahn, 1973; Herwig, 1980; Kennedy, 1980; Marder, 1961, esp. chs 6 and 7; Steinberg, 1965; Steiner, 1973; Woodward, 1935). In this case, Germany provided the initiating action by deciding to build a major navy, and Britain reacted in order to preserve its position as the leading naval power. Britain was able to contain the challenge by outbuilding the German naval programme, first in terms of quality, by introducing a more powerful type of battleship known as *Dreadnought*, and later, in terms of the quantity of Dreadnoughts constructed. For nearly a decade before the outbreak of war this arms race produced clear instances of the action-reaction dynamic in terms of Germany copying British design innovations, and Britain deciding its annual naval construction programme on the basis set by the rate of warship building in Germany.

The action-reaction model does not depend on the process by which technological innovation causes continuous improvement in military technology. But if such innovation exists, it certainly becomes part of the action-reaction dynamic. Even if the quality of military technology was static, and evenly distributed in the international system, the action-reaction process could still be the mechanism by which states competed militarily in purely quantitative terms. Increases in the number of soldiers or battleships in one state would still create pressure for responsive increases in other states. For this reason, the action-reaction model can more easily be applied than the other two to cases that occurred before the onset of the industrial revolution (Joynt, 1964, pp. 24–5). At least one author takes the view that arms racing has only become a distinctive international phenomenon since the industrial revolution unleashed the forces of mass production and institutionalized innovation into the international system (Huntington, 1958, pp. 41, 43). The importance of this insight will be developed in Chapter 8.

The action-reaction model stems primarily from the anarchic political structure of the international system: each state is a potential threat to others, and so each has to take measures to ensure its own survival, independence and welfare against encroachments by others. Anarchy at the level of the international system is therefore a form of political relations that tends to produce military competition among states along action-reaction lines. When the competition reflects a power struggle between states, as before both recent world wars, it can be intense and highly focused. Power struggles usually reflect an attempt by one or more states to increase their influence and control in the international system at the expense of others already well entrenched. They are thus likely to produce arms races in which the revisionist states hope to change their status either by winning the race without fighting, or by building up their military strength for a war with the status quo powers.

Even when there is no specific power struggle, or only a weak one, the action-reaction process still works at the level of maintenance of the military status quo. States will always have some sense of who they consider to be possible sources of attack even when they see the probability of war as being low. This perception will ensure an element of action-reaction in defence policy, albeit of a much more subdued kind than in an arms race. For maintenance of the military status quo as for arms racing, action-reaction expresses itself not only in the size of armed forces, but also in the type of forces acquired, and the level of concern about modernization and readiness for combat.

The action-reaction model therefore applies to the arms dynamic as a whole. One can see it working in specific cases like the Anglo-German naval race, where political rivalry generates a power struggle and an arms race. And one can see it working more generally in the international system, where the insecurity of life in the anarchy requires states to maintain armed forces at a level heavily influenced by the strength of other states. In reality, there is considerable blending of power and security motives in the behaviour of states. Most military instruments can be used for offensive as well as defensive purposes. It is therefore difficult for any state to distinguish between measures other states take to defend themselves and measures they may be taking to increase their capability for aggression. Because the consequences of being wrong may be very severe, the dictates of prudence pressure each state to adjust its own military measures in response to a worst-case view of the measures taken by others. Since each adjustment is seen by other states as a possible threat, even a system in which all states seek only their own defence will tend to produce competitive accumulations of military strength.

The set of circumstances that produces this tendency is known as the *security dilemma* (Buzan, 1983, ch. 7; Herz, 1950, 1951, 1959, 231–43. It is a dilemma because states cannot easily take measures to strengthen their own security without making others feel less secure. If others feel less secure they will take countermeasures that will negate the measures taken by the first state. That state in turn will feel pressured to restore its preferred ratio of strength by further increases in its own armaments. The logic of the security dilemma is thus closely related to that of the action-reaction model.

The idea of the action-reaction model is simple, but its operation in practice is complex. The basic model illustrates the conceptual simplicity. It contains two states A and B. A starts the process by increasing its strength, say, by adding 50 000 men to its army. B perceives this as a threat, and reacts by increasing the size of its own army, perhaps by more than 50 000 if it sees A's move as raising the probability of war. A can either accept the new balance at the now higher level of armament, or react to B's increase with a further increase of its own (Kodzic, 1975, p. 204). The pattern repeats until one side gives up, or a new balance acceptable to both is reached, or the issue is resolved by war. In this model there is a clear initiator (A), an uncomplicated two-party relationship (A and B), a clear and similar idiom that is the same on both sides (numbers of men), and a clearly differentiated sequence of moves (A, then B, then A). The model says little about motives other than that each side feels threatened by the other. Neither does it indicate whether the two actors are aware of, and seeking to control, the process in which they are engaged.

In reality, however, the only thing that may be clear is the general fact that the behaviour of states is driven by their sense of external threat. The specific details of the action-reaction process between states may be difficult to identify. This point needs to be considered in detail, because the validity of the action-reaction model is widely questioned on the grounds that its specific process is often difficult to see in relations between the superpowers. First the *idiom* of action and reaction will be examined: that is to say, the types of action that states can take within the process. Then other variables in the pattern of response can be identified, particularly magnitude, timing, and the awareness of the actors of the process in which they are engaged. Finally, it is necessary to look at the motives of the actors, which can have a considerable influence on the other variables in the action-reaction process. The action-reaction model is the best place to consider motives, because it is the one in which the conscious behaviour of actors is given the largest scope. Both the domestic structure and the technological imperative models are more structural in orientation. They give greater weight to the movement of large events by a myriad of unco-ordinated, incremental actions in the layers of social and political organization below the top political leadership.

## 6.1 THE IDIOM OF ACTION-REACTION

The idiom of action and reaction can take many different forms. The simplest is like that of the pre-1914 naval race, where two states compete in terms of a single, similar weapon system, and where the strength of the rivals can be compared directly because the weapons are designed to fight each other. Action and reaction in terms of the same weapon system can also be seen between the superpowers in terms of intercontinental ballistic missiles (ICBMs). In this case, though, the picture is complicated by the fact that, while some ICBMs are intended to fight each other, most are intended for bombardment of other targets. The idiom may be in terms of dissimilar weapons systems, or sets of systems, such as anti-submarine, anti-aircraft or anti-missile systems versus submarines, bombers and missiles. In such cases the calculation of relative strengths is much more difficult because of the large uncertainties that always surround estimates of how different, but opposed, weapons will work in combat. The idiom may not be single weapon systems, but instead be in terms of the over-all arsenals of states, with each trying to measure its general warfighting capability in terms of that of the other (Baugh, 1984, ch. 4; Rattinger, 1976). The difficulty of making such estimates is illustrated by the interminable debates within the North Atlantic Treaty Organization (NATO) about what force levels are necessary to deter or defeat a Soviet invasion of Western Europe (Bundy *et al.*, 1982; Rogers, 1982).

If the idiom is armed forces, then the distinction between qualitative and quantitative factors becomes important (Gray, 1971a, pp. 46–8; Huntington, 1958, pp. 65–89). States will compare not only the numbers of their weapons, but also their quality. If quality is even, then numbers are crucial, but if one side has a qualitative edge, then numbers may matter less. The Germans, for example, had a qualitative edge in 1914 in terms of the speed with which they could mobilize their army. This edge enabled them to offset the large numbers of troops possessed by their opponents, especially Russia. For a time during the late 1940s and 1950s the United States was able to use its qualitative edge in nuclear weapons to offset the larger Soviet armies deployed in central Europe.

In an environment of sustained technological advance, qualitative factors will always be present in a military balance, and the action-reaction dynamic will usually have both a qualitative and a quantitative dimension. This mix is illustrated by the endless discussions about the balance of strategic missiles. Raw numbers are important, as indicated by the setting of various ceilings in the Strategic Arms Limitation Talks (SALT) and other arms control negotiations. Yet qualitative factors such as accuracy, throw-weight, survivability, and numbers of warheads carried have also been major elements in the attempt to assess, and regulate, the military balance between the superpowers. Huntington makes the interesting argument that qualitative arms races are less war-prone than quantitative ones. His logic is that increases of quantity provide a known ability to fight, whereas constant changes in quality both undermine the value of quantitative accumulation and increase the difficulty of calculating the outcome of a resort to arms (Huntington, 1958, pp. 71–9).

When the action-reaction dynamic is in terms of over-all military strength, then defence expenditure may become in itself an idiom of interaction. It may also serve as a measure of the interaction (Holist, 1977). Attempts to use expenditure as a measure of the action-reaction dynamic between the United States and the Soviet Union have not met with much success (Fewtrell, 1983, p. 11; Kugler *et al.*, 1980; Russett, 1983b, pp. 17–18). As will be seen later, this quantitative approach has been central to the attempt to formulate a mathematical model for arms racing.

When reliable data can be obtained, defence expenditure is perhaps more useful to indicate the difference between arms racing and maintenance of the military status quo, than it is to measure a specific action-reaction dynamic between states. For this purpose, absolute levels of defence expenditure are less important than defence expenditure expressed as a percentage of the gross national product (GNP). If defence expenditure is a constant or declining percentage of GNP, then one is probably observing maintenance of the military status quo, especially where GNP itself tends to rise at a steady, but not spectacular, rate. Although absolute amounts spent will tend to rise, the increase will mostly reflect the rising costs of modern weapons compared with the older generations they replace. But if defence expenditure is rising as a percentage of GNP, then the state is increasing the level of its military activity at the expense of its other activities. Such an increase cannot be sustained indefinitely. Its appearance indicates either a shift away from maintenance of the military status quo towards arms racing, or else a state caught in the squeeze of economic growth too weak to support its desired range of defence commitments. Although very useful as an indicator of the intensity of the arms dynamic, the measure of defence expenditure as a percentage of GNP has to be used with caution. Different rates of growth can have a large impact on interpretation of the figures. Slow or static growth of the figure in a rapidly expanding economy like Japan's may disguise a considerable military expansion. A rise in the figure for a static or slow-moving economy like Britain's may indicate more a holding action than an expansion of military capability.

The idiom of action-reaction can take a variety of other forms, economic and political, as well as military. So long as the idiom remains military, the process is still within the arms dynamic. Action and reaction options other than increases in military strength or expenditure are available. States can, for example, change the deployment patterns of their armed forces in ways that make them more threatening and/or less vulnerable to an opponent. The stationing of long-range theatre nuclear weapons (LRTNW) by NATO in Europe, and the deployment of missile submarines off the North American coast by the Soviet Union, are examples of forward deployments that are part of the action-reaction dynamic. A decision to adopt a launch-on-warning (LoW) policy for ICBMs might also be a response to increases in the attacking strength of one's opponent.

States can also change their strategic doctrine in response to actions by an opponent. Such doctrines are a key element in actual military strength, as the Germans demonstrated with their imaginative use of *Blitzkrieg* in the early years of the Second World War. Changes in doctrine, like the American shift towards warfighting strategies of deterrence starting in the 1970s, can carry just as much weight in the eyes of an opponent as increases or decreases in the size and quality of armed forces (Brown, 1973, pp. 12–15; Gray, 1976, p. 7; Lambeth, 1981).

When the idiom moves into the economic and political domains, the action-reaction process of the arms dynamic joins the more general one of foreign policy, and the subject shifts from Strategic Studies to International Relations. The area of overlap cannot be ignored. Restrictions on trade may become part of the action-reaction process, as in the longstanding attempts by NATO to prevent militarily useful civil technologies like computers from reaching the Soviet Union. General shifts in perception, and therefore in the character of political relations, also play an important role in the action-reaction process. Shifts towards (or away from) more negative and hostile views of an opponent can mark a major shift towards (or away from) arms racing within the arms dynamic. Such a shift occurred in Britain towards Germany during the late 1930s, and in the United States towards the Soviet

Union during the mid-1940s. A political 'action' may also trigger a military 'reaction', as when states increase their military strength in response to an unleashing of revolutionary energy in a rival. Similarly, an increase in military strength may follow as a response to the use of force by one's opponent in such a way as to suggest that the probability of conflict is rising. The move towards higher military spending in the United States during the early 1980s can be interpreted in part along these lines as a reaction to the use of force by the Soviet Union in Afghanistan. This kind of interplay is where the arms dynamic blends into the broader political patterns of foreign relations.

One cannot assume that states will display *consistency* in the idiom of their actions and reactions: in other words, that their responses will be made in the same idiom as the actions that triggered them. The Soviet response to the large-scale deployment of ICBMs by the United States during the early 1960s was consistent: the Soviet Union deployed large numbers of ICBMs in the late 1960s and early 1970s. But the Soviet response to the earlier deployment by the United States of large numbers of bombers was not consistent: the Soviets built anti-aircraft defences and pushed development of ICBMs. The current American response to the Soviet build-up of ICBMs is also not consistent. Instead of adding to its own ICBM numbers, the United States is trying to open up the new technology of strategic defence. Consistent responses are more likely when the rate of technological innovation is low, and when the weapons concerned are ones that can be expected to fight each other, such as tanks, battleships and fighter aircraft. Non-consistent responses are more likely when technological innovation offers opportunities to degrade the effectiveness of existing weapons systems. They are also more likely when existing defensive capability looks more attractive than a matching offensive capability, or when resource constraints force one side to take unorthodox measures to stay in the competition. An example of the latter was when the Soviet Union deployed missiles in Cuba in 1962. Non-consistent responses tend to make the calculation of relative strengths more difficult.

## 6.2 THE VARIABLES OF MAGNITUDE, TIMING AND AWARENESS IN THE ACTION-REACTION PROCESS

To the variety of idioms in which the dialogue of the arms dynamic can be pursued must be added the variables that attend the process of action-reaction itself. These variables are: *magnitude*, in terms of what proportion the reaction bears to the triggering action; *timing*, in terms of the speed and sequence of interaction; and *awareness*, in terms of the extent to which the parties involved in the process are conscious of their impact on each other, and whether they govern their own behaviour in the light of that consciousness. As with idiom, these variables are almost always more complicated in reality than they are in the basic models of the action-reaction process. In addition, as Gray warns (1976, ch. 3), there is a persistent danger in the analysis of the arms dynamic of falling into the assumption that one's opponent is a mirror image of oneself in terms of the perceptions, reasoning and political structures that underlie actions. Such an assumption can lead to serious errors of analysis and prediction.

### 6.2.1  Magnitude

The magnitude of possible reactions within the arms dynamic covers a wide range. In theory, the reacting state can respond by outdoing its opponent, by matching it, by making a lesser move, by ignoring it, or by reducing its own strength (Buzan, 1983, pp. 194–6; Gray, 1971a, pp. 59–65). The prudent logic of the security dilemma, and even more so that of overt power struggles, suggests that reactions will tend to be larger than the actions that trigger them. If the dynamic progresses by mutual over-reaction, then moves to outdo one's opponent can range from pre-emptive war to acquisition of greater forces. A classic example of the latter is Britain's announcement in 1912 that it would out-build Germany in Dreadnoughts by a ratio of 8:5, and build two equivalent ships for every extra one that the Germans added to their existing programme of naval construction.

But the logic of over-reaction is by no means immutable, and there are many circumstances that can lead to responses of lower magnitude. Of particular importance in interpreting the significance of responses are the relative starting positions of the rival states. Starting positions can be roughly equal, as they nearly were in terms of Dreadnoughts between Britain and Germany in 1906, or they can be unequal, where one side starts with a lead. Examples of very unequal starting positions include the case of Britain and Germany in the older style battleships up to 1905, and the United States and the Soviet Union in terms of long-range nuclear weapons during the 1950s and 1960s. Where the rivals are equal, any substantial action quickly changes the balance between them. When they are unequal, the leader may be able to tolerate some disproportion in the magnitude of the measures taken by itself and its rival. Huntington suggests that the danger of war in arms racing is at its highest when the dynamics of the race are close to resulting in a shift in the balance of power (Huntington, 1958, p. 60). If he is right, equality of military strength between rivals is an unstable condition because only small changes are needed to shift the balance of power.

The idea of a sufficiency, or surplus capacity, of force, which becomes prominent when nuclear weapons are in play, may also affect the logic of action and reaction. In particular it may negate Huntington's point about the instability of parity. Past a certain point, additional destructive power offers diminishing returns in military capability. When force levels have passed the point of surplus capacity, the incentives to match increases by one's opponent are not as strong as they are with conventional weapons, where additional numbers more obviously increase relative capability.

Lower magnitude responses may also indicate a lack of resources or political will on the part of the challenged state. Or they may indicate a reasoned political judgement that the arms dynamic should be allowed to generate a peaceful change in the international balance of power and status. Such a judgement reflects a decision that new realities in the international system are so basic as to be very difficult to stop, and not so adverse that they are worth opposing by war. An example of this latter case is the willingness of the United States to accept the Soviet Union as a military equal during the SALT negotiations.

Although the idea of measured responses is clear enough in theory, in reality it is often very difficult to find reliable measures by which actions and reactions can be compared. The naval race is a rare instance where comparison was easy because its idiom, Dreadnoughts, was both simple and consistent: counting numbers of equivalent ships gave an accurate measure of relative strength. Few other interactions within the arms dynamic are as accommodating as this one. As Israel has demonstrated on several occasions, counting numbers of weapons may mislead more than it informs if there are significant qualitative differences in the forces deployed by rival states. The sources of qualitative difference are numerous and almost impossible to assess, ranging from morale, leadership, and training, to the robustness and sophistication of weapons technology (Buzan, 1983, pp. 204–5). If the weapons are nuclear, then force comparisons may begin to lose meaning once both sides have sufficient forces to ensure destruction of the opponent's society even after those forces have themselves been heavily attacked. Numbers also reveal little if there is low consistency in the types of forces deployed. We have no accurate means except war of comparing the relative strength of unlike forces, even when they are opposites like submarines and anti-submarine weapons. Even the use of aggregate defence expenditure as a measure for comparison poses problems. Governments do not always release complete or accurate figures, and even when they do, comparing the real value of expenditures across different currencies and different economies leaves a large margin for error. The most conspicuous example of this problem is the comparison of Soviet and American defence expenditure, which despite much effort has yet to be satisfactorily resolved (*Military Balance*, annually).

Not having clear measures of military strength is a problem for both analysts and policy-makers. It makes it difficult for either of them to assess the process of action and reaction with an acceptable level of accuracy. To the extent that calculation is imprecise, concepts like parity have no practical meaning. If states cannot know whether they are ahead of, behind, or equal to their rivals, then the logic of prudence and fear will increase their incentives to overinsure, and thereby further fuel the process of action and reaction.

### 6.2.2  Timing

The variable of timing poses even greater difficulties of measurement than that of magnitude. It is perhaps the major weakness in attempts to supply the action-reaction model to the study of the arms dynamic. The basic model assumes a clear sequence of action and reaction like that in a chess game. In theory, such a process should display a distinct pattern of move and counter-move which would enable the pace of the action-reaction cycle to provide one measure of the intensity of interaction. Slow versus rapid patterns of response would give a useful insight into the character of the arms dynamic, and might help to distinguish racing from maintenance.

In some cases this clear sequence model does reflect reality. It gives a fair view of the arms races that preceded the First and Second World Wars. In such cases it suggests some valuable insights: delayed responses, like that of Britain and France to Germany during the 1930s, will lead to very intense arms racing when the attempt to catch up is finally made (Huntington, 1958, pp. 58–63). It seems likely always to be significant at the start of a race, as when Britain reacted to the German naval programme in 1904, and the Soviet Union reacted to news of the American atomic bomb in 1945 (Holloway, 1983, ch. 2). It may also apply to elements of a race that it otherwise does not fit, as in the NATO deployments of cruise and *Pershing II* missiles in response to Soviet SS-20s, and the subsequent Soviet deployments of LRTNW in Eastern Europe as a response to the NATO move.

In other cases, however, and particularly in relation to the rivalry between the United States and the Soviet Union, the model does not fit the facts. Since concern about the Soviet-American case dominates contemporary thinking about arms racing, the action-reaction model has fallen into some disrepute. The difficulty with the model is not obvious, since it seems clear from the rhetoric, the rivalry, and the military policies of the two superpowers that they are without doubt, and in an important way, acting and reacting to each other. The problem lies in the nature of the timing. Rather than interacting with each other in a discernible sequence of stimulus and response, the two superpowers are engaged in the paradoxical business of *anticipatory* reaction (Gray, 1971a, pp. 71–3; Nincic, 1982, pp. 11–19). In other words, the superpowers are not reacting so much to what the other does, as to what each estimates that the other will do in the future. When such 'reactions' are simultaneous, the process can only be called action-reaction in the very broad sense that the over-all reference for the actions of each is defined by the threat from the other.

Some analysts use the term *spiral model* to identify the process of simultaneous, anticipatory interaction, the image being one of two actors locked into a smooth, continuous, and self-reinforcing pattern of mutual military stimulation (Jervis, 1976, ch. 3; Russett, 1983b, p. 69). One can find examples of spiral model behaviour in earlier arms races. In 1908–9, for example, Britain succumbed to fear of how many Dreadnoughts Germany might build if the Germans did not stick to their prescribed naval programme, but instead built secretly up to the full capacity of their shipyards. Britain laid down eight Dreadnoughts, so creating a concrete 'reaction' to something the Germans might do, but in the event did not.

The spiral model is, however, more characteristic of the contemporary arms dynamic for two reasons, the first to do with technology, and the second to do with the duration and character of military rivalries. Modern technology creates strong pressures towards anticipatory behaviour because of the long lead times required to bring a weapon system from conception to deployment – as much as 10 to 15 years for a normal weapon system like a supersonic bomber, more for really exotic projects like SDI (Allison and Morris, 1975, pp. 122–3). Under these conditions, major decisions have to be made about future military deployments far in advance of knowledge about what the actual military and political environment will look like when the weapons became operational.

Added to this technological factor is the distinctive duration and character of the superpower rivalry. Unlike most previous arms races, that between the United States and the Soviet Union is very longstanding. Most earlier arms races were relatively short affairs (Huntington, 1958, p. 43), which either ended in war, or else faded away because shifts in the balance of power resulted in changes of perception as to which country was the primary rival. The race between the superpowers cannot easily take either of these routes. The prospect of nuclear war makes direct military conflict between them a completely irrational, if not wholly unthinkable, way of resolving their rivalry. The fact that the two superpowers still dominate a bipolar international system means that there are no other comparable rivalries that could cause their arms dynamic to fade away. Because of these constraining factors, the United States and the Soviet Union are locked into a military rivalry from which the traditional escape hatches are closed. It is not surprising under these conditions that the military rivalry between them has settled into a deeply institutionalized form that does not fit the classic action-reaction model of arms racing. Neither side has much incentive to race for victory, and each can be fairly certain that it can, if necessary, prevent the other from gaining a decisive military advantage. Each can anticipate with virtual certainty that the other will be its principal rival for decades to come.

Under such conditions, the timing element of action-reaction becomes almost impossible to distinguish. Mutual, anticipatory 'reactions' tie the arms dynamic closely to the general process of technological innovation, which, among other things, tends to enlarge the grey area between maintenance of the military status quo and arms racing. In an institutionalized arms race, the driving force of the arms dynamic is found increasingly within states, the external action-reaction element of rivalry being so dominated and distorted by internal factors as to be scarcely distinguishable in its own right (Allison and Morris, 1975; Gray, 1976, pp. 18–22). Thinking along these lines carries us into the domestic structure and technological imperative models of the arms dynamic, which will be explored below.

### 6.2.3 Awareness

How aware are the actors of the process in which they are engaged? In particular, do they understand their impact on each other, and do they try to manipulate the action-reaction dynamic either to their own or to mutual advantage? (Schelling, 1966, ch. 7). The action-reaction model highlights the dangers of actors who are not aware of their impact on each other. It is a virtual truism of states that, like most individuals, they are more aware of the threats that others pose to them than they are of the threats that they pose to others. This unbalanced perception lies at the heart of the security dilemma. Because of it, each state is likely to overreact to the threats it sees from others, and underestimate the threat that its own actions will pose to others. In the context of an action-reaction dynamic, such behaviour leads to an escalatory cycle of provocation and overreaction.

If actors are sensitive to their impact on each other, then there is potential for managing the relationship so as to pursue balance and avoid overreaction. Such management can be approached co-operatively, in the form of negotiated agreements to restrain the arms dynamic, or unilaterally, in the form of actions by one side designed to avoid overstimulating the threat sensitivities of the other. The logic of the various responses to military means explored in Part IV rests on the ability of states to take a more sensitive view of each other's security requirements. The peculiarly locked condition of the superpower arms dynamic also encourages the parties to be aware of each other. Among other things, the institutionalization of a long-term rivalry that cannot rationally be solved by war provides considerable incentives for joint management. As Gray points out, awareness also has its dangers (Gray, 1971a, p. 56). If one side is more keen to manage the arms dynamic than the other, it makes itself vulnerable to having its enthusiasm exploited, and its relative strength weakened. Hawkish opinion in the United States sees the SALT process of the 1970s in this light. When suspicions arise that an attempt to manage the arms dynamic is being cynically exploited by one side, then the arms control process can itself become the mechanism that heightens the intensity of arms racing.


## 6.3   MOTIVES

Motives within a rivalry can have a major impact on other variables within the action-reaction process. It is, for example, reasonable to conjecture that the action-reaction dynamic between two status quo rivals each interested in maintaining its position through deterrence will be much less intense in terms of the pace and magnitude of its interactions, and much more restrained in its idiom, than a dynamic between two rivals both interested in changing their position, and both prepared to fight a war in order to do so. The relations between India and Pakistan, between Israel and the Arab states, and amongst the great powers during the late 1930s, all approximate to the more extreme case of rivalry. The relationship between the United States and the Soviet Union can be interpreted in terms of the mutual deterrence, status quo, case. Because of unavoidable uncertainties in assessing motives it can, however, also be interpreted as a mixed case, with one power seeking stability and deterrence, and the other seeking change and willing to risk war. With the advent of a more hawkish administration in the United States since 1980, the superpower relationship can even be seen as a case of both sides wanting change, although though both still remain heavily constrained from the option of war.

Despite the obvious importance of motives in the action-reaction dynamic, the element of uncertainty makes their role difficult to assess. On purely conceptual grounds, it might be suggested that two pairs of distinctions capture the most important elements of motive within the action-reaction process. The first pair concerns the military balance between the actors, and the distinction is whether their motives are to *change* it or to *preserve* their existing positions. The second pair concerns the military objectives of the actors, and the distinction is whether their motives are to pursue an ability to *fight* or an ability to *deter*. Other things being equal, it would seem probable that the dominance of change and/or warfighting motives would push the arms dynamic towards arms racing, while the dominance of preservation and/or deterrence motives would lead more towards maintenance of the military status quo. Looked at in this way motives run close to the traditional distinction between status quo and revisionist states (Buzan, 1983, pp. 175–86).

If any major state seeks to change its international status as a high priority, then the probability rises that it will seek to increase its military strength. Its moves in this direction will lead to an arms race with those whose interests are challenged by its ambitions. This was certainly the case with Germany prior to both world wars, and with Japan during the 1930s. It appears still to be the case with both sides in the Middle East, though not between Egypt and Israel since the 1973 War. Pursuit of an ability to fight is also likely to lead to arms racing because warfighting preparations generate open-ended military needs. When war is considered to be a rational instrument of policy, then there is no absolute ceiling on the force requirements of either side. The needs of each are determined according to the capability of the other in a potentially endless cycle of action and reaction. The existence of exaggerated cycles of overreaction may even be a signal that war is increasingly likely to occur (Rattinger, 1976, p. 526).

Conversely, if preserving position is the main priority for *all* parties in the rivalry, then only the pressure of the security dilemma pushes them towards arms racing. Possibilities then exist for keeping the arms dynamic at the level of maintenance of the military status quo. But if one party seeks change, then the status quo states face the much stronger arms racing pressure of an explicit power struggle. If the military objective is deterrence, then there are possibilities for avoiding the open-ended competitive accumulations of a rivalry in which war is an acceptable instrument of policy. As shown in Part III, deterrence can in theory be achieved by possession of an absolute capability to devastate one's opponent. Such a capability is considerably less sensitive to increases in an opponent's strength than is the case in warfighting rivalries. Again, however, the moderating effect of the deterrence motive is much stronger when all parties hold it than if it is held by only one side in the rivalry.

There are two problems with this otherwise attractive and useful line of reasoning. The first is that states often hold mixed motives within the categories just discussed. The second is that it is frequently impossible to identify reliably which motive an opponent holds. Although change and preservation motives appear to present a mutually exclusive choice, it is probably true that most states hold a mixture of both. These motives cannot be detached from the constraints and opportunities posed by the distribution of power in the international system. A state may only be wedded to preservation objectives because it has reached the limits of its power and so is incapable of creating change. Likewise a state may be attracted to motives of change because its influence and status in the international system are lower than its level of relative power.

Motives are ephemeral. They can change with circumstances, and more to the point, they can change because of changes in capability. When motives become subordinate to capability, then the erstwhile governing factor becomes subordinate to the elements of power that it is supposed to control. It is easy to see how this problem affects relations between the superpowers. The current distribution of capability forces each into a preservation position. But because of their ideological conflict, neither can ignore the possibility that the other would switch to change if some momentary weakness of the opponent, or some momentary advantage created by developments in military technology, offered the opportunity. Change and preservation motives are thus not opposites. They can be combined in a hierarchy of choice where capabilities and opportunities determine which one will dominate.

The second problem with motives is the difficulty of distinguishing between them. The best example of this difficulty poses one of the major dilemmas in contemporary strategy, namely that it is much easier to make the distinction between warfighting and deterrence motives in theory, then it is to make it in practice. In practice, the military capabilities for warfighting and for deterrence may be very similar. If so, actors are left in the uncomfortable position of trying to determine the motives of their opponents directly, rather than having the more secure option of inferring them from capabilities.

The United States has had this problem in relation to the Soviet Union for a long time. From what the Soviet leaders say, their policy appears to be aimed at avoiding war, and therefore at deterrence. But their military doctrine and deployments both emphasize warfighting (Holloway, 1983; Lambeth, 1981). This combination does not necessarily indicate hypocrisy or deception, though it might do so. It can be justified both by the argument that a stout warfighting capability is the most effective means of pursuing deterrence (Gray, 1976, chs 3, 5, 6; 1984), and by the argument that warfighting capability is a necessary second priority in case deterrence fails. This line of argument combines the problem of indistinguishability of motives with that of mixed motives. The combination generates such ambiguity as to make impossible the reasoned use of motives in assessments of one's opponent.

In the context of superpower relations, this ambiguity of motives has been getting worse. As will be seen in Part III, American policy has moved towards the Soviet model of deterrence through the threat of warfighting. These policies of the superpowers, and the interaction between them, are making the boundary between deterrence and warfighting motives increasingly difficult to identify.

The difficulties created by the mixing of warfighting means with deterrence ends are discussed further in Part III. For the present, one can conclude that while motives appear to be an important element in the action-reaction process, they pose insuperable difficulties for both analysis and policy because they cannot be either isolated or identified accurately. If the response to this uncertainty is to assume the worst, then valuable opportunities for co-operation may be lost, and the operation of the security dilemma may be intensified sufficiently to cause arms racing. If assumptions about motives are too optimistic, there is a danger that one's opponent will interpret conciliation as weakness, and by seeking to exploit the situation create the conflict that the conciliatory behaviour was aimed at avoiding.

These problems, along with the others outlined above, explain why the action-reaction model has fallen out of favour despite its many attractions. Although its basic logic has force, its specific ideas are frequently difficult to apply to particular cases. In addition, there are many cases where the model does not seem to provide anything like a complete explanation for observed behaviour. Frustration with the model, especially amongst those concerned to understand the arms dynamic of the superpowers, has therefore driven enquiry away from interaction factors between states, and towards domestic ones within them.

# 7 The Domestic Structure Model

The domestic structure model rests on the idea that the arms dynamic is generated by forces within the state. It is, in an important sense, derived from, and complementary to, the action-reaction model. It functions as an alternative to it only in the sense that the two models compete for primacy of place in ability to explain observed behaviour within the arms dynamic. In a narrow sense, the literature on the domestic structure model is quite new, dating from the 1970s, and the failure of the action-reaction model adequately to explain what goes on between the superpowers. In a broader sense, however, it is simply an extension of the longstanding tradition that seeks to explain the behaviour of states primarily in terms of their domestic structures and affairs (Waltz, 1959, chs 4, 5).

The proponents of the domestic structure model do not argue that the rivalry between the superpowers has become irrelevant, but that the process of the arms dynamic has become so deeply institutionalized within each state that domestic factors largely supplant the crude forms of action and reaction as the main engine of the arms dynamic. The external factor of rivalry still provides the necessary motivation for the arms dynamic. But when 'reactions' are anticipatory, the particularities of military funding, procurement and technology are largely determined from within the state. The interesting question about this model is therefore not whether it is better than the action-reaction model in some general sense, but what proportion of observed behaviour each model explains for any given case. What structures and mechanisms within the state become the carriers of the arms dynamic?

This view of the domestic structure model fits nicely into the historically unusual character of the superpower arms race sketched in Chapter 6. It is hard to imagine that any state finding itself locked into a long-term rivalry would not adjust its internal structures to account for the rivalry as a durable issue. On this basis, there is every reason to think that institutionalization, and therefore internalization, is a natural function of longevity in an arms races. Unfortunately we have too few historical cases to put this hypothesis to the test. An additional factor encouraging internalization is the emphasis on deterrence motives in the superpower rivalry. Deterrence requires forces in being, which in turn generate large organizations with military interests as permanent actors within domestic politics.

Most of the studies that support the domestic structure model focus on the case of the two superpowers (Allison and Morris, 1975; Holloway, 1983, chs 6–8; Kaldor, 1982; Kugler *et al.*, 1980; Kurth, 1973; Mosley, 1985; Nincic, 1982; Russett, 1983b; pp. 86–96). This is partly a matter of priority, because of the intrinsic importance of the superpower case. It is partly by default, because information from other cases is harder to come by, though at least one author looks at the European states (Rattinger, 1975). Strong opposition to the general logic and validity of the model is rare. Since much more information is available about domestic structure variables in the United States than in the Soviet Union, the American example dominates the literature. The importance of the American case makes the exercise worthwhile, but requires us to keep in mind questions about how applicable the whole model is to other cases. Because the superpower case dominates the literature, one cannot help noticing how much of the existing material on the domestic structure model applies only to states that are major producers of arms. As was explained in Part I, such states are few in number. The relevance of the domestic structure model for the greater numbers of non-producers and part-producers remains largely unexplored.

## 7.1 THE AMERICAN CASE

The American case of the domestic structure model offers a whole range of factors to explain the arms dynamic. The principal ones are: the institutionalization of military research, development, and production; bureaucratic politics; economic management; and domestic politics. The normative question that underlies consideration of these factors is how they should be seen. Are they a reasonable response to the requirements of deterrence in a long-term rivalry? Or are they a distortion of the national political economy, that serves powerful vested interests, and that, whatever the validity of its origins, has become a self-serving mechanism which promotes and perpetuates the rivalry that justifies it?

The institutionalization of military research and development (R&D) plays a major role in the domestic structure model (Baugh, 1984, pp. 86–93, 107–15; Gray, 1976, pp. 39–43; Nincic, 1982, pp. 19–25; Thee, 1986, chs 3, 5). This role relates closely to the discussions of the technological revolution in Part I, and of the technological imperative model in Chapter 8. What makes it distinctive within the domestic structure model is the measures that states take when the rhythm of technological development forces them to take a long view of military procurement. As Pearton argues, the increasing involvement of the state in military R&D is a historical trend that began to gather force in the nineteenth century and culminated in the symbiosis of state and science in the nuclear age (Pearton, 1982). In the modern era, military technology is so capital intensive, and takes so long to develop, that any state wishing to remain at the leading edge has no choice but to create, or encourage, a permanent R&D establishment. No state can become a fully independent arms producer without its own R&D base, and since technological improvement is a continuous process, the establishments that support it necessarily become permanent.

There is an element of the chicken-egg paradox here. On the one hand, R&D establishments are created because the complex and expensive nature of technology requires them. On the other hand, the establishments become mechanisms that set ever higher standards of expense and complexity, increase the pace of technological advance, and work relentlessly to make their own products obsolete. In promoting their own organizational security, they necessarily become promoters of technological change. Although their offerings are not always accepted for production, as witness such projects as *Skybolt*, the B-70 bomber, and the 1960s versions of anti-ballistic missiles (ABM), they do mount a continuous challenge to accepted standards of adequate military technology. Thus what starts as a response to a problem, becomes part of the process by which the problem is continuously re-created.

These establishments reflect the technological conditions stemming from industrial society. Yet they have also been instrumental in the process by which 'reactions' within the arms dynamic have become anticipatory, continuous, and self-reinforcing. Once the process of military R&D becomes institutionalized, an internal force is created within the state that not only responds to advances in technology, but in many sectors pulls them along. R&D establishments race with the leading edge of the technologically possible. In so doing they drive the qualitative element of the arms dynamic by a logic which is distinct from, though not uninfluenced by, the logic of rivalry between states.

Despite its domestic roots, and its self-contained logic, the institutionalization of military R&D can in one sense be viewed as part of the action-reaction model. States competing at the superpower level must have an R&D establishment in order to be in the game at all. Rivalry between states justifies the enterprise of R&D. But the American R&D establishment competes more directly against the continuously receding leading edge of the technologically possible than it does against the Soviet Union. Where one side is more proficient at innovation, it can force the pace for the other by trying to base its security on the military advantage of a qualitative edge in technology. The United States has, with very few exceptions, proved to be more proficient at technological innovation than the Soviet Union. It has consequently sought to maintain a qualitative lead, not only for its intrinsic military advantage, but also to compensate for its difficulty in matching the quantity of Soviet military deployments. The SDI can be seen as the latest in a long line of leading American innovations that started with the Atomic Bomb in 1945.

The Soviet Union tends to follow American innovations like the multiple, independently manoeuverable re-entry vehicle (MIRV), ballistic missile submarines and cruise missiles. Occasionally it will take an independent course, as when it largely skipped heavy bombers and moved straight to ICBMs during the 1950s. By a combination of its own work and spying on the West it manages not to fall too far behind. It can draw even in areas like armoured vehicles, where the technologies are relatively mature, and the rate of change is slow. The Soviet R&D establishment seems to have its agenda set rather more by what happens in the West than by any general assault on the frontiers of the possible (Holloway, 1983, pp. 147–50). Although coming second is not a wholly comfortable role for the Soviet Union (Fewtrell, 1983, pp. 25–6), it has the advantages of making the opponent carry the costs of leading the innovation process, and of being relatively easy to sustain at a position not so far behind the leader as to jeopardize one's military credibility.

Thus although the instutitionalization of R&D does drive the arms dynamic internally, in line with the domestic structure model, it also echoes the action-reaction model. Rival states must hold their relative positions in relation to a constantly moving leading edge of technological quality. The process of such rivalry is smooth and continuous because it is structured into permanent organizations working in long time-frames. One effect of this institutionalization is to complicate the task of differentiating arms racing from maintenance of the military status quo.

The logic that drives the instutitionalization of R&D is both linked to, and similar to, that for military production. Production and R&D often share close organizational links in high technology industries. States face the same need to maintain military production capabilities in being as they do to maintain a permanent R&D establishment (Kaldor, 1982, pp. 60–5; Kurth, 1973, pp. 38–42; Russett, 1983b, pp. 80–6). Maintaining military production capabilities in turn requires government support for the whole range of basic industries on which military production depends, so bringing a wide range of industrial interests into the picture (Sen, 1984).

The need to maintain a standing capacity for arms production is reinforced by the conditions of long-term rivalry and deterrence policy that face the superpowers. A long-term rivalry requires not only a degree of permanent mobilization in case there is a rapid move towards conflict, but also the capacity to expand production quickly if the country gets drawn into peripheral wars like those in Korea and Vietnam. A policy of deterrence also requires a substantial degree of permanent mobilization in order to keep the necessary retaliatory forces in being and up to date. In addition, a high level of activity in the R&D sector will speed up the cycle of obsolescence, and so require production capability to keep up with the flow of replacement weapon systems. Under these conditions, states cannot afford to demobilize or dismantle their military production capabilities as they might have done in the past, when simpler technologies meant that civil industry could more easily be converted to military production. In other words, it is becoming hard to envisage any state being able to add to its stocks of weapons through domestic production during the course of a major conflict.

Because of the need to keep production facilities in being, the argument connects at this point with the discussion of the arms trade and industry in Chapter 3. Given this need, governments have to generate both sufficient volume and sufficient continuity of orders to keep their military industries going. This is not just a matter of keeping plant in being, but also of maintaining skilled teams of workers. The arms trade is one way of achieving this goal, but it cannot be applied to strategic weapons like missile submarines, ICBMs and heavy bombers which are almost never transferred to other countries. The other way is to provide a volume of orders for one's own armed forces that is sufficiently large and regular to keep in being an armaments industry of the desired size and scope. In this way the imperative to maintain capacity results in the creation of an internalized push for arms production up to a level sufficient to meet the needs of the industry. That push will produce a pattern of arms production that bears no direct relation to any action-reaction dynamic with a rival power, even though the need to maintain a capacity of a given size is defined by the existence, and the character, of the external rival.

Considerations of this type help to explain why there is little discernible pattern of specific action-reaction in the armaments acquisitions of the superpowers, and why their internally driven arms dynamic results in such large arsenals. The result is a locked cycle. The existence of a long-term rivalry justifies the need to maintain substantial military R&D and production capability. Maintenance of that capability requires both continuous arms production and an institutionalized process of technological innovation that is encouraged by the state. The result is to cast the rivalry into a military competition that cannot easily be stopped because both sides of it continue their activity on the basis of a largely independent structure of domestic organizations. The element of action-reaction occurs mainly in the general size of arsenals, and in the pace at which the qualitative leading edge of technology is pushed forward.

Other lines of argument in the domestic structure model repeat this theme of semi-independent internal pressures for arms production. These pressures relate to external factors only inasmuch as the existence of a rival power provides a necessary framework for them. Much of this argument concerns the organizational and bureaucratic momentum that characterizes the process of large-scale government in general. Studies of the arms acquisition process in the United States (Allison and Morris, 1975; Gray, 1976, ch. 2; Gray, R. C., 1979; Kurth, 1973) all point to a major role for the momentum that arises out of the desire to simplify and stabilize the process of government, and out of the conservative character of large organizations.

Organizations like the armed services develop fairly fixed views of their missions and the mainstream weapons systems that they prefer.

These views are shaped as much by national historical experience, and by the traditions of the individual services, as by considerations of what the opponent is doing. Service views play a major role in what systems get built. The US Air Force, for example, has a long-standing attachment to bombers. This attachment owes at least as much to USAF traditions and self-image as it does to the rather strained argument that bombers add necessary flexibility to a long-range bombardment capability that is more cheaply achieved with ICBMs. At its mildest, the conservatism of the armed forces results in types of weapons being kept in service longer than the evolution of technology would dictate. Examples of this range from horse cavalry through battleships to manned heavy bombers. At worst, it results in the syndrome that Mary Kaldor labels 'baroque technology', (Kaldor, 1982) in which favoured weapons are developed to such a pitch of complexity that their ability to function in combat becomes doubtful. Aircraft like the F-111 and the F-16 tend in this direction, and much of the criticism of SDI is on grounds that it is far too complex to work reliably. Even inter-service rivalry gets channelled into a routine 'fair shares' principle of budget allocation. The whole power of governmental momentum arises from the desire of big bureaucracies for continuity in their affairs. It is perhaps best summed up as a factor in the arms dynamic by Gray's observation that 'the best guide to the level of next year's [military] budget is the level of this year's budget' (Gray, 1976, p. 38).

The interest of political leaders is also served by having predictable military budgets, and therefore contributes to the shaping of military procurement by organizational momentum. If military budget decisions can be made routine, then less time has to be spent arguing over them. More planning stability can then be given both to organizations concerned with military affairs, and to programmes that compete with military requirements in the annual process of budgetary resource allocation. Domestic political interests can also impinge on the budgetary process in several ways that stimulate the arms dynamic. The government may decide to use increased military spending as a means of stimulating demand within the economy. This technique is especially useful in a country like the United States, where Keynesian measures of economic stimulation might, in themselves, attract ideological opposition. Military spending tends to be less controversial than welfare measures and other public works, and the government is more in control of the variables that govern the need for defence measures (Russett, 1983b, p. 85). The international system nearly always obliges by providing threats that are real enough to be exaggerated if the need to do so for economic reasons arises.

Political factors can influence military spending more directly, particularly when electoral considerations come into play (Gray, 1971a, pp. 74–5). Military procurement decisions can make a big impact on patterns of employment and income in specific electoral districts or constituencies. Whether in terms of new investment and new jobs, or the maintenance of existing plans and jobs, such decisions cannot avoid entanglement in the political process by which individual politicians and political parties seek to enhance their electoral appeal. On a larger scale, electoral considerations can shape the way that parties campaign on military issues (Baugh, 1984, pp. 101–3; Gray, 1976, pp. 33–6). The American presidential campaigns leading up to the Kennedy Administration in 1960 and the Reagan Administration in 1980 are instructive in this regard. In both cases the winning candidate raised alarms about military weakness created by their predecessors, and promised to build up the armed forces. It is always difficult to separate genuine concern from calculation of electoral advantage in such cases. What cannot be denied is that pointing to foreign threats is almost always an available, and frequently an effective, means of getting political support.

There is an obvious parallel interest among the organizations concerned with R&D and production, those concerned with consuming military goods, and the politicians with their economic and electoral concerns. This parallel interest underlies the idea of a 'military-industrial complex', coined by President Eisenhower, which generated a mostly polemical literature during the early 1970s. The term still has a somewhat ill-defined common currency, but its implication of a conspiracy to militarize the national interest was never proved convincingly. The concept did, however, have the merit of pointing to the importance of domestic structural inputs into the arms dynamic. It led to the more detailed studies of the invididual components of domestic structure reviewed here, and it drew attention to the fact that the process of arms acquisition had a logic of its own. That logic did not always clearly serve the national interest, and it was both strong enough and independent enough to be an important part of the problem defined as arms racing.

This general line of argument can be expanded upwards from mere electoral considerations, and applied to the functioning of the whole state as a political organism (Burton, 1984; Gray, 1976, pp. 31–3; Kaldor, 1985). The basis case here is that states are relatively fragile political structures, and that the task of governing them is made possible in some cases, and easier in others, by cultivating the unifying force of external threat. Such threats will thus be positively sought out and amplified by governments even where the objective basis for them is weak. Without them, domestic divisions and dissatisfactions would rise to higher priority on the political agenda, either threatening the status of the ruling élite, or making the process of government more difficult. Such arguments have an obvious relevance to politically weak states like Pakistan, where the religious basis of the military and political rivalry with India helps to hold together a country otherwise threatened by serious ethnic and ideological splits. They also apply, albeit in a milder fashion, to military postures designed to emphasise national prestige, such as the French *Force de Frappe*. Some writers interpret the superpower relationship in this light, where the unifying stimulus of rivalry helps to disguise stale ideologies and economic systems incapable of living up to the expectations of their populations (Burton, 1984; Kaldor, 1985).

This view is sometimes referred to as *autism* (Dedring, 1976, pp. 79–81). Autism is intellectually related to Marxist insights into the behaviour of states. Marxists see capitalist states as inherently aggressive ('imperialist' in Lenin's usage) because of the expansionist, competitive, and exploitative nature of their domestic class structure and its associated structure of political economy (McKinlay and Little, 1986, chs 6 and 9). Among other things, capitalist states generate arms production because of their needs to use the surplus capital that they generate.

To the extent that the autism view is correct, the consequences for the international system are serious. Individuals whose behaviour is generated more by their internal processes than by their interaction with their environment are usually defined as insane. Excessive egocentrism in the behaviour of states is an almost certain path to friction and paranoia in relations among them. If the logic of autism is taken to extremes, it makes the domestic structure model of the arms dynamic virtually autonomous, and therefore an alternative, rather than a complement, to the action-reaction model. If the arms dynamic is driven powerfully from within states, then it becomes much more difficult damp down. Any state that reduces its own military strength in hope of a response from its rival will be disappointed if its rival's armaments are determined more by internal than by external factors.

## 7.2  HOW APPLICABLE IS THE DOMESTIC STRUCTURE MODEL TO OTHER CASES?

Since the features of the domestic structure model are largely drawn from the arms dynamic between the superpowers, they have obvious relevance for that case. But the fact that the literature draws predominantly on the American experience makes it dangerous to assume that the model can be applied as it stands to other countries and other cases. To begin with, there are some obvious differences even between the United States and the Soviet Union. While there may be useful parallels between the superpowers in terms of military production requirements, governmental momentum, military lobbies, and the logic of autism, there are clear differences in terms of terms of R&D style, history, military tradition, economic management, and political pressures (Holloway, 1983, chs 6–8; Jahn, 1975). The Soviet Union is not driven by the same deeply-rooted market forces that make technological innovation such a feature of the American political economy. It does not have the pluralist organization that allows non-governmental organizations to become powerful domestic actors. Neither does it have the competitive party structure and non-government press that makes public opinion an important factor in Western debates about defence policy and military procurement. In one sense it can be argued that the Soviet Union does not have a military-industrial complex because there is no independent set of military interests within it. In another sense it can be argued that the whole country is a military-industrial complex because military and governmental interests are locked together both organizationally and in terms of shared views.

There are also important differences between the United States and the other Western democracies, even though some of the political parallels are more in harmony than they are between the superpowers. In many of these countries, the electoral appeal to foreign threats is much less attractive than it is in the United States. With a few exceptions, the arms industry is also weaker in relation to the economy, and more under state control. The logic of R&D and production is therefore proportionately less applicable to decisions about military procurement in these countries than it is in the United States.

If we try to carry the domestic structure model to the arms dynamic of the part-producers and non-producers in the Third World, the content of the model may need very substantial re-working. While the idea of internal generation of the arms dynamic probably remains valid for most countries, at least in part, the form it takes varies widely according to the type of political economy in the state concerned. The most generally applicable elements of the domestic model are the existence of organizational pressures from the military establishment on weapons procurement, and the domestic insecurity logic of autism. Even these common factors will vary greatly from country to country. Organizational pressures from the military, for example, will take quite different forms in states where the military runs the government than in states where the military is subordinate to civilian political leaders. In addition, quite a lot of Third World countries are so politically weak that domestic security problems define their principal requirement for armed force. This adds a strong practical dimension to the autism case, for it means that the demand for weapons is determined by the insecurity of the government in relation to its own citizens (Buzan, 1987). This factor is present to some degree in all countries. It is relatively insignificant in the politically stable states among the Western group, more significant for states in the middle range, like India and Brazil, and dominant for weak states like Sri Lanka, Chad and Sudan.

In countries where the arms industry is small, or non-existent, many of the most powerful forces evident in the American case will not operate. In the absence of an arms industry there can be no R&D or production sector push, little electoral factor in the siting of arms industries and the disposition of procurement orders, and no Keynesian demand management of the economy to drive the arms dynamic from within. In such countries, military procurement requires imports, and is therefore more clearly at odds with the economic interests of the state than in cases where procurement supports a domestic industry. It seems fair to conclude that the idea of a domestic structure input into the arms dynamic will have a nearly universal validity, but that the particular form of it will be different in each country. Use of this model thus requires caution against over-generalization from the American case, and sensitivity to the quite different features that will mark other cases, especially those involving Third World countries.

# 8 Completing the Picture

## 8.1 THE TECHNOLOGICAL IMPERATIVE MODEL

The technological imperative model derives in large part from the material on the technological revolution discussed in Part I. It can therefore be presented here quite briefly. The reason for posing a third model is not to offer an alternative to the other two, but to identify a fundamentally independent element of the arms dynamic that is not fully captured by either action-reaction or domestic structure. That element is the qualitative evolution of technology as a whole. As has been argued already, military technology is not separable from the knowledge and technique that underlie the larger body of civil technology. At most, it represents a distinctive and specialized sector within that larger body, albeit one that is often located at the leading edge of qualitative advance in many areas of engineering, materials development, and electronics.

Although the leading-edge position of military technology gives it some influence over the shape and timing of technological advance, the military sector cannot outrun, or detach itself from, the shape and pace of the whole. In other words, it is just as true to say that the military sector is an offshoot of the civil one, as it is to argue the reverse. The fact that both propositions are true underlines the intimacy of the linkage. Indeed, except at the highest levels of specialization, it is hard to locate major dividing boundaries between the civil and military sectors, and it is not always clear in the early stages of development whether a technology will have a military application. In some cases, developments in the civil sector lead those in the military. Historical examples here include motor vehicles, metal ships, and the early phases of aircraft. In other cases, military purposes lead, as with the development of rockets, radar, nuclear power and the later evolution of aircraft. In yet other cases, such as computers, lasers and telecommunications, civil and military pressure for development are both strong, with neither being a clear leader. Almost all of the major military technologies have close links to those in the civil sector regardless of which leads. It does not seem credible to argue that unless bombers, tanks, missiles and nuclear weapons had come first, the civil sector of industrial society

105

would not have developed automobiles, passenger aircraft, satellite launchers or nuclear reactors.

This linkage is important to the arms dynamic for two reasons: first because it means that a large element of the pressure for qualitative technological advance is not located in the military sector; and secondly, because it means that the military sector cannot escape the implications of a relentless qualitative advance over which it has only partial control. Deborah Shapley colourfully characterizes this relentless advance as 'technology creep' (Shapley, 1978). One way of looking at the technological imperative as a main input into the arms dynamic is in terms of the idea raised in Chapter 2 that all industrial societies have a latent military potential. If we assume a disarmed major industrial country in which no military sector exists, there would still be a powerful industrial technology, and an institutionalized process of qualitative advance. If that country had to arm itself for some reason, a set of military applications would quickly come forth from the existing technological and industrial base. One can approach this exercise by imagining the disarmed country first with a technological level similar to that of the industrial countries in the 1920s, and then with a level similar to the present. At the 1920s level, the civil base would easily give rise to a whole array of chemical weapons, both poisonous and explosive, and probably to the idea of aircraft as a delivery system, but it would not generate thoughts of nuclear weapons, lasers or precision-guided munitions. With the knowledge and technology base of the present, the idea of nuclear weapons would be unavoidable, as would the idea of using rockets to deliver them. Japan provides a partial example of this latter case. Though it is by no means disarmed, Japan does not have a large arms industry. No one doubts, however, that Japan could rapidly convert its impressive R&D and productive capacity to military purposes should its political consensus on the issue change.

One cannot evade the fact that there is a general process of technological advance that is only partially driven by the military, but which has profound military implications. This process is probably strongest in capitalist societies because of their commitment to technological innovation as an engine of economic growth. Sustained growth not only means higher profits, but also makes easier the job of managing politics in the presence of a markedly unequal distribution of wealth. Even in non-capitalist industrial societies, however, there is a deeply embedded commitment to the pursuit of technological innovation for civil purposes.

Defining technological change as an independent variable exposes a major component of the arms dynamic that is not covered by the other two models. Neither the action-reaction process, nor the institutionalization of military R&D within the domestic structure of states, explains more than a fraction of the qualitative advance that is such a major feature of the arms dynamic. The stimulus of international rivalry, and the permanent organization of military R&D, certainly contribute to the process of technological advance. They increase the amount of resources available to fuel the process, and they select areas of military utility for intensive development. These are important considerations that make a major impact on the whole pattern. Their contribution is easily sufficient to justify the other two models, but they do not set the basic rhythm that determines the march of technology. By themselves they cannot offer more than a partial explanation for the arms dynamic that we observe. A large percentage of the behaviour that is commonly identified as arms racing stems directly from the underlying process of technological advance. When countries compete with each other in armaments, they must also compete with a standard of technological quality that is moving forward by an independent process of its own. When they institutionalize military R&D, countries are seeking to exploit, and not be left behind by, a process that is already under way in society as a whole. They may be able to steer the process to some extent, and influence its pace, but they are basically riders, and not the horse itself.

The technological imperative model provides a depth of view that is all too often lacking in thinking about arms racing. Huntington hints at it when he identifies arms racing as a phenomenon of industrial society, (Huntington, 1958, pp. 41–3) but he does not go into the matter in any detail. Some of those who have written about the history of military technology, particularly Brodie and Brodie (1973), and Pearton (1982), make the connection between civil and military technology clear, but do not explicitly relate that insight to the problem of arms racing. A few of the better writers on arms control do identify this issue clearly (Bull, 1961, ch. 12; Howard, 1985, pp. 11–12). The idea of a world military order also contains elements of the technological imperative model. It draws attention to the arms dynamic as a global phenomenon in which all countries are caught in a worldwide pattern of military forms and standards determined by the doctrines, styles, and technologies of the major arms producers. By focusing narrowly on military technology as a thing in itself, however, most purveyors of this useful view underplay the profound links that the phenomena they observe have to the larger pattern of technology as a whole. Perhaps only the recent work of Thee comes anywhere close to identifying the technological imperative as a major independent variable in the arms dynamic (Thee, 1986).

Incorporating the technological imperative model into our understanding of the arms dynamic produces a fully balanced view of arms racing. Adding in a massive current of *independent* technological advance to the other two models creates a sense of continuous process that is more deeply institutionalized even than that of the domestic structure model. This depth stems from the fact that the technological imperative is based globally rather than within single states, and because it relates to the totality of technology rather than to the military sector alone. Such a view has major implications for arms control and disarmament, which will be taken up in Part IV.

## 8.2   RELATING THE THREE MODELS

Most writers on arms racing now accept that the action-reaction and domestic structure models are complementary, and that understanding the phenomenon requires looking at it through both perspectives. In order to get a full picture of the arms dynamic it is necessary to add the technological imperative model to this existing set, and draw out the ways in which each of the three models interacts with, and influences, the other two.

### 8.2.1   Technological Imperative

The technological imperative model is important because it defines a condition that is so deeply structured as to be effectively permanent. Because of its deep structure, the technological imperative has a similar function to that of anarchy, except that it sets the technological rather than the political context in which the other two models function. For the action-reaction model, the technological imperative sets a context in which the technological conditions determining military power and security are subject to continuous change. This permanent instability adds to the existing uncertainties of life in the international anarchy. States cannot be sure that their existing weapons will remain effective. They face the constant worry that their rivals will gain a military advantage by being the first to achieve a decisive technological breakthrough. Such conditions create relentless pressure on states to lead, or at least to keep up with, the pace of change by continuously modernizing their armed forces. Large R&D establishments are necessary to ensure the capability of responding to both anticipated and unanticipated developments in the military capability of adversaries.

If states fail to keep up with the pace, then the effectiveness of their armed forces will decline quite rapidly in relation to those who do. If they succeed in keeping up with the leading edge, then the probability of being caught at a disadvantage is minimized. But if they do meet the challenge then they embark on a process that produces an endless flow of new weapons, and possibilities of new weapons. That process can hardly avoid exciting the security dilemma among other states. The technological imperative thus forces states to behave in a way that looks like arms racing, but where the principal motive is as much keeping up with the leading edge of technological standards as it is keeping up with other states. When the pace of technological innovation is high, one result is to blur the boundary between maintenance of the military status quo and arms racing.

As noted earlier, one of the ways in which the continuous change of the technological imperative complicates the calculations that states have to make about how their military forces relate to each other, is in terms of the offensive and defensive quality of the prevailing weapons systems. The shifting standard of the technologically possible can render profound changes in the character of the dominant weapons of the day. These changes sometimes result in defence being easier than offence, as with barbed wire and machine-guns during the First World War, and sometimes in offence being easier than defence, as with the union of nuclear weapons and missiles during the 1950s. The problem of which condition prevails, and for how long, not only affects relations between individual rivals, but also the stability of the international system as a whole (Gilpin, 1981, pp. 59–66; Gray, 1971a, pp. 56–7; Jervis, 1978; Quester, 1977). When the defensive is dominant, aggression is more difficult, and military security easier to achieve, than when technological conditions favour the offensive. It follows also that if the defence is dominant, then resources invested in defence will go further than equivalent amounts invested in offence, and vice versa. The general progress of technology sometimes favours the one, and sometimes the other, and there is relatively little that states can do to alter quickly the character of whatever technology prevails at a given time.

The main impact of the technological imperative model on the domestic structure one is in the setting of technological change as a permanent problem for state military planners. Because military planners have to expect technological change, they have little alternative but to institutionalize the process of change within the state, either in terms of permanently organized R&D, or in terms of regular imports of up-to-date weapons from better-equipped producer states. This qualitative treadmill affects all states, whether producers or non-producers. It is one of the most conspicuous features of the post-1945 arms dynamic. Although action-reaction and domestic structure factors do play a substantial role in it, it is important not to lose sight of the fact that both sets of factors are themselves heavily conditioned by the independent process of the technological imperative.


## 8.2.2  Action-Reaction

The action-reaction model probably identifies a general stimulant to the broad process of the technological imperative, although the case is difficult to make directly. Because the international political system is fragmented and competitive, it might be argued that more resources are pushed into advancing technology than would otherwise be the case. In this view, insecurity and/or lust for power become motives for directing resources into technological innovation instead of consumption. The fact that the highly fragmented and competitive state system of Europe was the birthplace of the technological revolution gives weight to this view. It can also be argued, however, that in terms of the international system as a whole, political fragmentation leads to a relative stifling of the technological imperative. Points here include: the huge duplication of effort in national research programmes; the diseconomies of scale inherent in national economies; and the wasting of resources in competitive national military consumption. It is hard to judge which of these contradictory effects of action-reaction on the technological imperative is dominant.

It is easier to trace the positive impact of action-reaction on the technological imperative through the mediating effect of the domestic structure model. The action-reaction model clearly provides a strong motive for states to institutionalize military R&D, but only if the underlying expectation of permanent technological change already exists. If technology was static, then the pressure from action-reaction would impinge only on production capability as states sought to ensure that their rivals could not gain a decisive advantage by exploiting superior capacity for military production. It is thus the combination of pressures from the action-reaction and technological imperative models that generates powerful incentives for states to create permanent military research, development and production sectors wihin their economies. Once established, these sectors become both an independent input into the arms dynamic, and a part of the idiom in which states compete with each other. Competition therefore creates pressure to push the process of technological innovation, and so feeds into the technological imperative as a whole.

### 8.2.3 Domestic Structure

The domestic structure model in turn influences both of the other models. The institutionalization of military R&D, as described above, is part of the larger process that produces the technological imperative. There is no paradox in arguing that the military-industrial complex is both a response to, and a part of, the general condition of technological change. The fact that it is both binds it into a self-reinforcing circular relationship which explains not only the strength of its position within the state, but also the strength of opposition to it on the grounds that its activity reproduces the conditions that require its own existence. This latter charge is true, but it is often a misleading truth. People too easily assume that the military-industrial complex is *wholly* responsible for the process of technological change. In fact, as has been argued, it merely reinforces, and to some extent shapes, a process of change largely determined by other, much broader, social forces.

Because the domestic structure model evolved as a response to the deficiencies of the action-reaction model, the question of its impact on the older model has received a lot of attention in the literature, and is well understood. Both models offer a cause for the speed at which states accumulate weapons and improve their quality. Although in theory the two models can therefore be seen as alternatives, in practice the question is almost always what balance of influence exists between them for any given case The interaction is more complicated than a straight division of explanation, because the presence of domestic structure factors disrupts the process by which the action-reaction model is supposed to work. The existence of an internally-driven element of the arms dynamic dissolves the boundary between action and reaction. In so doing, it makes reaction into a continuous process rather than an episodic one, and reduces the sensitivity of each side to the specific actions of the other. Increases or decreases of strength by either side may elicit little or no response from the other if armaments programmes are locked into a set of domestic structures. When responses do occur, they will be influenced in form, substance and timing by the internal machineries through which they must pass, perhaps so heavily that it is difficult to discern them as responses at all, whether in terms of idiom, magnitude or timing.

To the extent that each side is internally driven, neither can easily manage the rivalry by making conciliatory moves. Such moves would encounter opposition from organizational vested interests within the state making them. If they were made, the other state would have difficulty responding to them because of the momentum of its own internal processes. The existence of domestic structure variables thus tends to lock the action-reaction process by institutionalizing it within states. Once locked in this way states are less able to influence either their own behaviour or that of their opponent in the arms dynamic. The result is that the arms dynamic becomes less of a conscious interaction between rivals and more of an automatic process moving in parallel within them.

The domestic structure model can also generate political consequences for the action-reaction one (Gray, 1976, pp. 100–2). To the extent that the domestic model is accepted as the dominant explanation for the arms dynamic, proponents of more arms procurement can argue that higher levels of arms will have no effect on the opponent because his level of arms is determined internally. Thus hawks in both superpowers can argue that implementation of their preferred arms programmes will not cause responses from the other superpower because the arms dynamic within the rival is determined by the domestic pressure of its military-industrial complex. If both sides think in this way, and the action-reaction process works to the extent that both find any status less than 'equivalence' unacceptable, then the political use of an analytical idea will result in a steady rise in over-all force levels.

# 9 Problems in Studying the Arms Dynamic

The use of a three-model composite for analysing the arms dynamic, though an improvement, by no means solves all the problems attending the study of this difficult phenomenon. This chapter will look at the major ones remaining: the difficulties of using the distinction between arms racing and the maintenance of the military status quo; the barriers to the development of a theory of arms racing; the 'level of analysis' problem in understanding cause-effect relations; and the impact of arms production on the arms dynamic between states.

## 9.1 WORKING WITH THE DISTINCTION BETWEEN ARMS RACING AND THE MAINTENANCE OF THE MILITARY STATUS QUO

The distinction between arms racing and maintenance of the military status quo, is necessary to explain the range of behaviour that we observe in the peacetime military procurement of states. That range causes immediate difficulties with any attempt to make a general fit between the behaviour we observe and the idea of a race: as one writer observed, the superpower relationship is 'more of a walk than a race' (Kahn, 1962, p. 332). While states may well be interacting with each other in their military procurements, they can do so in pursuit of a wide variety of objectives, many of which fall well short of racing (Buzan, 1983, pp. 194–6; Gray, 1971a, pp. 57–65). They may, for example, merely wish to hold an equal, or even an inferior position, and have to keep up with the normal pace of modernization in order to do so. In other words, much of the military procurement behaviour of states is simply the routine business of maintaining military forces as a hedge against the uncertainties of life in the international anarchy. Doing this requires that states respond both to what other states do, and to what the general advance of technology makes possible. The process of that response will, over the long run, both shape, and be shaped by, the domestic structure

114

of that state. Such behaviour is clearly not 'racing', but is none the less strikingly similar in form to behaviour that is racing.

The similarity of idiom between arms racing and maintenance of the military status quo is by definition inescapable, especially in the qualitative dimension of the arms dynamic. If a state routinely introduces a new fighter to replace older ones that are coming to the end of their designed lifespan, that new aircraft will naturally reflect improvements in technology that have become available since the previous generation was built. However different in motive and consequence, that behaviour is no different in form from a qualitative arms race in which one side seeks to gain an edge by pushing the pace of qualitative improvement against its rival. The distinction between racing and maintenance is usually clearer in the quantitative dimension, though even there it may not be obvious. A build-up of numbers may well indicate a racing desire to increase military power. But it may also result from the introduction of a new type of weapon, like Dreadnoughts or ICBMs, whose numbers need to be built up from zero as a normal part of maintenance of the military status quo in an environment of technological change.

Because the idiom of maintenance of the military status quo is by definition similar to that of arms racing, identifying the boundary between the two is easier in theory than in practice, a common problem with concepts in the Social Sciences. The advantage of adding the idea of maintenance of the military status quo is therefore not gained primarily in terms of easing the difficulty of defining when an arms race exists. The gain is in the idea that armed states are a normal feature of the international system, and therefore that there must be a baseline of routine behaviour against which to assess the more extreme behaviour of arms racing. The role of maintenance of the military status quo as an idea is therefore to condition approaches to the understanding of arms racing in general, as well as of particular arms races, by inserting into the enquiry the idea that one needs to find out what is normal before one can identify what is extreme.

The conditions that define normal maintenance of the military status quo behaviour almost certainly cannot be generalized across different cases. What is normal in any given case will depend on the nature of prevailing technologies, on the pace and scope of technological change, on the character of prevailing military doctrines, and on the character of prevailing attitudes towards the probability, feasibility and desirability of war. Objective comparison of these qualities across cases poses insuperable difficulties. The best one can do is to apply general ideas to the understanding of particular cases. It does not seem reasonable, for example, to equate the problems of maintenance of the military status quo in a period when rapid technological change is redefining the character of major weapons systems, with those in a period when dominant weapons systems are relatively stable. Maintenance of the military status quo is more difficult in periods of major changes in dominant weapons, like the shift in warships from wood and sail the iron and steam between 1840 and 1870, and from bombers to ICBMs in the 1950s. It is easier in periods of relative continuity, like the 1960s and 1970s when the ICBM held unchallenged supremacy in the strategic nuclear relationship.

### 9.1.1   The Superpowers: Arms Race or Maintenance of the Military status quo

There are weighty debates as to whether the arms dynamic between the United States and the Soviet Union should be considered as an arms race (Nacht, 1975; Wohlstetter, 1974). It is no surprise therefore that the military relationship between the superpowers displays the distinction between arms racing and maintenance of the military status quo at its most useful in terms of understanding what is going on. The superpower case is also worth examining because it reveals one of the difficulties of the distinction in terms of defining a clear boundary between the racing and maintenance ends of the arms dynamic spectrum. If it is a race, then it seems remarkably low key. Although the level of arms is high, nearly all of the quantitative indicators of weapon stockpiles are stable or declining. Ballistic missile warhead numbers are a steady growth area, but new ones are smaller than old ones, and so the aggregated total of their explosive yield has declined. Defence expenditure is fairly high, both in absolute terms, and, especially on the Soviet side, as a percentage of GNP. But it is not, especially in the West, at anything like crisis levels in terms of its effect on civil consumption and investment. Neither does it show any steady tendency to rise as a percentage of GNP, as one would expect it to in response to either quantitative expansion of forces or a concerted drive for qualitative superiority. Sometimes it rises, as in the 1980s, and sometimes it declines, as in the 1970s. Although the early stages of the superpower relationship looked like an arms race, with the Americans surging ahead in strategic nuclear strength, and the Soviet Union struggling to catch up, by the mid-1960s the United States seemed willing to accept the Soviet Union as a nuclear equal, and gave clear proof of that acceptance in the SALT agreements. The elements of racing were reduced to American doubts about whether the Soviets would accept equality, or simply use it as a waystation on the road to superiority, and to uncertainty whether the United States itself could live permanently with the reduced status of equality.

There is no doubt whatever that both superpowers could, if they felt it necessary, allocate much higher fractions of GNP to defence, albeit at a social cost, than they have done over the past four decades. To the extent that arms racing is supposed to be an aspect of wartime behaviour carried on during periods of peace, there must therefore be serious doubt as to whether the superpowers are arms racing. Only the Soviet Union could be said to be anywhere close to a war economy, and both sides could substantially compress R&D time scales, and greatly increase the pace and scale of military production, if they felt the need to do so. In other words, current levels of activity leave plenty of room for the superpowers to threaten each other with a real arms race.

If the superpower relationship is to be called an arms race, then it is strikingly different from the races that preceded the last two world wars. In those cases, the sharp expansion of military forces and expenditures was much more obvious, not least because they took place in a climate of opinion which saw war as a usable, likely, and in some quarters even desirable, instrument of state policy. If this comparison is evaded by the argument that the superpowers are now in a qualitative arms race, the problem arises of distinguishing between the normal pace of the technological imperative, which is quite high, and the addition to it that would represent real arms racing behaviour. Many of the technological advances that have made an impact on superpower military relations do not seem much out of line with the inescapable advance of technology as a whole. This is not to deny that large resources have been devoted to developing military applications of technology, nor to discount the effect that technological leadership in the military sector can have on civil sectors such as commercial aircraft. It is simply to point that the scientific and commercial attractions of civil applications for such things as computers, aircraft and rockets would probably have produced a similar general pace of scientific and technological advance even in the absence of a military sector. After all, it was

President Kennedy who set in train what amounted to a civil technology 'race' to put a man on the moon. Jet bombers, ICBMs, MIRV, cruise missiles, and the whole variety of tactical precision-guided munitions all use technology that is not far removed from applications in an equally fast evolving civil sector.

SDI, with its promise to devote large resources to promoting exotic technological breakthroughs in areas of little civil interest, is significant because it is one of the few qualitative moves that looks like arms racing behaviour. SDI undoubtedly does contain a major element of technological challenge by the United States to the Soviet Union. In political terms, it is a means by which the United States can threaten to withdraw the recognition of military equality that it extended to the Soviet Union during the 1970s. Much of the SDI research, however, is in the field of information technology, including advanced software and fifth generation computers. It is this general leap in an area of technology also important to the civil sector that worries the other Western states. SDI thus demonstrates an aspect of the domestic structure model inasmuch as the military rivalry with the Soviet Union provides a useful lever to get a reluctant Congress to allocate large resources to basic research areas with broader economic implications.

If the superpower relationship looks to be less than an arms race, it is still considerably more than the bottom line of maintenance of the military status quo. In many ways, the idea of maintenance does seem to describe essential features of the relationship. Military budgets and arsenals are reasonably stable, the pace of qualitative advance is not much out of line with that in the rest of society, at least in the West, and there is much talk about equivalence as a common standard. The doctrine of deterrence also lends itself to the idea of maintenance. One could make a case that maintenance of the military status quo under contemporary conditions – in other words, dominated by the availability of fast delivery, long-range, mass destruction weapons; quite high levels of real political hostility; rapid technological advance; and military doctrines of deterrence – would have to look something like what the superpowers actually do.

This case has several shortcomings. Perhaps most obvious is that the level of arms is much too high for minimum deterrence. The two superpowers are more sensitive to each other's military doctrines and deployments than they would be for simple maintenance of the military status quo. There is too much enthusiasm, especially in the United States, for encouraging the military application of dubious options like MIRV and SDI that become available through the process of qualitative advance. Although the two superpowers do accept a general equivalence, this seems to be more a matter of accepting the inevitable than of embracing the idea for its intrinsic merit. As a consequence, there is no firmly accepted balance of power, and each state seeks whatever opportunities it can find to exploit the weaknesses of the other. The United States challenges Soviet ability to sustain the technological pace. The Soviet Union keeps pressure on the United States through the quantity of its military deployments, and by preserving a massive offensive theatre capability, both conventional and nuclear, against Western Europe. Although neither side desires war, their hostility is sufficient that neither rules it out. Consequently each thinks in terms of warfighting, is sensitive to the measures that the other takes in that regard, and plans its own force levels in terms of a possibility of war.

The only reasonable conclusion is thus that the case of the superpowers falls into the grey area between maintenance of the military status quo and arms racing. The case has strong enough elements of both to preclude its being clearly defined as either. Plenty of room still exists for an intensification of the American-Soviet relationship into an arms race. Plenty of room also exists in the other direction for winding the rivalry down towards basic maintenance of the military status quo. The fact that the major pattern of superpower behaviour is in terms of maintenance, but that it is at a rather high level of armament, suggests that the grey area is occupied by a series of levels at which maintenance can occur. The minimum level would have to be defined according to the circumstances of the case under consideration. In this case it might be set according to the various ideas in circulation for minimum deterrence policies between the superpowers discussed in Part III. Maintenance options would exist at a range of higher levels of armament, but it would still be important to differentiate these from the less stable condition of arms racing, where one side is trying to change the military balance, and the other is resisting that effort. The borderline position of the superpower case does not mean that the relationship is unstable. It does underline the nearness of the superpowers to arms racing, and therefore the importance of continuous measures to prevent any escalation of their arms dynamic.

## 9.1.2  Conclusion

By adding maintenance of the military status quo to arms racing, it
is possible to create a more balanced perspective on the whole issue
of peacetime military relations between states than is available
through the idea of arms racing alone. Arms racing gives no sense of
what constitutes normal peacetime military relations between states,
and consequently tends to push thinking towards extreme
interpretations. These generate unhelpful and substantially false
choices, like those that dominate so much of the public debate,
between the unacceptability of arms racing and the impossibility of
general disarmament. With a broader perspective, the problem can
be more accurately stated, and a range of more precise questions
asked about what should and can be done.

Substituting the duality of maintenance of the military status quo
and arms racing for the single idea of arms racing changes the nature
of the research agenda, and may open up lines of enquiry more
fruitful than those that have emerged from arms racing by itself. For
example, it raises questions about what conditions define the
problem of maintenance of the military status quo in any given
period, and why relationships of maintenance sometimes turn into
arms racing. It also adds an interesting dimension to the traditional
range of questions about the relationship between arms racing on
the one hand, and war, arms control, disarmament and deterrence
on the other. It seems worth hypothesizing, for example, that
situations of maintenance of the military status quo will be less likely
to lead to war, and more likely to be amenable to arms control, than
will arms races. This might be stated in reverse, that when war is
thought to be probable, behaviour will shift towards arms racing,
and when war is thought to be improbable, it will shift towards
maintenance of the military status quo. Deterrence policies aim to
reduce the probability of war, and are therefore likely to generate
maintenance of the military status quo, albeit perhaps at high levels
of armament. The identification of maintenance of the military
status quo as a norm of behaviour in the international system also
makes the case for disarmament as an alternative to arms racing
much more difficult to carry, as we will see in Part IV.

The purpose of this long exercise in establishing the idea of the
arms dynamic is, therefore, to redefine the idea of arms racing
sufficiently to enable it to play its proper central role in strategic
thinking. Only if a firm and realistic grip can be established on the

mechanisms that govern the peacetime military deployments of states do we have the necessary basis on which to approach the subjects of defence, disarmament, arms control and deterrence.

## 9.2 PROBLEMS IN DEVELOPING A THEORY OF ARMS RACING

The range of behaviour within the arms dynamic, added to the natural complexity of the phenomenon detailed above, has largely defeated the attempt to produce a coherent theory of arms racing. Although individual cases share common features, their idiosyncratic features are so dominant that generalizations have proved impossible to sustain. One can certainly find all sorts of tantalizingly similar behaviours across cases. The technological leap from mixed-gun battleships to all big-gun Dreadnoughts in 1905, and the subsequent British panic in 1908 about how many Dreadnoughts the Germans were building, finds a strong echo in the emergence of ICBMs in the 1950s, and the American worry about a 'missile gap' in favour of the Soviet Union. Despite such similarities, it has not proved possible to discover any general explanation of how arms races work. One can neither assume that one race will unfold like others, nor predict whether arms races will lead to war (Diehl, 1983; Intrilligator and Brito, 1984; Lambelet, 1975; Wallace, 1979, 1980, 1982). Existing knowledge is so crude that there is no basic set of agreed categories with which to undertake analysis. There are not even accepted criteria by which to ascertain that a situation of arms racing exists (Rattinger, 1975, pp. 571–2).

Even the normative status of arms racing is disputed. Despite the widespread negative connotation attached to arms racing, there are several writers prepared to discuss it as a useful substitute for war in the management of relations between states (Gray, 1974, pp. 232–3; Halle, 1984, pp. 23–5; Howard, 1983, pp. 17–20; Huntington, 1958, p. 83; Russett, 1983b, ch 3; Tsipis, 1975, p. 80). This normative ambiguity highlights the danger of politicization that so plagues discussion of the arms dynamic. The different models can be seen as representing different aspects of reality, but they can also be seen as political attempts to 'construct' reality by portraying it in a certain light. As already noted, the domestic structure model can serve the interests of those wishing to argue that arms increases by their side will not stimulate 'reactions' from a rival. The action-reaction model fits into the needs of those advocating arms control, and the technological imperative model could serve the needs of those wanting to argue that nothing can be done about the whole process. Indeed, as has been argued, the term arms racing itself often reflects a political choice about how to characterise the issues under discussion. The ease with which ostensibly empirical analytical devices can be used for political purposes is thus one of the principal difficulties impeding the debate about arms racing.

As with other social phenomena like war, inflation and power, there is enough similarity among cases of arms racing to indicate that one is looking at a coherent class of things, but enough diversity among separate instances to prevent the formulation of simple or reliable statements about cause and effect. Existing knowledge does not justify the label of theory, since not even the basic step of ranking the explanatory power of the three models can be convincingly undertaken except on a case-by-case basis. The models serve to organize questions, and to act as a framework for analysing specific cases. At best they perhaps represent a sufficient aggregation of explanatory ideas to be labelled a pre-theory.

The difficulty of theorizing about the arms dynamic is reflected in the shape of the literature. On the traditional side, Colin Gray has made the most comprehensive attempt to tackle the problem of basic categories (Gray, 1971a, 1974, 1976). The earlier work of Samuel Huntington also still represents a significant contribution along traditional lines (Huntington, 1958). The result of Gray's effort is an interesting and suggestive set of lists: seven reasons why states arms race, ten descriptive categories, five strategies, five outcomes, eleven process dynamics and six patterns of interaction. Although one can question the tightness of Gray's categories, the very length and number of his lists confirm the point that arms racing is too diverse and complex a phenomenon to allow for much generalization. Differences in technology, historical circumstance, and motive across cases are so great as to leave little hope that the comparative method will yield firm cause-effect relations for either explanation or prediction of the phenomenon as a whole. At best, the traditional approach leads towards an analytical framework, like the one elaborated here, which provides a menu of ideas and categories for application to particular cases. Such a menu does not easily generate theory because it seldom provides categories that can be found equally in all cases.

A rather different, but in the end no more successful, approach to a theory of arms racing is that taken by the many writers who have built on the pioneering mathematical work of Lewis Richardson (1960). Richardson tried to reduce the essentials of the action-reaction model to a small number of quantifiable variables that he could express in terms of equations. In doing so he opened up the method of trying to understand the arms dynamic by approaching it in terms of highly simplified, but rigorous, mathematical models of its basic interactions. Limitations of space forbid any detailed explanation of Richardson's models here. Anatol Rapoport (1960, chs 1–2) probably still offers the clearest introduction for those otherwise intimidated by quantitative methods, and Richardson's work is extensively reviewed and discussed in the literature (Bellany, 1975; Busch, 1970; Lambelet, 1975, pp. 123–4; Luterbacher, 1975; Smoker, 1964). The great merit of Richardson's approach is that it offers a systematic way of exploring relationships between discrete factors in the arms dynamic. Richardson, for example, distinguished between arms races that would feed on themselves, and ones that would tend to die down, according to the balance between specified variables within the state and the action-reaction process. Such insights are a valuable stimulus to analysis. The use of formal models with highly restricted assumptions about the variables in play is often a useful way of opening up and exploring patterns of relationships that would be neither obvious nor easy to handle if one tried to trace them through the jumbled complexities of historical evidence. As a fruitful way of thinking in the abstract, the Richardson school can claim considerable success.

Its difficulty has been in trying to bridge the gap between highly simplified abstract models, and analysis of cases in the real world. Three problems have prevented this attempt from having much success. The first is that the Richardson approach is tied to the imperfections of the action-reaction model. Richardson's models assume that action-reaction is not only the major driving force of arms racing, but that it is a deterministic relationship (Busch, 1970, pp. 196–7). That assumption does not fit well with the observed behaviour of the superpowers, which seems to proceed on the basis of a considerably more complicated and diverse set of factors.

The second problem stems from the first in that the rigour of the models cannot be sustained once their highly simplifying assumptions are relaxed sufficiently to incorporate the complexities of the real world. In the models, one can assume rational actors, perfect information, uncomplicated two-party situations, and a set of actions and reactions that occur in a clear sequence of cause and effect. In the real world, actors are not always rational calculators; information is seldom perfect; states are concerned in their arms policies not only with more than one opponent, but also with allies; and reactions are not always in strict sequential relationship with the actions that are supposed to cause them (Brubaker, 1973, pp. 203–4; Busch, 1970; Luterbacher, 1975, pp. 212–15; Rattinger, 1976, p. 529).

Reliance on such assumptions is an unavoidable necessity of using quantitative methods. But the validity of assumptions is very hard to sustain in applications of the models to real cases. Some assumptions, like that of rationality, attract charges of serious misrepresentation of reality. Attempts to adjust the logic of the models to the complexity of real situations also run into awkward intervening variables. How, for example, does one disentangle the impact of peripheral wars like Vietnam from the pattern of military procurement and expenditure in the over-all arms dynamic between the United States and the Soviet Union? (Rattinger, 1975, pp. 572–3). Although these attempts often give interesting insights along the way, they tend to result in increasingly less clear-cut, and more confusing, conclusions (McGuire, 1965, 1968, pp. 249–53). As things stand, the rigour and logic of the models can only be purchased at the price of gross oversimplification. Enriching the variables to try to capture reality destroys the clarity that makes the models useful in the first place.

The attempt to engage the models with real cases raises a third problem, which is the difficulty of obtaining reliable quantitative measures with which to link the power of the equations to conditions in the real world. Richardson's use of defence expenditure as a measure of arms racing, though obviously convenient, is widely thought to be too crude for applied studies (Bellany, 1975, pp. 120–4; Luterbaker, 1975, pp. 200; Rattinger, 1976, p. 502). But finding more specific measures has proved extremely difficult (Busch, 1970, pp. 230–3; Gillespie *et al.*, 1979, pp. 256–7; Luterbacher, 1975, pp. 200–2). Here the method runs into a problem that afflicts all quantitative approaches to the study of International Relations. Reliable data is hard to get for many countries, especially regarding sensitive areas like defence expenditures. Even the study of superpower relations is hampered by lack of firm, comparable data about the Soviet Union. Much of the data that is available is hard to compare even within the same time period. Measures of GNP, for example, are notoriously inaccurate for countries still possessing a large barter economy that does not register in calculations of monetary value. Few reliable data sets extend far back into history, and even where they do, it is hazardous to assume that values have the same significance across historical periods.

Problems with data can require elaborate statistical operations to try to achieve comparability (Gillespie *et al.*, 1979, pp. 256–7). Such operations not infrequently lead to controversies about excessive manipulation of data leading to bias in the analysis (Luterbacher, 1975, pp. 212–15). The use of statistical techniques seems prone to generate arguments about method because, 'apparently insignificant research choices can collectively influence results in a profound way' (Diehl, 1983, pp. 210–11). In the case that gave rise to that remark, one author found a 90 per cent correlation between arms racing and war, and another found that 77 per cent of major power wars were not preceded by an arms race (Diehl, 1983; Wallace, 1979, 1980, 1982). The frequency of such disputes, as well as the specialized language in which they are necessarily conducted, go a long way to explaining why there is relatively little communication between those studying arms racing using the Richardson method, and those whose focus is on historical case studies, or more traditional analysis in the style of Gray and Huntington. This lack of communication is to be deplored, because one of the brighter features of the arms racing literature is the way in which debate about the action-reaction and domestic structure models has stimulated, and been stimulated by, research into the details of the arms dynamic between the United States and the Soviet Union.

## 9.3   THE LEVEL OF ANALYSIS PROBLEM

Both the traditional and the Richardson approaches to the arms dynamic face a problem that is common to many areas of International Relations, which is to determine the level of analysis on which one seeks to explain observed phenomena. The classical form of this problem is whether one seeks explanations at the level of individual states or at the level of the international system (Singer, 1961). One can also add the level of individuals, as Waltz did when he enquired into where the root causes of war might be found: in human nature; in the nature of states; or in the anarchic structure of the state system as a whole, (Waltz, 1959). Unless the level of analysis is kept clear, it is impossible to come to coherent conclusions about relationships of cause and effect. With the arms dynamic, the level of analysis problem is additionally complicated because the phenomenon is technological as well as political. As a consequence, we find explanations being offered on a range of levels. Reviewing these levels is a useful way of putting the different explanations of the arms dynamic into context.

The lowest level is the domestic structure model, in which the arms dynamic is explained by what goes on inside individual states. The extreme form of this view is autism, which sees the process as almost exclusively internalized within the state. As noted earlier, this level of explanation fits into a long-standing tradition by which the behaviour of states is analysed in terms of their domestic structures and events. The advantage of this level is that it offers access to a rich body of detail relevant to specific cases. Its main disadvantage is that the wealth of idiosyncratic detail makes the search for generalizations more difficult.

The next level up is the action-reaction model, which seeks explanation in the pattern of relations between specified states. There is a methodological dispute within this level about whether the arms dynamic should be considered in terms of pairs of states (dyads) or larger sets of states. The dyadic assumption is essential for the Richardson school, because without it quantitative approaches would become unmanageably complicated. Some traditionalists also defend it on the grounds that action-reaction requires that specific security or status issues exist between arms racing states (Huntington, 1958, p. 42), but others reject it as a distortion of reality (Gray, 1971a, pp. 45–6). The analytical issue is whether one sees a multistate arms race like that preceding the First World War as a single phenomenon binding together two coalitions of states, or simply as a large number of separable dyads that happen to be occurring in parallel. One of the hazards of the dyadic assumption is revealed in the debate between Wallace and Diehl noted above. Wallace used a dyadic assumption, and was therefore able to find a large number of arms races ending in war because the bulk of his cases came from the mass of dyads preceding the two world wars. The problem is a serious one. The logic of dyads has some force, and greatly facilitates analysis. Yet the idea of generalized, multiparty arms races clearly captures important elements of some cases, though only at the cost of making systematic analysis much more difficult.

On the system level, we can find the same generalized explanation for arms racing that Waltz found for war, namely that the anarchic structure of the international political system provides a deeply-rooted environment that does nothing to prevent, and something to encourage, such behaviour. System structure does not explain or predict particular cases. It does predict that a system in which independent units are responsible for their own security against each other will generate the security dilemmas and power struggles that give rise to the arms dynamic. So long as the anarchic structure persists, arms racing behaviour will be likely, though not inevitable if factors on other levels work strongly and uniformly against it.

A variety of historical theories at a high level of generalization also contain explanations relevant to arms racing. Lenin's theory of imperialism (Lenin, 1916), for example, posits a cycle of increasing competition amongst capitalist states for the world pool of markets and resources. In a quite different vein, Robert Gilpin argues for a cyclical process of rise and decline in the hegemonic powers that underpin much of the order in the international system. He argues that hegemonic powers play a key role in diffusing technology to the rest of the international system, and also that the decline of the hegemony creates periods of instability when the ordering forces in the international system are weak and the pressures for change strong (Gilpin, 1981). Theories of this type suggest that arms racing will be more common and more intense under some kinds of historical condition than under others. They are not theories of arms racing in themselves, but they offer insights which, if valid, need to be taken into account in any over-all understanding of the arms dynamic.

The technological imperative model is also a system level explanation, albeit in the technological rather than in the political realm. The idea of a technological revolution as a global phenomenon transcends both individual states and relations between them. It identifies a process of qualitative advance that is rooted in the whole body of scientific knowledge, and which drives a standard of technology that affects the military position of all states. The process by which this revolution continues to unfold and spread is a fundamental part of the arms dynamic, and a key input into arms racing. In understanding the arms dynamic, the fact that states have to assess their military procurements in relation to the standard of the technological leading edge is as important as the fact that they also have to assess their military capability in relation to each other.

## 9.4   ARMS PRODUCTION AND THE ARMS DYNAMIC

The interplay of these levels of analysis in the three-model composite points to the need for a new distinction in analyses of the arms dynamic between relationships in which the participants are themselves major producers of arms, and those in which they are primarily importers. This distinction applies to the arms dynamic as a whole, but is particularly important in cases of arms racing. There will be grey area cases in which the participants are part-producers, and, more rarely, in which one side is a producer and the other is a non-producer. But we can use the terms *primary* to designate an arms dynamic between major producers, and *secondary* to designate one involving only lesser part-producers or non-producers. Most of the existing literature about arms racing has stemmed from concern about relations among great powers, and therefore assumes that races are primary. Yet decolonisation, and the diffusion of modern weapons through the arms trade, has created a whole new arena in which the arms dynamic is largely secondary in character. As argued in Chapter 3, the diffusion of production capability is a slow process, and many countries will remain dependent on arms imports for the foreseeable future.

Surprisingly, the few writers who have taken an interest in cases of secondary arms racing have largely ignored the fundamental difference of condition with which they are dealing (Gillespie *et al.*, 1979; Rattinger, 1976). Gray's notion of 'hierarchy' (1971a, pp. 53–4) gets no closer than the half-truth that secondary arms races are simply local proxy manifestations of races among the great powers. Kaldor's idea of a 'world military order' goes no further than describing the process of technological diffusion, and the uniformities of military technology that it is creating in the international system as a whole (Kaldor, 1982, ch. 5). These views are valid as far as they go, but they do not give the full picture. They ignore, or discount, both the real independence of the arms dynamic amongst Third World countries, and the very substantial difference that being dependent on imports rather than on production makes to the whole process of peacetime military interaction between states.

If a secondary arms dynamic is to any large extent a proxy event for a great power rivalry, then the first obvious difference is that such a dynamic cannot be considered as a strict dyad. At least four states will be involved: the two local clients and their two great power sponsors. Even if the secondary dynamic is largely a local affair, one cannot remove the influence of arms suppliers. The arms dynamic between India and Pakistan is certainly more independent than proxy, but the embargo on arms supplies by the United States and Britain in 1965 had a major impact, especially on Pakistan. External suppliers affect secondary arms dynamics by determining the amount and the quality of the weapons supplied. They can easily inflate a secondary dynamic into an arms race by pumping large supplies to one side at low cost, as the superpowers have done in the Middle East and South Asia. They can also try to restrict the quality and/or quantity of arms made available, though, except for the special case of nuclear technology, this is difficult in a buyer's market.

Perhaps the main point of difference between primary and secondary arms races in terms of arms supply is that in a primary race the rate, volume and quality of supply is constrained by the productive capacity of the rivals themselves, whereas in a secondary race these variables are under the much looser constraint of what suppliers will agree to provide. A pace of supply set by productive capacity is much more predictable in every way than one set by markets. In a primary race, the rivals will usually have a reasonable knowledge of the maximum production capabilities of their opponents. Major qualitative transformations in forces like MIRV or SDI will amost always give plenty of warning, and take a long time to deploy in numbers substantial enough to change the military balance. That warning time gives the rival power an opportunity to respond in some way that will preserve the military balance. By contrast, in a secondary race, where total numbers of weapons are usually, but not always, much smaller than for great powers, new weapons can be introduced rapidly, unexpectedly, and in unknown quantities. The Soviet Union, for example, has made massive transfers of weapons to Egypt, Syria, Somalia and Ethiopia within short periods of time. Such injections can change a local military balance very quickly. Since the potential for them is a constant condition of life for states dependent on arms imports, there seems every reason to expect that secondary arms races will be much more volatile, and much more difficult to manage, than primary ones. In other words, the technological imperative is in one important sense easier to live with when it is internalized within states in the form of independent production capability, than when it isn't.

Another major contrast between primary and secondary arms dynamics is the role of domestic structure. As already suggested in

Chapter 7, the absence of institutionalized military R&D and production creates a wholly different configuration of domestic factors in non-producing countries from those in producer states. That difference should affect the balance of factors among the three models quite substantially. Although the nature and extent of the difference is a matter for research, it seems reasonable to hypothesize that the domestic structure model will have proportionately less influence in secondary arms dynamics than in primary ones. In other words, secondary arms races will be more determined by action-reaction and technological imperative factors than by domestic structure ones.

## 9.5   CONCLUSION

Taken together, these problems have contributed to the existence of a weak literature at the heart of the cluster of subjects that make up Strategic Studies (Gray, 1976, pp. vii–viii; Rattinger, 1975, pp. 571–2; Schelling, 1963, pp. 465–78). This weakness has both political and intellectual consequences. On the political side, it means that there is no check on the widespread emotive use of the term arms racing in public debate. Such use exploits a seed of truth to cultivate a forest of misunderstanding about both defence policy and international relations. That misunderstanding in turn makes the operating environment of the field as a whole more difficult. On the intellectual side, it creates a debilitating ambiguity at the core of the subject. To the extent that arms racing is not fully understood, many other major elements of the strategic debate also cannot be understood. Thinking about arms control and disarmament lacks a clear referent if one is not sure about the processes and consequences of arms racing. Finding agreement about the probability of war, and about how to reduce it, is almost impossible without some consensus on the significance of the arms dynamic. And thinking about deterrence, both as theory and as policy, cannot be detached from understanding of the arms dynamic to which it is intimately linked. The present weakness in understanding of arms racing, in other words, should not be an excuse for neglect of it in the future.

The reinterpretation of arms racing into the broader framework of the arms dynamic provides a foundation for the rest of the book. A process has been defined that underlies and influences the whole range of military relations among states. That process is deeply rooted in both the political structure of the international system and the scientific and technological drive of what is now a global civilization. Its most extreme form is arms racing, which is widely, but not universally, held to be a dangerous and undesirable condition. Its regular form is maintenance of the military status quo, which some see as a necessary, and even desirable, consequence of preserving independent states, and others see as wasteful, undesirable, and potentially dangerous. These conflicting attitudes towards the arms dynamic run through the whole strategic debate, influencing positions on defence, deterrence, disarmament, and arms control, which are the subjects of Parts III and IV.

# Part III

# Deterrence

# 10 Introduction:
## Deterrence and Defence

### 10.1 RETALIATION VERSUS DENIAL IN DETERRENCE STRATEGY

One of the principal sources of confusion – and therefore of dispute – in the debates about deterrence arises from the relationship between defence and deterrence. Some authors treat the two as distinct, alternative, and in some ways incompatible, approaches to policy (Art, 1980, pp. 5–7; Halle, 1984, pp. 23–33; Snyder, 1971, pp. 56–7; Waltz, 1981, pp. 4–5), while others argue, or assume, that there is a broad overlap between them (Gray, 1982a, pp. 84–92; Hoag, 1962; Lodal, 1980, p. 155). This difference has major implications for what is meant by the term deterrence. It has both definitional and political roots, and one needs to have a very clear understanding of it before trying to tackle the intricacies of the deterrence literature.

The definitional problem is easier to understand if it is approached using the more precise distinction between *retaliation* and *denial* as military strategies. Retaliation involves the infliction of punishment on an opponent in response to an attack. The punishment need not take place within the same area as the attack that provoked it. Its principal purpose is to inflict reciprocal cost. The threat of nuclear bombardment that the superpowers hold over each other in the event of nuclear attack is a clear example of retaliatory policy. Denial involves direct resistance by force to the attempt of another to attack areas that are under your control. The essence of denial is to block an attack by physical opposition to the forces making it. The effort of NATO to mount armed forces in Europe sufficient to delay or stop a conventional invasion by the Soviet Union is a denial policy.

In military terms, denial and defence have virtually identical meanings. Those who treat deterrence and defence as alternatives are assuming that deterrence is likewise synonymous with retaliation. In this view, the terms defence and deterrence thus reflect the unambiguous distinction between denial and retaliation. This narrow

135

view is questionable. As will be seen in detail in Chapter 12, the essence of deterrence is the making of military threats in order to prevent another actor from taking aggressive actions. Deterrence is about stopping unwanted actions *before they occur*. Nothing in that definition restricts the threats to retaliation. There is no reason why the threat of a stout defence cannot fulfil the requirements of deterrence. Logically, therefore, the concept of deterrence encompasses both denial and retaliation. Its proper opposite is not defence, with which it runs partly in parallel, but what Schelling has called *compellence*, which is the active use of force either to make your opponent do something (like retreat), or stop him from continuing some action that is already underway (like attacking you) (Art, 1980, pp. 7–10; Schelling, 1966, p. 69ff.).

By this reasoning, deterrence is a statement of a strategic end, and retaliation and defence/denial describe two different ways of pursuing that end. The issue of ends and means in deterrence strategies will be considered in detail in Chapter 13. For the moment, the essential point to register is that retaliation and denial represent two major threads in the debate about deterrence strategy. In some eyes these threads are complementary, and the term deterrence is used in a way that incorporates them both. In other eyes, they are seen as contradictory, and the term deterrence is used more narrowly to refer exclusively to threats of punishment by retaliation. In this narrower view, defence is seen as a strategy that is different from, and frequently incompatible with, deterrence. The difference between these two views has profound implications for the military means and strategies by which deterrence is implemented. If deterrence is purely retaliatory, then its logic leads to a rejection of strategic defences, but if it includes denial, then it may well be logical to deploy strategic defences.

If one takes the broad view of deterrence, then the concept blends easily into traditional strategies for national defence. Although the term deterrence did not become important in strategic debate until the early years of the nuclear age, the idea that strong defensive forces would prevent opponents from attacking has always been a central element in strategic thinking. Fortified borders like the Maginot Line exemplify deterrence by denial in traditional military strategy. The idea that deterrence could be achieved by threats of punishment other than those associated with denial only came to fruition when nuclear weapons provided much larger means of destruction than had hitherto been available. Only then did the term itself become a major element in strategic thinking. The elements of a capability for deterrence by retaliation were building up during the 1920s and 1930s with the development of long-range aircraft armed with chemical and high-explosive bombs. These developments, however, were neither potent enough nor sufficiently dramatic to break the mould of traditional strategic thinking in the way that nuclear weapons did.

The development of deterrence theory, and thus of the whole literature on deterrence, hinges on the distinction between deterrence by denial/defence, and deterrence by retaliation/punishment. In the West, and particularly in the United States, thinking about deterrence developed initially out of enthusiasm for the new strategic possibilities of deterrence by retaliation. Much of deterrence theory and literature is thus rooted in the distinctive logic of this view. In the decades since the first flourish of enthusiasm for pure retaliatory strategies, deterrence theory has come under sustained pressure to incorporate more and more elements of denial. Western thinking is now split between those who still favour a deterrence strategy predominantly based on the logic of retaliation, and those who wish to see the logic of denial given priority. The evolution of deterrence theory in the West therefore now covers the whole range of issues arising from the two different approaches to deterrence, and the interplay between them. The term deterrence is appropriate even for the stronger denial views, because the overarching threat of nuclear devastation makes war avoidance the central priority for both strands of thought.

In the non-Western nuclear powers, the Soviet Union and China, no comparable enthusiasm for the logic of deterrence by retaliation ever developed. Nuclear weapons made their impact on strategic thinking in these countries in a context dominated by traditional defence priorities, and by a political unwillingness to entertain the idea that national security could be based on mutual vulnerability with one's opponent. Both China and the Soviet Union favour deterrence by denial (Segal, 1983–4, pp. 22–5). They do so strongly enough that the idea of deterrence does not emerge as clearly distinct from their general preoccupations with defence, and does not have the separate identity, the theoretical elaboration, or the policy importance that it does in the West.

Because of this difference of attitude, Western thinking about deterrence has been much more wide-ranging than that coming from the Communist powers. Until well into the 1970s, the denial approach of the Communist powers and the retaliatory approach of the West shared little common ground. Since then, the logic of deterrence by denial has become much more prominent in Western thinking. This convergence does not mean that deterrence thinking has become identical between East and West, but it does mean that the two sides no longer inhabit strategic universes that share very few common assumptions. It also means that the next three chapters can concentrate mainly on the richer and more accessible Western literature without missing the logic that informs the Soviet and Chinese views.

## 10.2   DETERRENCE THEORY AS A WESTERN ARTIFACT

Deterrence is a distinctive concept because it gives priority to war prevention as a strategic objective. The fact that retaliatory deterrence theory has achieved such prominence in the strategy of the West is no accident, but reflects both the historical position and the social conditions of the Western powers. In turn, the character of Western, and particularly American, society has influenced the way in which deterrence has been conceived and implemented.

The advent of nuclear weapons imposed a particular historical timing on the emergence of deterrence, and given that timing, it is not surprising that the construction of a relatively free-standing deterrence theory has been largely an Anglo-Saxon pursuit. This is partly because the United States was the dominant military power in the West, but partly also because the Western winners of the Second World War were primarily Anglo-Saxon: the United States and Britain, with Canada and Australia as smaller participants, and France as a kind of half-winning outsider. The Western winners of the Second World War inherited the problem of security management in the international system. They faced a situation radically altered from that of the period before the war. The key differences were the emergence of the Soviet Union as a single major opponent whose threat united them all, and the introduction of nuclear weapons into strategic calculation. These were the conditions that dominated the development of Western deterrence theory, and which explain why the United States became its principal home. The Americans not only had to head the opposition to the Soviet Union, but they also possessed a substantial lead in the development and deployment of nuclear weapons. Deterrence theory thus developed primarily in response to the policy problems of the American state. It has wider Western roots both because the American problem was how to ensure the security of the other Western states against the Soviet Union, and because Britain, and later France, developed their own nuclear forces. Despite American predominance, there was in an important sense a single strategic problem confronting the West as a whole. That single problem meant that there was a multinational basis for the development of deterrence theory in the West.

Probably the most important consequence of these origins was that deterrence theory developed within a political context defined by status quo policy concerns. American economic and military hegemony, and the general dominance of Western culture, was challenged principally by the military and ideological power of the Communist Bloc. Although the decolonization movement challenged the right of the West to direct political control in the Third World, it only challenged the over-all hegemony of the West when Third World countries threatened to align themselves with the Soviet Union. Because the West was almost everywhere dominant, its security outlook took the classical status quo form of preserving position. Although political hostility to Soviet ideology was strong in the United States, there was little mainstream support for military aggression against it even in the days before the Soviet Union acquired a credible nuclear force. After the experience of the Second World War, Western societies were not in a militarily aggressive mood. War had lost its appeal as an instrument of state policy for anything except the most basic issues of national survival, and domestic welfare concerns headed the political agenda.

This politically and militarily defensive outlook harmonized neatly with the war-prevention imperative generated independently by nuclear weapons. As an additional bonus, nuclear weapons fitted well into the predisposition of advanced capitalist societies to prefer capital intensive technologies as the basis of their military strength. War prevention was not only required because of nuclear weapons; it was preferred because of the West's political position, and it complemented its technological inclinations. The combination produced a strong normative orientation within Strategic Studies towards security defined in terms of stability: as Gray notes, stability is the 'master concept' of American strategists (Gray, 1982a, p. 11). Yet as Carr observed even before the nuclear age, security is the watchword of the status quo powers. Their attempt to define their own interests in universal terms is not a moral position but a part of power politics (Carr, 1946, pp. 79–105). Nevertheless, the military conditions of the nuclear age have added a new dimension to the traditional policy ploys of the status quo powers. Although Carr's point accurately identifies one self-interested political foundation of Western deterrence theory, it does not do justice to the real universality of interest in avoiding all-out nuclear war that also underlies the concept of deterrence.

The distinctively Western and Anglo-Saxon character of deterrence theory is underlined by the dominant role that civilians have played in its development. This role came about not just because of the relative openness of Western, and particularly American, society, but also because the nature of the subject encouraged it. Encouragement took two forms: one arising from the new instruments of warfare, and the style of war they made possible; the other from the logic of strategy aimed at war prevention.

Even during the Second World War, before the nuclear age, the new instruments of war required the broad involvement of civilian experts in operational planning. This was particularly true of air power, which was too newly developed and too rapidly evolving to have much military tradition of its own. Air power involved sophisticated technology. It raised questions that were outside the normal realm of military expertise, such as what the targeting priorities should be for strategic bombing of the enemy's war economy. In addition, the programme to create nuclear weapons brought large numbers of scientists into contact with questions of military strategy, and ended the isolation of the scientific profession from government (Pearton, 1982, Part IV; Tsipis, 1985, ch. 1). After the war, the combination of nuclear weapons and air power not only ensured a continued role for civilians in strategy, but made their expertise central to the military power of the state. Nuclear weapons and their delivery systems could not be built, maintained or sensibly targeted without the involvement of scientists, technicians, economists and many others from the civil sector.

The logic of a strategy aimed at war prevention also opened the way for civilian strategists because it discounted the claim of the military professionals that only they held the expertise necessary for strategic thinking. The goal of war prevention meant that nuclear strategy was concerned primarily with the period before war broke out, rather than, as in traditional strategy, after. The point of deterrence strategy was to stop one's opponent from using force in the first place, not to defeat an attack after it had started. Since the expertise of the military was in using weapons to fight, the demands of nuclear strategy opened up a new field – in which nobody could claim prior expertise – of using weapons primarily to threaten. Nuclear strategy was more directly political than traditional strategy because it sought to work on the decision-making of political leaders, rather than to compete with the military skills of rival military commanders. As Freedman puts it:

> The essence of the strategy . . . was that any use or threat of use of nuclear weapons should be seen as a supremely political act, reducing the potential relevance of purely military considerations. They did not devise new strategies for the military but strategies for politicians.
>
> (Freedman, 1981, pp. 176–7)

The civilians brought with them a wide variety of intellectual skills from the natural and social sciences. They also brought an open-mindedness which enabled them to assess the nuclear situation in a manner unencumbered by the weight of military tradition. Anyone who doubts that this has made a difference, given the way that deterrence thinking has become preoccupied with military hardware, need only compare its product to Soviet thinking about military strategy. The Soviet Union, whose strategic thinking is dominated by military professionals, never separated war-prevention from preparation for warfighting. Consequently, Soviet leaders do not share the Western view of deterrence as an independent strategic concept. Where Western nuclear strategy displays the subtle, though sometimes excessive, influence of economic logic, the Soviet version still reflects the intellectual stamp of the artilleryman (Holloway, 1983, ch. 3 and pp. 150–4; Lambeth, 1981).

The skills of the civilian strategists resulted in the use of more systematic and calculating methods for thinking about military problems. The tools of systems analysis and game theory were applied to problems ranging from the design of deterrence policies to the procurement choices for new weapons systems (Brodie and Brodie, 1973, ch. 10; Enthoven and Smith, 1971; Freedman, 1981, ch.12; Schelling, 1960). Civilian involvement in nuclear strategy also ensured that the debate would be public. Part of the field remained academic, tending towards a relatively detached, theoretical and long-term view of deterrence. Another part developed in closer contact with the American policy-making process, where entrepreneurial consultants focused on the short-term, technical, and often classified issues that the pursuit of deterrence policy raised for governments. These issues frequently concerned procurement decisions for military hardware. As Gray observes, the sociology of Strategic Studies reflected the openness of American society, which enabled the community of strategists to enjoy career mobility both within and outside government (Gray, 1982b, p. 2). The civilian influence on deterrence theory thus made a significant impact on both the substance and the style of the debate about nuclear strategy.

The next chapter will trace how this peculiarly Western deterrence theory evolved from 1945 to the present day, stressing how the impact of both political and technological developments influenced its course. Chapter 12 will examine the logic of deterrence, and the kinds of variables that make deterrence easier or more difficult to achieve. Chapter 13 will take up four major debates that have featured in the discussion of deterrence ever since the theory first attained prominence as a justification for military policy.

# 11 The Evolution of Deterrence: Theory and Policy since 1945

Gray identifies three periods in the development of Western nuclear strategy – the First Wave, the Golden Age, and the Third Wave – and these provide a useful framework within which to organize a description of how deterrence theory and policy have evolved since the opening of the nuclear age in 1945 (Gray, 1982a, pp. 15–17).

## 11.1 THE FIRST WAVE

As several commentators have noted, a handful of British and American strategists writing immediately after the end of the Second World War laid down most of the basic ideas that were later to become the core of Western deterrence theory (Booth, in Baylis *et al.*, 1975, p. 34; Gray, 1982b, ch. 3; Herken, 1984, pp. 15–18. For the detailed intellectual history, see Freedman, 1981). These early writers included Bernard Brodie, Jacob Viner, Vannevar Bush, William Borden, Basil Liddell Hart, and P. M. S. Blackett.

The work of the First Wave writers was primarily an intellectual response to the advent of nuclear weapons. Starting from the single datum of a major increase in the power to destroy, these writers tried to work out the theoretical consequences for international relations of the deployment of such weapons by the major powers. Despite its high quality, this early thinking made little impact precisely because it was theoretical: no major deployments of nuclear weapons had yet occurred. Nothing could illustrate more clearly the close link between the development of deterrence theory and the evolving character of the Western security problem than this failure of the First Wave to generate a significant debate. The work of the First Wave attracted little interest because it did not address issues of immediate policy concern. The First Wave writers were thinking ahead to a time when both the United States and the Soviet Union would possess nuclear weapons. During the later 1940s the

143

United States had a nuclear monopoly, though the number of atomic bombs in its arsenal was still small. Its rivalry with the Soviet Union was therefore seen in traditional defence policy terms of building a position of superior strength. The immediate urgencies of the Cold War left little inclination to worry about a situation of nuclear parity that many hoped was as yet a considerable number of years in the future.

The first wave was a false dawn, not in terms of its ideas, but in terms of its timing. Deterrence theory would only make an impact on policy and on public awareness when the realities of nuclear relations created a policy need for ideas about strategy in an environment in which one's opponent also possessed nuclear weapons.

## 11.2   THE GOLDEN AGE

There is not the space here to trace the whole complex story of Golden Age thinking in detail. Interested readers can find the historical intricacies well laid out by Freedman (1981), and a historically detailed critique from the right in Gray (1982b). This chapter only outlines its main ideas, and traces how the development of those ideas related to the changes in technology and the balance of power that set the evolving security problem of the West.

### 11.2.1   The Coming of Bipolarity as the Background to the Golden Age

By the mid-1950s the international environment had changed substantially from that in which the First Wave writers worked. Many of their ideas had to be reinvented when Strategic Studies blossomed into its 'Golden Age' during the decade from the mid-1950s to the mid-1960s. The Soviet Union had tested a nuclear device in 1949, ahead of expectations, and by the mid-1950s was well into the nuclear race. Nuclear-armed rivalry was imminent, a situation which obviously made the West's problem of war prevention much more difficult than it had been during the first post-war decade.

The policy problem that triggered the Golden Age appeared in the concrete form of a hostile opponent acquiring apace the military technology that had hitherto given the West a decisive military edge. Against a more powerful opponent, the problem of how to prevent war took on greater urgency for two reasons. First, the loss of nuclear monopoly undermined the whole logic of threat by possession of superior destructive power which the West had so far counted on to dissuade the Soviet Union from military aggression. What use would American's nuclear threats be when the Soviet Union could make nuclear counterthreats? And secondly, nuclear mutuality made real the theoretical conditions foreseen by Brodie and others in the First Wave, and earlier by Bloch and Angell, where war became so destructive to fight that almost no conceivable policy objective of the state would justify resort to it. It was against this background that the new style of strategic analysis called for by Brodie finally came into its own.

The coming of nuclear mutuality provided the general backdrop for the flowering of deterrence theory. But it was the Eisenhower Administration's 1954 announcement of 'Massive Retaliation' that provided the link between academic strategy and public policy which was to prove such a durable feature of Strategic Studies. The doctrine of Massive Retaliation reflected a desire to use American nuclear superiority to offset the Soviet advantage in locally deployed conventional forces in Europe and Asia. It was motivated in good part by the unsatisfactory experience of the Korean War, in which the use of conventional forces to fight a limited war had proved expensive, politically divisive, and militarily indecisive. The problem was that the doctrine depended on a unilateral nuclear advantage that the United States could not sustain for more than a few years. As the Soviet Union began to deploy nuclear forces of its own, the American threat to meet Soviet aggression with nuclear retaliation would not only lose credibility, but also raise the unacceptable risk of triggering a nuclear war. The logic of Massive Retaliation was backward-looking in relation to the way the nuclear balance was actually, and rapidly, unfolding during the mid-1950s. Its flaws and hazards provided an ideal foil for the line of analysis opened up by the First Wave writers (Gray, 1982b, ch. 4). The Golden Age of deterrence theory seemed golden not just because some of its thinking was original, but because of the high level of political attention that it attracted.

The policy problem of the West remained constant in terms of defining the Soviet Union as the core threat to security. It also remained constant within the West in terms of continued American leadership, although France made significant moves towards a semi-independent posture. These continuities, however, were disturbed by two lines of change: a steady relative increase in Soviet military strength; and a rapid development in the technology of nuclear weapons and their delivery systems.

As a result of these changes, the decade of the Golden Age marked a period of profound transformation in the character of military relations between the United States and the Soviet Union. At the beginning of it, the United States had a massive nuclear superiority based on an arsenal of several thousand atomic bombs carried by fleets of modern, medium- and long-range jet bombers. The Soviet Union had only a few atomic bombs, and no delivery system capable of mounting a mass strike on the United States. By the middle of the 1960s both sides had deployed hundreds of ICBMs, and fusion warheads were available with explosive yields more than a thousand times larger than the fission bombs dropped on Japan. Although the United States still had a substantial advantage in nuclear strength over the Soviet Union by the mid-1960s, the Soviet Union had clearly reached the point where it could inflict a devastating blow on the United States in return for any attack the Americans might make on them. Since the attack would be delivered by missiles, there was not even any hope, as there was against bombers, of mounting an effective defence. Although the United States still had an edge in many aspects of quantity and quality of nuclear forces, the two superpowers were equal in the sense that neither could physically prevent the other from delivering hundreds of thermonuclear warheads onto its territory. What had been a highly lopsided two-party balance of power in the mid-1950s, was, by the late 1960s, a bipolarity of effectively equal nuclear vulnerability.

This momentous transition from a nearly unipolar nuclear power system to a solidly bipolar one was both the context for, and the stimulant of, the Golden Age. In one sense, deterrence theory was an abstract, non-partisan, and theoretical response to the concrete reality of nuclear bipolarity. In that sense, the theory had a claim to be objective in a way that transcended the policy interests of either superpower. Yet the whole development of the theory can only be understood when that detached and theoretical stream is blended into the over-all perspective of the Western policy problem. Although the fact of nuclear bipolarity did have a certain objective reality about it, the view from the two parties was not the same, and an independent deterrence theory based on retaliation developed within only one of them.

For the Soviet Union, the significance of bipolarity was extremely positive. It meant that they had broken out of an intolerable position of unilateral vulnerability into the comparatively congenial atmosphere of mutual threat. Indeed, so great was their euphoria that it stimulated Khrushchev to make a rare revision to basic Leninist doctrine. Khrushchev repudiated Lenin's theory that war between imperialist and socialist states was inevitable. He did so on the grounds that Soviet nuclear strength was sufficient to deny the imperialist states victory in war. Because they would not be able to win, they would not attack (Khrushchev, 1961, pp. 8–10; Lenin, 1964, p. 79; Zimmerman, 1969, p. 169).

For the West, the shift to bipolarity represented a major deterioration of position. This was true both for the United States as military leader, and for the Western Europeans, who saw the change as weakening the deterrence umbrella that the United States had so easily and comfortably extended over them during the 1950s. Within a decade, the United States slipped from being militarily invulnerable and superior, to being vulnerable, and merely the first among equals. Yet despite this slippage the United States still carried the huge security burden, acquired when it was superior, of defending the status quo for the West. In particular, it had still to prevent the Soviet Union from reaping political advantage from its strong military position against Western Europe. Deterrence theory, despite its objective elements, developed very much in response to this Western view of the problem.

### 11.2.2 The Central Ideas of Golden Age Theory

The central ideas of Golden Age deterrence theory were based on the emerging realities of nuclear bipolarity, both in the objective terms of the distribution of military power in the international system, and in the subjective terms of the Western policy problem. Indeed, those realities fixed a pattern of assumptions which still defines much of the subject. The most basic assumption was that the problem of nuclear strategy could be analysed in terms of relations between just two major powers. This assumption validly reflected reality during the decade of the Golden Age. Only China and France have since raised any challenge to it, and the superpowers have maintained their dominant position by accumulating nuclear arsenals on a scale so vast as to deny easy entry to any aspirant to their club. The two-party assumption is central to most contemporary deterrence thinking and, as will be seen in Chapter 12, it marks a logical limitation of virtually the whole literature on nuclear strategy.

The second basic assumption was that the union of nuclear weapons and missiles gave such a big advantage to the offensive that no over-all defence of homelands would be possible. Even if some attacking warheads could be destroyed, and some targets hardened or hidden to survive attack, the infrastructure of society in terms of its cities, industries, and transportation and communication networks would remain highly vulnerable even to a few dozen warheads.

The third basic assumption was that the two parties in the nuclear relationship would be actively hostile to each other. This was definitely the case throughout most of the Golden Age decade, which coincided with the last half of the Cold War. The assumption was given durability by the ideological as well as power character of the rivalry between the United States and the Soviet Union. Marxist, and even more so Leninist, doctrine inclined the Soviet leaders to see East-West relations in conflictual terms. In the West, and especially in the United States, post-war Soviet behaviour in Eastern Europe, the near East and Korea quickly led to the Soviet Union inheriting the image of aggressive totalitarianism created by the Fascist states during the 1930s (Yergin, 1978). The realities of Cold War hostility were so intense as to be beyond questioning. Western perceptions of innate Soviet aggressiveness magnified the significance of increasing Soviet military power. The unquestioned assumption of hostility inherited from this period was to have a powerful and long-term impact on the development of deterrence theory.

The combination of these assumptions about bipolarity, vulnerability and hostility led directly to some of the core insights and wisdoms of Golden Age deterrence theory. The conclusion of most immediate importance was that the technological requirements for nuclear forces under conditions of bipolarity were much more demanding than those for the one-sided nuclear relationship enjoyed by the United States up to the late 1950s. For one-sided deterrence, the nuclear forces of the deterrer needed only to be able to reach the opponent and penetrate his defences. But under bipolar conditions, nuclear forces that were themselves vulnerable to nuclear attack would simply invite the opponent to attack them first, a problem made worse by the short flight times of ICBMs as opposed to bombers. Bombers that could not get well airborne within the warning time available for an incoming missile attack would have no credibility as a retaliatory force. Neither would unprotected liquid-fuelled ICBMs whose fuelling process took longer than the entire flight time of an attacking missile (Wohlstetter, 1959). Under conditions of bipolarity, the only use for nuclear delivery systems that were themselves vulnerable was first strikes.

If both sides had vulnerable forces, then the technical characteristics of their relationship would make the outbreak of war highly probable. Each side would have strong incentives to strike first, and the side that did so had real prospects of rapid and total victory. The conclusion drawn was that nuclear forces must be made as invulnerable as possible. If mutual deterrence was to work, each of the two nuclear powers must possess a secure second strike force – that is, an arsenal large enough and protected enough so that it could inflict a devastating retaliation on the opponent even after having been subjected to a massive attack itself. The conditions of bipolarity thus demanded a whole new range of protective technologies. Missiles needed to be buried in hardened silos and hidden in submarines. Early warning systems were required to give bombers enough time to get away from their bases. Serious thought needed to be given to the command and control system for nuclear forces, and to what should happen if the political leadership was obliterated in a surprise 'decapitation' attack (Bracken, 1983).

This conclusion about the importance of technological variables in nuclear rivalries underpins much of Golden Age strategic theory. The key insight of the Golden Age theorists was that if the military condition of secure second strike forces could be met, then the *technical* characteristics of deterrence would profoundly transform the general conditions of rivalry between the two opposed powers. If both sides possessed a substantial secure second strike, then each would hold the other's society under threat of 'assured destruction' (AD). The situation between them is described in a term that produced the most famous acronym in the field: 'mutually assured destruction' (MAD). If MAD existed, the danger of first strikes against nuclear forces (counterforce strikes) would recede, and both sides would have strong incentives to avoid war despite their hostility.

The logic of MAD pointed to a neat technical fix by which a potentially unstable rivalry could be forced into a stable configuration. In addition, it created a situation in which the rival powers would find themselves sharing a common interest arising out of their mutual concern to avoid war. If neither side could gain advantage from striking first, and both would suffer huge damage to their homelands in any all-out conflict, then both would have strong reasons to prevent war from breaking out for accidental or trivial reasons.

The conceptual elegance, power to dampen rivalry, and apparent practicability of MAD explain its widespread intellectual and political appeal. From a Western perspective, MAD had a great deal to recommend it as a response to the problem of bipolarity. Because its logic derived from the basic structure of the situation, it had a universal ring to it which seemed to ensnare the Soviet Union into a status quo framework. MAD was not only a doctrine to be followed, but also a description of a situation from which there appeared to be no escape. So long as a secure second strike could be maintained, the Soviet Union would be forced to accept war avoidance as a shared goal, and the pursuit of stability as a shared interest. Although the loss of invulnerability was painful to the United States, an outcome of military paralysis that supported the status quo was considerable compensation.

The logic of MAD also opened up interesting and politically important new ways of thinking about the management of military rivalry. If the paralysis of MAD was unavoidable, then the rivals might share interests deeper than mere war prevention. War prevention alone created common interest primarily in terms of crisis management, and the avoidance of automatic escalation either from some local confrontation or from accidents involving nuclear forces. But if both sides accepted MAD not only as reality, but also as doctrine, then much broader possibilities for co-operation emerged. The logic of MAD was so compelling that many Golden Age strategists simply assumed that both sides would have to adopt it as doctrine.

If MAD was accepted as doctrine by both sides, then arms control became a major additional area of common interest. The idea of arms control was one of the innovations of the Golden Age (Bull, 1961; Singer, 1962), and it derived directly from the logic of MAD. MAD rested on deterrence by the threat of punishment. That threat in turn rested on the vast increase in destructive power made available by nuclear weapons. Given that there was no effective defence against a nuclear attack on society, the threat to punish required only a finite military capability. One of the best known estimates of how much would be enough to threaten AD reckoned that 400 one megaton-equivalent delivered warheads would kill 30 per cent of the Soviet Union's population and destroy three-quarters of its industrial capability (Enthoven and Smith, 1971, p. 207).

Figures of that kind could be used to define the force requirement for a policy of MAD in a way that would not be possible if strategy was based on the open-ended requirements of a threat to fight a nuclear war. If both sides pursued deterrence by threat of punishment, then it would be in their mutual interest to negotiate ceilings on force levels. It would also be in their interest to keep those ceilings low by agreeing not to deploy either defensive measures or counterforce first-strike capabilities, either of which would increase the size of the force necessary for AD. The promise of arms control was to preserve the essential stability of MAD at the lowest possible cost to both sides, and with the least amount of uncertainty about the credibility of the AD threat. Arms control was a complete departure from the traditional appeal for management of the arms race by disarmament. It offered a way out of the unproductive impasse that had characterized disarmament negotiations during the 1930s and 1950s. Arms control started from the premise that weapons were an important part of the solution, and not just a definition of the problem. The arms control approach was not necessarily to reduce numbers of weapons, but rather to encourage deployments that enabled MAD to be preserved in the simplest and most stable ways, and to block deployments of weapons that undermined either side's ability to maintain a threat of AD. The logic of arms control will be explored more fully in Part IV.

## 11.2.3 The Problem of Extended Deterrence

Despite its many attractions, the elegant and compelling framework of MAD and arms control contained a major weakness in relation to the West's policy problem. The logic of MAD assumed two rivals each trying to deter the other from attacking it. The problem was that the United States had not only to deter attacks on itself, which was relatively easy, but also to deter attacks on the many allies it had accumulated all around the periphery of the Soviet bloc. In particular, it had to deter a Soviet attack on Western Europe, whose markets and industrial resources made it the key to the global balance of power. Given that Western Europe lay directly under the shadow of Soviet military power, this task looked difficult. Since neither the Europeans nor the Americans were willing to seek deterrence by denial, which would require them to match Soviet conventional strength, Western Europe's security had somehow to be preserved within the framework of nuclear deterrence. To do so, however, risked undermining the symmetry on which the whole logical edifice of MAD as doctrine rested.

Extended deterrence (ED) was the worm in the apple of Golden Age theory. The American commitment to extend deterrence to Western Europe had been acquired at a time when the military superiority and invulnerability of the United States made the task quite straightforward. The question was how to maintain this commitment under the drastically altered circumstances of nuclear bipolarity. As more than one analyst has suggested, this question was the main underlying theme of the whole evolution of nuclear strategy right through to the 1980s (Freedman, 1981, p. xvi; Ravenal, 1982, pp. 31–5). The logic of MAD led to a convincing paralysis in the use of force by the superpowers directly against each other's homelands, but it left considerable ambiguity as to how far and how effectively this paralysis extended to the protection of secondary security interests.

The United States, because it was the status quo power, had a lot more secondary security commitments than did the Soviet Union, and so felt the pressure of this ambiguity keenly. Since it could not realistically defend all of its commitments by conventional military means – a conclusion reinforced by the experience of the Korean War – the United States had powerful incentives to find strategies that would enable it to cover these commitments with its nuclear forces. Since the onset of nuclear bipolarity, this policy problem has never been satisfactorily resolved either in theory or in practice. The attempt to do so has generated a weight of contending argument so immense as almost to bury the original core of Golden Age strategic logic.

Two sets of contradictory views lie at the heart of the debate about ED. These will be explored in detail in Chapter 12, but it is useful to sketch them in here because of their centrality to the development of deterrence theory. The first set concerns different assessments of how seriously the ambiguity in MAD about ED should be taken. Opinion divides between those who see ED as a gaping hole in MAD which invites aggression, and those who see it as a marginal uncertainty with more theoretical than practical significance. In reality, opinion occurs across a complicated spectrum between these two poles, but the over-all character of the debate is easiest to capture through its extremes. Those of the first view conclude that a pure MAD policy is inadequate for ED, and that the hole must be plugged by doctrines of limited war, and by deployment of additional forces to make threats of limited war credible. This view leads strongly towards the insertion of denial factors into deterrence policy. Those of the second view are inclined to give more weight to the deterring effect of anything which raises the probability of a nuclear war. They therefore tend to stick as closely as possible to basic MAD doctrine, arguing that the risk of escalation will deter even for secondary objectives. This more complacent view of MAD and ED is seen as especially relevant where American commitment to secondary objectives is very obviously strong, as it is for Western Europe and Japan.

The second set of contradictory views on ED occurs within the majority whose views on the first set are that ED requires forces and doctrines additional to those necessary for MAD. The question is not only how extensive these forces need to be, but also whether they should be conventional, or whether they should include nuclear weapons. A purely theoretical perspective favours conventional forces for denial that are sufficient to fight limited wars on a scale proportional to the importance of the objective. But theory here faces strong and persistent pressure from the policy realm. Within the Western powers, provision of conventional forces on the requisite scale for denial of the Soviet Union would encounter insurmountable political obstacles. As the history of NATO illustrates, this political obstacle has repeatedly thrown the issue back into the context of nuclear strategy (Boutwell *et al.*, 1985).

Nuclear solutions require a doctrine of limited nuclear war (LNW), and an array of nuclear weapons suitable for tactical and theatre warfighting. Both of these have been available since the 1950s, and the temptation to develop them as the solution to ED has not been resisted. The appeal of LNW is that the basic measures for it are relatively easy and inexpensive to implement when compared with the measures necessary for denial by conventional forces. It provides a way for the United States to do something about its ED commitments without having to confront the political difficulties of mustering larger conventional forces. There are, however, many problems with LNW. Perhaps the three most prominent are as follows. The first is that the extra nuclear forces required for LNW undermine the possibility for achieving MAD at the relatively low force levels required for the basic punishment strategy of AD.

Secondly, the threat of LNW risks disconnecting ED from core deterrence by offering the opponent a contained war at a lower level of risk. Logically a policy of LNW might therefore weaken ED rather than reinforcing it. Thirdly, LNW might not be controllable: once started it might escalate to full-scale war.

A brief reflection on these problems illustrates why the issue of LNW has come to occupy such a prominent place in deterrence theory. Even the last two problems mentioned above produce an unresolvable circularity when considered together. If we move from the second to the third, then it seems that LNW increases the risk of nuclear war by offering a false promise of limited conflict. But if we move from the third to the second, the uncertainty about uncontrollable escalation seems to restore the credibility of the LNW threat by linking it back to core deterrence. It does so, however, only at the cost of raising questions about why the whole LNW policy is necessary as an intermediate stage between peace and all-out war under MAD.

These complex logical cross pressures affected debate about limited war strategies right from the early days of the Golden Age, and they still determine the main lines of argument. But although the problem of limited war was discussed as a main theme of the Golden Age (Freedman, 1981, chs 7, 8; Halperin, 1963; Osgood, 1957), its full significance did not develop until well into the 1970s. The policy conclusion arrived at during the Golden Age decade was that something needed to be done. The answer came in the form of 'flexible response', an idea that has guided American policy since the early 1960s despite many changes in name. Flexible response rested on possession of a range of military options, both conventional and nuclear. These were intended to deter aggression, in part by denial, at all levels, and to mount a forward defence if deterrence failed (Freedman, 1981, pp. 285–6). But flexible response, as the name implies, simply reflected, rather than solved, the many ambiguities and contradictions raised by the question of how to reinforce ED under conditions of nuclear bipolarity. It avoided strict either/or choices between conventional and nuclear means, but only at the cost of requiring endless reinterpretations by successive American Administrations. Those reinterpretations have set much of the agenda for deterrence theory right down to the present day.

During the Golden Age, however, the still substantial superiority of America's nuclear forces muted the difficulties raised by ED. The worm had not yet broken the skin of the apple, and so the Golden

Age was dominated by the fusion of theory and policy in MAD and arms control. The idea of limited was was recognized as a major issue, and the fact that it pointed directly back towards the traditional logic of denial and warfighting was obviously contradictory to the main thrust of Golden Age thinking. But this development had not yet come to dominate the strategic debate. The Golden Age thus marked the high point of the attempt to base strategic theory on the novel idea of deterrence by threat of retaliation.

## 11.3 AFTER THE GOLDEN AGE: A THIRD WAVE?

The Golden Age drifted to a close in the mid-1960s. It ended not because there were no issues left to discuss, but because all of the basic concepts and vocabulary necessary for the debate about nuclear strategy had been worked out. Thinking about deterrence after the Golden Age was essentially about adjusting this body of ideas and policies to the changing circumstances of superpower rivalry. The principal lines of change were the same as those that had motivated the Golden Age: the relative gain of Soviet military power on the United States; and improvements in the technology of nuclear weapons and their delivery systems.

### 11.3.1 The Relative Gain of Soviet Military Power

Although the changes in superpower relations after 1965 were not as profound as the transformations of the Golden Age decade, they were sufficient to trigger major assaults on the orthodoxy of MAD from two different directions. Gray has labelled one of these assaults the Third Wave (Gray, 1982a, pp. 15–17). The essence of it has been to challenge MAD by extending the logic of LNW into a full-scale denial doctrine of extended deterrence by threat of warfighting. The influence of this view on deterrence theory in the United States has been increasing since the early 1970s. The other assault rests on the idea of mounting a defence against nuclear attack which is sufficiently effective to allow escape from the whole logic of mutual deterrence by threat of retaliation. This idea is highly dependent on technological capabilities. It had its first outing in the late 1960s, faded into the background with the ABM Treaty of 1972, but was revived by President Reagan's 'star wars' speech in March 1983. Although these two assaults on MAD are conceptually distinct, there is a strong tendency for them to merge if the technology for nuclear defence can be made only partially effective.

MAD was vulnerable to assault because of its conceptual weakness on the issue of ED, and it was this weakness that offered opportunity to the proponents of deterrence by denial. In addition, these critics of MAD benefited from the way in which developments in superpower relations undermined some of the assumptions that infused Golden Age thinking. Of particular importance here was the continued growth of Soviet military strength relative to that of the United States. This growth had already produced the parity of mutual vulnerability, the shock of which was a principal trigger of the Golden Age. By the end of the 1960s a second shock was becoming evident based on the arrival of general equivalence in the size and capability of the nuclear forces deployed by both sides. Golden Age logic did not anticipate this shock because its reasoning stressed the fundamental equality of vulnerability to AD, and discounted the significance of forces surplus to that requirement.

When it actually arrived, however, equality of forces undermined the attractiveness of MAD to the United States in several important ways. It removed the buffer of superiority that had seen the United States successfully through the Cuba missiles crisis, and which had generally made the loss of invulnerability easier to bear. It made the problem of ED look much more difficult by removing the West's ability to offset Soviet conventional strength with superior nuclear resorces. It also drove home the point that the Soviet Union had never accepted MAD as a doctrine. The convergence of strategic logic on which many Golden Age thinkers had counted was not occurring. Instead, the Soviet leaders were sticking with a doctrine of deterrence by denial. This doctrine, involved not only denying military victory to the West, but also preparing to survive, and if possible win, a nuclear war (Arnett, 1981; Holloway, 1983, chs 3, 5; Jukes, 1981; Lambeth, 1981).

In Western eyes, the Soviet commitment to the traditional strategic objective of military victory sat uneasily beside the idea that the basic Soviet commitment was to deterrence by denial. Although the denial threat of warfighting could support deterrence ends, it could also support an intention to break out of the nuclear paralysis. When combined with increasing Soviet strength, this doctrine raised fears in the United States that the Soviet Union might be attracted by the option of a counterforce first-strike against American ICBMs. If successful, such a strike might break the logic of MAD by leaving the American President with a choice between surrender and a pointless and suicidal retaliation against Soviet cities. It was not even clear that the Soviet Union planned to stop their accumulation of weapons at equivalence. This possibility left the United States facing the prospect that it might soon find itself in a position of military inferiority.

For all these reasons, the arrival of actual parity made MAD look much more problematic as a basis for American nuclear policy than it had done a decade earlier. It was politically difficult for the United States to accept military equality, and probably impossible for it to accept inferiority, on the basis of an abstract doctrine that was clearly not accepted by its opponent. This difficulty was enhanced by the continued strength in the United States of an aggressive and hostile perception of the Soviet Union. In crude political terms, a measure of superior strength seemed essential to maintain the security of the status quo against an opponent committed to ideological change. To rely on the logic of MAD from a position of inferiority looked like a confession of weakness, the more so because of the many vital ED commitments for which the United States was responsible.

This continued shift of the military balance against the United States defined one major aspect of the policy problem that shaped deterrence theory after the Golden Age. From the early 1970s onwards, therefore, the strategic debate turned increasingly away from thinking about deterrence by threat of punishment, and towards thinking about deterrence by threat of warfighting. The logic of MAD with its ultimate threat of deterrence by punishment remained at the heart of nuclear strategy, but became obscured behind ever more elaborate LNW strategies aimed at both enhancing ED, and countering any Soviet thoughts of winning by means of a counterforce first strike. These strategies have evolved in a mutually supporting relationship with the increasingly numerous and sophisticated nuclear warheads deployed by the United States (Cordesman, 1982). Their rationales range across a considerable spectrum. The simplest ones involve a desire to bolster the credibility of ED under conditions of parity. The argument is that if the United States is to be able to deter Soviet aggression against its major Western partners, it must have intermediate options between doing nothing and declaring all-out war. The most ambitious

rationales involve escaping from parity by recapturing a margin of
superiority over the Soviet Union so as to establish 'escalation
dominance' at any level of nuclear warfighting (Gray, 1984).

By the 1980s, the evolution of these limited warfighting doctrines
was complete enough to have filled in virtually the whole theoretical
spectrum between no war and all-out nuclear exchange. In so doing,
it steadily shifted both the practical and the theoretical emphasis of
deterrence thinking towards denial strategies based on threats of
warfighting. Deterrence by threat of punishment remained in place
as the ultimate threat at the top of the escalation ladder. Yet the
locus of deterrence was moved forward in time from that ultimate
threat to the likely starting point of escalation in the lower levels of
conflict that might arise from ED. The purpose of the exercise was
still war prevention, but the threat was LNW. Its logic aimed at a
difficult combination. On the one hand, LNW options sought to
push the ultimate threat into the background, both because it lacked
credibility under bipolar conditions, and because it was thought to
raise the danger of war if the ultimate threat was too close to the
front line of policy options. On the other hand, LNW kept the
ultimate threat in the foreground by linking it to extended deterrence
through the threat of escalation, whether controlled or not.

These developments raised a host of complex theoretical and
technical problems for deterrence theory which will be examined
more closely in Chapters 12 and 13. LNW policies both contributed
to, and were encouraged by, the failure of arms control negotiations
to fix low levels for nuclear forces. They were envigorated by the
breakdown of arms control and détente in the late 1970s. In a
curious way, the triumph of denial doctrines over MAD fulfilled the
Golden Age expectation of convergence in nuclear doctrine between
the United States and the Soviet Union. But it fulfilled it in reverse,
with the Americans shifting towards the Soviet view rather than the
other way around. In this sense Gray is correct to identify this
development as a Third Wave. It does represent a departure from
the optimistic simplicities of MAD. In its most extreme versions, it
embodies a willingness to embrace the quite different, and much
more complicated, logic of deterrence by threat of warfighting. Yet
one must be careful not to lose sight of the fact that much of this
Third Wave still rests on the conceptual foundations of the Golden
Age. Third Wave thinking continues to reflect Golden Age
assumptions about bipolarity and hostility. It has not, as Jervis
argues, successfully escaped from the problem of vulnerability

(Jervis, 1984). The new thinking has not so much replaced the logic of MAD, as overlaid it with a mass of qualifications and elaborations.

## 11.3.2 Changes in Military Technology

The second major factor shaping strategic thinking after the Golden Age has been the continued evolution of military technology. As with the shifting balance of military strength, the biggest change in technological factors also occurred during the Golden Age when the union of ICBM and nuclear weapon conferred a massive advantage on the offence and made the defence of societies impossible. It has been the burden of deterrence theorists that they have had to conduct the search for basic theory within an environment of continuous technological change. This has meant that a lot of work within the field has had to be devoted to analysing the consequences of technological developments for prevailing theories and doctrines. Technological developments provided the basic conditions for the theory of deterrence, and the whole enterprise is permanently vulnerable to additional developments which change those conditions. Major upheavals of the type represented by the advent of nuclear missiles are infrequent, but they have to be watched for. In the period between them, adjustments have to be made for developments that alter some conditions without overturning the basic premises of existing theory.

In the two decades since the end of the Golden Age there have been many technological developments which required that theory and doctrine be adjusted. There has been one clear view of a future technology that might overthrow the whole framework of deterrence theory. The best example of new technology requiring adjustment to doctrine is the combination of developments that led not only to the placing of several independent warheads on one missile (MIRV), but also to the accuracy of those warheads beginning to approach effective perfection. The accuracy of such weapons meant that hardened silos were no longer an effective way to protect land-based ICBMs. The number of warheads on each attacking missile enabled the attacking party to destroy a number of opposing missiles several times greater than the number of missiles required to make the attack. This new technology reversed the previous situation, which was that an attacker using single warhead missiles would need to use more missiles to make the attack than were destroyed by it (because of misses, malfunctions, etc.). This development thus increased the ability of each side to mount counterforce first strikes against the nuclear forces of the other, and thereby increased the difficulties and uncertainties of both sides in maintaining land-based secure second strike forces.

A great deal of energy within Strategic Studies has gone into analysing the consequences of this type of technological development. Because technology is so important to strategy, much of the literature of the field since the Golden Age has been absorbed by the endless procurement debates that accompany major acquisitions of weapons systems in the United States. The anti-ballistic missile (ABM) debate of the late 1960s and the debate about the *MX* ICBM of the late 1970s and early 1980s are only the most outstanding examples of this process, others being over various versions of supersonic bombers, cruise missiles, and the single-warhead *Midgetman* ICBM. Although the theme of technological change is central in thinking about deterrence, one should not lose sight of the fact that nuclear weapons provide a major element of continuity. It is the destructive power of nuclear weapons that sets the whole paradigm of deterrence.

The one set of technologies coming out of this process that looked potentially able to transform the deterrence paradigm was ballistic missile defence (BMD). Should such a technology ever become really effective against all the major strategic delivery vehicles (SDVs) – bombers, cruise missiles, ballistic missiles – then the nuclear revolution would be negated, and the whole problem of strategy would have to be redefined in some new Golden Age. President Reagan's Strategic Defence Initiative (SDI) put the possibility of that transformation firmly onto the strategic agenda in the early 1980s. Yet only the bare beginnings of the technologies that might make it a reality are available, and there are serious doubts about whether a sufficiently perfect defence can ever be mounted (Drell *et al.*, 1984; Glaser, 1984; Schlesinger, 1985). It may be chasing a chimera to hope that any combination of technologies can overcome the immense offensive power of nuclear weapons against societies. What seems more likely is that the rhetoric of escape from deterrence will succumb to costs and technical problems. A scaled-down interest in SDI will merge with, and reinforce, the denial school of thought that has arisen out of the application of LNW to the problems posed by extended deterrence (Gray, 1976, pp. 170–4; 1984; Hoffman, 1985; Jastrow, 1984; Lodal, 1980). The logic of this merger will be examined in Chapters 12 and 13.

## 11.4  THE FUTURE OF DETERRENCE

Western deterrence theory grew out of, and fed into, the process of nuclear policy-making principally in the United States. As the theory took shape in response to major shifts in technology and the balance of power, it influenced, and was influenced by, the formulation of American nuclear policy. This close association between the abstract academic activity of strategic theorizing, and the concrete process of making nuclear policy, marked deterrence theory from the beginning and remains one of its distinctive features. There is no reason to expect these basic working conditions of the subject to change, and therefore every reason to expect that the future of deterrence thinking will, like its past, consist of continuous adaptation and periodic transformation of theory.

New technologies will continue to redefine such problems as maintaining secure second strike forces, and posing credible threats to fight limited nuclear war. SDI may eventually transform the whole basis of deterrence, and the attempt to develop it will generate a host of interim implications both for MAD and LNW. The major shifts in the balance of power between the United States and the Soviet Union are probably over. Since neither will let the other gain a permanent military advantage, and neither can stop the other from matching its deployments, they seem fated to oscillate permanently around the ambiguous status of parity. This relative inertia in place of the dramatic past shifts in this variable may provide deterrence theory with a period of comparative stability in terms of its assumptions about the balance of power.

Nuclear multipolarity, however, looms in the future as a long-term threat to this stability. It cannot be too many decades before the real prospect of three or more strategic nuclear powers requires a fundamental reconsideration of nuclear strategy. The assumption of bipolarity in strategic deterrence seems unlikely to hold past the early part of the twenty-first century. This trend towards multipolarity rests most firmly on developments in China, which has already established its political and military autonomy in relation to the superpowers. The rather less certain movements towards more independent attitudes in Western Europe and Japan on global issues may also turn out to be significant for it. A more unified Europe or a more independent Japan may decide to loosen its military dependence on the United States, or the United States may become less willing to subsidize their security.

One interesting point of speculation raised by the long-term prospect of multipolarity is what impact it will have on the evolution of deterrence theory. The ethnocentrism in Western strategic thinking so cogently criticized by Booth (1979) arose in part because the United States was the first country with a pressing policy need to think through the implications of nuclear weapons. The relatively exotic theory of deterrence by threat of retaliation that resulted has not been received with enthusiasm outside the Western group of states. Given both the magnitude of American dominance during the period of Golden Age thinking, and the state-centred character of strategic thinking, it was not unnatural that American strategists conflated the universal and the parochial aspects of nuclear deterrence theory. The arrogance of the Golden Age has already given way. Western deterrence theory is now an uneasy and contested amalgam of retaliation and denial. The Soviet view of deterrence is no longer simply dismissed as antediluvian, but is now acknowledged as a valid, if not attractive, alternative (Ermath, 1978; Segal, 1983–4). The question is what view of deterrence would be taken by new entrants to the ranks of strategic nuclear power. Would they be attracted by the Golden Age logic of MAD, or would they opt for the more traditional denial approach of the Soviet Union? The factors that will bear on their decision are the subject of the next two chapters.

# 12 The Logic of Deterrence

## 12.1 BASIC LOGIC: WHAT PRODUCES INACTION IN OPPONENTS?

The logic of deterrence, like that of chess, is much more complicated than the basic principles that define it. The simple statement of basic deterrence principles is clear, and capable of universal application: one actor prevents another from taking some action by raising the latter's fear of the consequences that will ensue. Deterrence implies the existence of two parties, the deterrer and the deterree. Its object is to stop the deterree from taking actions against the interests of the deterrer. Its mechanisms are *threats* – the posing of adverse consequences for the deterree that will outweigh the gains of the contested action – and *calculation* – the ability of both deterrer and deterree to weigh costs and benefits in a similar fashion.

Because the objective of deterrence is inaction, it can be difficult to assess the effectiveness of deterrence policies. Has the deterree remained quiescent because the deterrer's policy has been effective? Or has inaction resulted simply from the deterree's motives? Is the deterree indifferent or even averse towards the actions about which the deterrer is worried, and therefore would not take them whether actively deterred or not? This question frequently cannot be answered with any certainty, although examples can easily be found to illustrate the range of possibilities. The United States is indifferent about taking over control of Canada, and therefore Canada does not have to mount a substantial deterrence policy against that contingency. India wants no more Muslims and no more poverty than it already has, and therefore does not need to be deterred from annexing Bangladesh because it is averse to taking the action in the first place. North Vietnam, by contrast, was highly motivated to reunify with the South, and was neither deterred by formidable American military threats, nor compelled to stop by American military action.

If one asks how strongly motivated the Soviet Union is to dominate or invade Western Europe, credible cases can be made for all options, with no clear means of deciding reliably amongst them. Under such ambiguous conditions, prudence dictates the mounting

163

of some deterrence. Once deterrence is undertaken, it becomes easy to slip into the assumption that inaction is only a result of deterrence policy. Because they cannot be known reliably, the other incentives bearing on the deteree's behaviour are often ignored or discounted in thinking about deterrence. If the worst-case assumption that the deterree would attack if not deterred is taken for granted, then deterrence appears to be more difficult than it is in reality.

The effectiveness of deterrence, and the ease or difficulty of implementing it, thus depend on two sets of factors: first, the strength of basic motivation in the deterree towards the action, and the probability that he would undertake it in the absence of specific deterrence measures; and secondly, the logic of costs and gains which results from taking the action in the presence of deterrence measures against it. In practice, there is a mixed area at the boundary between these two sets. Any military action will risk some costs, and therefore a measure of deterrence, perhaps considerable, exists between states whether it is made specific or not. Deterrence logic assumes that there is a significant risk that the deterree will attack unless the costs to him of doing so are raised, and that raising costs will lower his desire to attack. If his basic motivation to take the action is high, then deterrence measures will need to be substantial if they are to be effective. If his basic motivation is low, then modest deterrent measures will suffice. Perceptions of the deterree's level of motivation may themselves be strongly conditioned by the ideological stance of the deterrer (McKinlay and Little, 1986, chs 8, 10).

A further variable here is the deterree's tolerance for costs. If the deterree is 'soft', and sensitive to costs, then he will be easier to deter even if his incentive to attack is high. The Soviet Union should find it easy to deter even hawkish American leaderships for this reason. If the deterree is 'hard', and willing to accept punishment in return for gain, then deterrence will be more difficult. China under Mao worked hard to establish just such a hard image of itself. The deterrer has therefore to calculate not only the deterree's possible gains from action, but also the strength of its desire to take the action, and its sensitivity to costs. Looking at basic motivation is essentially a political approach to deterrence. One is really asking how alienated the deterree is from the international status quo. A state will be more willing to use force to pursue change if all other paths to its aspirations are blocked, and if it thinks that force is likely to be used against it. Its incentives to use force will be lower if some paths to change remain open, and it sees the danger of being attacked as low.

On this basis, it is interesting to reconsider the case of the Soviet Union. As Rosecrance has observed (Rosecrance, 1975, pp. 25–6), the Soviet Union has reasons for considerable, perhaps even increasing, attachment to the status quo. It has a stake in preserving its empire and sphere of influence. It has good scope for pursuing its ideological goals through political means. It stands in little danger of calculated surprise attack. And it has been able to increase greatly its power and status within the existing framework. Although the Soviet leaders may be opposed to some of the dominant international norms, they have plenty of reasons to pursue change through peaceful coexistence, and no urgent need to resort to force. When added to the fear of war resulting from its historical experience, these considerations should make the Soviet Union, as MccGwire argues, relatively easy to deter (MccGwire, 1983, pp. 19–23). The Chinese accused the Soviet Union of becoming soft as long ago as the early 1960s, when they slated Khrushchev for 'goulash communism'.

The importance of taking these political considerations into account when assessing deterrence cannot be overestimated. If they are ignored or discounted, inaction will appear to result solely from deterrence measures. Such a perspective leads easily to an unbalanced and excessively militarized view of relations between states.

The other component of deterrence is the logic of costs and gains resulting from taking the action in defiance of specific threats against it. It is this component that receives the bulk of attention in deterrence theory. The deterree has to calculate the balance between the possible gains and the possible costs which result from taking, or *not taking*, given actions. Inaction cannot be assumed to be always benign for the deterree. In the early decades of this century, for example, many in Germany were aware that the modernization of Russia would soon foreclose any possibility of German hegemony in Europe. Part of Germany's motivation for war was thus a sense of being within a window of opportunity. Inaction would inevitably result in a worsening of Germany's position in the international hierarchy of power.

The calculation made by any deterree in relation to a deterred action has to weigh both the comparative value of costs and gains, and the level of probability that either will actually occur. The deterree's calculations thus encompass four basic variables:

1   the level of possible costs in terms of lost and damaged national assets, lost or suppressed ideological values, heightened threats, and diminished power, status and independence;
2   the level of possible gains in terms of expanded power, status, and/or territory, increased independence, reduced threats, and extended political influence;
3   the probability of possible costs being inflicted;
4   the probability of possible gains being acquired.

These four variables yield an infinity of possible combinations of values. To explore their logic we have to ignore two practical problems: first, that the values of costs and the values of gains cannot readily be put into the same terms; and secondly, that the actors involved will frequently not be able to assign the values relevant to their situation with much accuracy. These difficulties aside, it is apparent that some combinations give a clearly calculable outcome, while others do not. This can be illustrated as in Table 12.1 by assigning arbitrary values to the level of costs and gains on a scale of 0–100, and to probability on a percentage scale.

*Table* 12.1   The calculation of deterrence logic

| | Costs | | Gains | |
|---|---|---|---|---|
| *Effectiveness* | *Level* | *Probability* | *Level* | *Probability* |
| High | 80 | 90% | 20 | 10% |
| Low | 20 | 10% | 80 | 90% |
| Ambiguous | 70 | 10% | 30 | 90% |

In a situation where possible costs are valued at 80, possible gains at 20, the probability of costs is 90 per cent and the probability of gains is 10 per cent, the logic is clear and deterrence is very likely to be effective even if the deterree is hard, and his basic motivation to attack is high. If the numbers for costs and gains are reversed, the logic is still clear, but deterrence is unlikely to be effective unless the basic motivation of the deterree was already very low, or he was extremely soft. The logic becomes unclear when the values for levels and for probabilities go in opposite rather than similar directions. Thus if possible costs are high at 70 and possible gains are low at 30, but the probability of the high costs is very low at 10 per cent and the probability of low gains is very high at 90 per cent, the calculation produces an ambiguous result. Under such circumstances deterrence may not be effective against a strongly motivated deterree.

## 12.2  THE IMPACT OF NUCLEAR WEAPONS: IS NUCLEAR DETERRENCE EASY OR DIFFICULT?

Since deterrence now occupies such a central position in relations among the great powers, the question of whether it is relatively difficult or relatively easy to achieve may be the most important one can ask in the realm of contemporary strategic thinking. That the question is controversial is indicated by the tension between Golden Age deterrence theory and the warfighting theorists of the Third Wave. The former see deterrence as essentially easy to achieve, the latter as difficult. Whether one sees deterrence as being easy or difficult depends partly on one's assessment of the basic motivation of one's opponent(s). Mostly, however, it depends on how profound a transformation one thinks nuclear weapons have made in the logic of costs and risks.

Before the nuclear age, deterrence was difficult because prevailing military technologies made it hard to raise the possible costs above the possible gains. Germany and Japan, for example could reasonably make a military bid for power as recently as the Second World War. The gains to them of winning would have been large in terms of regional empire and world power. The nature of the then prevailing military technology did not suggest that the cost of losing would be either disproportionate to the stakes for which the military gamble was being played, or wholly catastrophic to the historic destiny of their nations. In the event, the costs of losing, though substantial, were bearable, and did not destroy them as nations. Total defeat cost some territory, casualties up to 10 per cent of the population, a few years of humiliating foreign occupation, a decade or two of economic hardship, and perhaps five or six decades of political emasculation in world politics (Organski and Kugler, 1977). Germany was divided into three parts, but one of these is still large enough to be the biggest economy in Western Europe. A similar calculation applies even within the nuclear age to non-nuclear countries, and explains the willingness of countries like Iran and Iraq to engage in long and costly wars.

Since the 1950s, the deployment of large arsenals of nuclear weapons has made such military gambles far more hazardous. Under nuclear deterrence, the possible costs are raised to inifinity – 100 on our arbitrary scale – or more simply, the obliteration of the state as a political and cultural entity. Under such conditions, possible costs are *always* much higher than possible gains, since within most value systems no gain could offset the complete destruction of the state and nation making it. The question is therefore whether the permanent and massive ascendancy of costs over gains makes deterrence with nuclear weapons easy?

Nobody seriously disputes the cost-imposing potential of nuclear weapons, and so the grounds for debate about the ease and effectiveness of deterrence shift to the question of degrees of risk. In other words, although there is no room for doubt that massive nuclear arsenals *can* impose unacceptable costs, there is still considerable room for doubt about whether they *will* be used to achieve that end, especially when deterrence is mutual. It is differences of opinion about the probability, or degree of risk, attached to costs that underlie the debate about whether deterrence is easy or difficult.

## 12.2.1  The 'Easy' School

Both sides agree that potential costs enormously outweigh possible gains. Those who think that deterrence is easy assume that the magnitude of the possible cost overawes considerations about the degree of risk. In other words, they assume that when potential costs become effectively infinite, as they have with nuclear weapons, then calculations about degree of risk become much less important. Under conditions of possibly infinite cost, the deterree's incentives to think about risks as a subject worthy of serious, practical calculation, drop so drastically that even low probabilities of incurring that cost will be sufficient to deter. Furthermore, there is likely to be a substantial negative spillover from infinite costs into the level of possible gain. Costs of that magnitude may well obliterate both the deterree and the prospect of gain. Such would be the case if the United States destroyed both the Soviet Union and Western Europe during the course of an East-West war. The 'easy' school assumes that at least moderate degrees of caution and responsibility govern the minds of decision-makers even where basic motivation is high. They therefore think that medium or even quite low risks of *total* loss will be sufficient to deter.

The 'easy' school also assumes that fanatical zeal for aggression is the exception rather than the rule in international relations. Although opportunism may be quite widespread, cases of high basic motivation in deterrees will be rare. Consequently, deterrence logic is generally operating against low and medium levels of basic motivation. This assumption is an important element in the position of the 'easy' school, because motivations for aggression at the level of opportunism are much easier to deter than are those at the level of fanatical commitment to change. Opportunists are, by definition, calculating, and are therefore more likely to be impressed by the possibility of infinite costs than are zealots. For the reasons already argued, the 'easy' school tend to view the Soviet Union as, at worst, opportunist in its motivation towards aggression.

In terms of the four basic variables given above, the case that deterrence is easy can be formally stated as follows:

If the level of possible costs comes close to meaning the total political and physical obliteration of the deterree, then –

    (a) the reliability and the salience of calculations about both the level of possible gains and the probability of acquiring them will drop substantially, thereby lowering the incentives for aggression;

    (b) the salience of calculations about the probability of costs being inflicted will be so heavily discounted by the fears arising from the magnitude of the possible costs, that even low probabilities will suffice to deter.

### 12.2.2 The 'Difficult' School

Those who think that deterrence is difficult give less weight to the impact of infinite costs, and more weight to the possibility of aggressive deterrees. They therefore see a significant relationship between costs and risks. They assume that actors will not just weigh possible gains against possible costs, but that they will also calculate the odds or risks involved. On these assumptions, even though possible costs (given nuclear weapons) will always outweigh possible gains, military aggression might still be worthwhile if the probability that the costs will be inflicted is sufficiently low. In other words, the 'difficult' school assumes that calculations of risk are not substantially discounted even when possible costs are raised to very high or infinite levels. They assume a gambling mentality in which good

chances of winning a partial gain will be sought even against the risk
of a total loss, provided the odds against the total loss occurring are
low enough.

In formal terms, the case that deterrence is difficult can be stated
as follows:

Even if the level of possible costs may mean the political and
physical obliteration of the deterree –

   (a) the salience of calculations about both the level of possible
       gains, and the probability that they will be acquired, will
       remain high so long as there is a good probability that the
       possible costs will not be inflicted;
   (b) the salience of calculations about the probabilities of
       incurring costs will remain high because low probabilities
       may offset the fact that possible costs outweigh possible
       gains, and so justify an aggressive gamble in situations
       where possible gains are substantial, and the probability of
       achieving them is high.

From this analysis, one can derive a clear indication of the policy
implications which arise from assumptions about whether deterrence
is easy or difficult.

### 12.2.3   The Policy Implications of 'Easy' versus 'Difficult'

If deterrence is easy, then the essential policy requirement is
possession of sufficient nuclear capability to threaten your opponent
with some form of 'infinite' costs. As noted in Chapter 11, even
against the largest states, a force of several hundred nuclear
warheads is sufficient to meet the standards of 'unacceptable
damage'. If a state can keep such a force convincingly secure against
disarming first strikes, then it possesses assured destruction (AD),
and therefore effective deterrence, against its opponent. Since the
effectiveness of the deterrent derives principally from the magnitude
of the threatened cost, policy-makers will not have to be excessively
concerned about their opponent's calculation of risks. Even fairly
rudimentary efforts to ensure the credibility of threats should suffice.

As Waltz argues, the emphasis of this logic is on the reasoning of
the deteree (that is, the potential aggressor). If the deteree has
doubts that his attack will be anything less than 100 per cent
successful in preventing a retaliation to assured destruction levels,

then the high potential costs will deter him (Waltz, 1981, pp. 4–5). The whole position of the 'easy' school rests on the assumption that *uncertainty* in the minds of the deterree's leaders will stop them from acting if possible costs are very high. Nuclear weapons make it quite simple to create such uncertainty, amplifying as they do the well-established unpredictabilities of war as an instrument of state policy. Several writers share the view that the essence of deterrence lies in the fear of war created by the existence of a surplus capacity of destructive power (Brodie, 1978, p. 65; Jervis, 1979, p. 299; 1979–80, pp. 617–33; Martin, 1980, pp. 11, 17; Steinbrunner, 1976, pp. 237–8). Since uncertainty is easy to create when possible costs are very high, the required conditions for effective deterrence are not difficult to meet in a nuclear age. In this view nuclear weapons have transformed strategic relations by making available a surplus capacity of destructive power. In the pre-nuclear age deterrence was usually difficult because potential costs seldom convincingly outweighed potential gains.

If deterrence is difficult, then policy requires not only sufficient capability to threaten high costs, but also measures to persuade one's opponent that the level of risk he faces is as close to certainty as possible. One's opponent is assumed to be constantly searching for possibilities of attack where the risks of having costs inflicted on him are low enough to justify gambling for possible gains. The assumption here is that nuclear weapons have made little basic difference to the operation of traditional Clausewitzian assumptions about the utility of war as an instrument of policy.

In order to deter such an opponent, risks must be kept high. Most of the ways of raising risks require expanded conventional and nuclear arsenals to give the deterrer a range of denial and retaliatory choices between doing nothing and resorting to all-out nuclear war. These options follow the logic of LNW outlined in the previous chapter. They make deterrent threats more credible because they give the deterrer a range of options in response to less than all-out provocations. It can also be argued that the larger arsenals required for flexible response strategies usefully raise the level, as well as the probability, of threats. Larger arsenals enable a range of specific targets beyond assured destruction to be threatened. These include the opponent's strategic forces, his political establishment, his conventional armed forces, and his transportation and communication networks. Those of the 'easy' persuasion see such additional threats as irrelevant, and even counter-productive. Yet if deterrence really is difficult, then raising possible costs above assured destruction may increase the effectiveness of threats.

The 'deterrence is easy' school assume that deterrence is made effective because of *uncertainties* in the mind of the aggressor. Those who think that deterrence is difficult, assume that it becomes effective only when the potential aggressor is confronted with the *certainty*, or near certainty of unacceptable damage. The need to create near certainty of risk is what makes deterrence difficult to achieve. If one holds these assumptions, then because deterrence is seen to be difficult to achieve, it is an uncertain and unstable path to security.

The 'easy' school thus concentrates on the importance of the constraint placed on the deterree by the threat of assured destruction. Its logic leads to the relatively simple policy of deterrence by threat of retaliation. The 'difficult' school worries more about the responsibilities of the deterrer in trying to keep the level of risk to the deterree as high as possible. A particular worry here is the deterrer's uncertainty about his own behaviour if the logic of deterrence has failed and he has been attacked. If the need to ensure that risks are nearly certain is taken as a requirement for effective deterrence, then a whole range of problems become prominent which have only low salience under the assumptions of the 'easy' school. These problems lead to policies of deterrence by denial. They have spawned such extensive and complicated literatures that they have come to occupy the central ground in deterrence thinking. Indeed, one could easily apply Mary Kaldor's condemnation of modern military technology as 'baroque' to much of this writing about deterrence (Kaldor, 1982).

## 12.3 INTERVENING VARIABLES IN DETERRENCE LOGIC

When looked at in abstract terms, as above, deterrence logic can lead to either 'easy' or 'difficult' conclusions about the implementation of deterrence policy in general. But deterrence logic is not applied in a vacuum. In the real world there are many conditions that enhance the ease or difficulty of deterrence policy. Sometimes the impact of these intervening variables is clearly towards either 'easy' or 'difficult'. The availability of nuclear as opposed to conventional military threats, for example, is crucial to the 'easy' case. But in other cases their impact is ambiguous, appearing to pull in both directions for different reasons. Those people who are very strongly persuaded by the 'easy' logic may still conclude that deterrence is easy even if several of the intervening variables seem to pull towards 'difficult'. This position requires that the impact of possibly infinite costs be seen as so compelling that it overrides all other considerations. A more cautious view would acknowledge that the 'easy' logic can be eroded by 'difficult' conditions, and that the efficacy of deterrence policy thus depends significantly on the nature of the conditions within which it is applied.

These intervening variables can be grouped under five headings: polarity, technology, geography, the political objectives of deterrence, and political relations. The ramifications of these variables can be extremely complex, and given limits of space, the discussion that follows should be taken as indicative rather than exhaustive.

## 12.3.1 Polarity

Polarity refers to the number of nuclear powers amongst which deterrence is in operation. The effect of polarity on deterrence logic is strong, but ambiguous. If, to keep matters relatively simple, one assumes that each additional pole of power represents a fully-fledged nuclear great power (that is, one with a secure second strike assured destruction capability against any other power), then the impact of polarity is as follows:

> With one nuclear power, deterrence is very easy so long as the danger of aggression is not from the nuclear power itself. For that reason, the transition from one to two nuclear powers is a danger point, because the first power may strike to prevent the emergence of a second (Intrilligator and Brito, 1979).
>
> With two nuclear powers, deterrence logic becomes considerably more complex. Each power is simultaneously both deterrer and deterree. In order to maintain credible threats of assured destruction (AD), each side must deploy secure second strike retaliatory forces that are substantially invulnerable to destruction by a first strike from the other side. This requirement means that bipolar deterrence is technologically demanding, as was seen in relation to the United States and the Soviet Union in Chapter 11. Both sides must take continuous pains to ensure not only the security of their retaliatory forces, but also their ability to

penetrate whatever defences the other might have. If they can do so, a situation of mutually assured destruction (MAD) obtains between them, and the basic logic of deterrence is sustained.

Bipolarity makes deterrence easier because it creates a general fear of mutual destruction which restrains both sides from resorting to major aggression. It can also be argued that the inherent simplicity of bipolarity makes deterrence easier, especially in comparison with multipolar deterrence systems. With two powers, the relationship of forces is clear, the complexities of a shifting pattern of alliances amongst the great powers are removed, and management of relations is possible using parity as a norm. Bipolarity also makes deterrence more difficult. If each side challenges the other's ability to maintain AD, then the technological requirements for MAD can become extremely demanding (see 12.3.2 below). The relative clarity of a two-party relationship can be disadvantageous in that it puts relations into zero-sum terms (the gains of either must be the losses of the other). Zero-sum relations can easily focus and concentrate hostilities (see 12.3.5 below). They can also encourage each side to seek advantage, and thereby lead to the pursuit of elaborate 'if-then' scenarios in search for weaknesses in one's own, or one's opponent's, position (see 12.3.4 below). Such scenarios make the calculation of deterrence logic complex, and deterrence policy difficult to implement.

The most famous of these scenarios is called the '*ex ante*, *ex post* problem' (Rosecrance, 1973, pp. 283–90; 1975, pp. 11–12; Steinbrunner, 1976, pp. 231–4). It envisages a counterforce attack by one side against the other in which the attacked state loses more of its forces than the attacker uses in his first strike. Such an outcome is plausible when the attacker is using MIRVed missiles. The question it raises is: Would the attacked state retaliate against the attacker, knowing that to do so would be suicidal, because the attacker still has sufficient forces to destroy its cities? This question focuses on the difference in logic before and after such an attack. What might seem a sound deterrence position before such an attack does not provide attractive options if it fails to deter. That fact can be seen as weakening its initial deterring credibility in the face of a highly motivated deterree willing to brave the first hurdle.

Those who think that deterrence is easy dismiss this type of thinking as irrelevant. The scenario only creates the problem for the deterrer by ignoring the very large initial fear that the deterree would have to overcome to make the attack in the first place. Those inclined to think deterrence difficult see the *ex ante, ex post* problem as important. They see it as revealing conditions in which the deterree might be influenced towards aggression by a reduced probability that infinite costs would be inflicted. Worry about this scenario was one of the main justifications for acquiring the range of retaliatory options necessary to fight LNW. Such options would ideally give the deterrer the ability to make a proportional counterforce response on the attacker's remaining forces while still leaving both sides holding each other's societies as hostage. What separates the 'easy' from the 'difficult' schools is their estimate of whether the deterree will gamble on the self-deterrence of the deterrer when the costs of being wrong are so high.

Conditions of three or more nuclear powers become more similar as numbers rise, and can be considered as a single group labelled multipolar deterrence systems. Multipolarity is traditionally thought to make deterrence more difficult, but the question has not really been given sufficient study. Some aspects of multipolarity also give strong support to the 'easy' case.

On the 'difficult' side, it can be argued that multipolarity makes MAD hard to calculate because each deterrer must account for more than one deterree (Rosecrance, 1972, p. 135). Multipolarity creates the possibility of aggressive alliances in which two or more powers gang up to threaten a disarming strike against one other (Rosecrance, 1973, pp. 287–9; 1975, pp. 29–31). It raises the dangers of attack from unidentified sources by giving suitably equipped powers the possibility of launching clandestine attacks against another from submarines. During a period of crisis between two powers, such an option might in theory be used catalytically by a third power to trigger a war between the other two (Brennan, 1972, pp. 13–23; Rosecrance, 1975, pp. 32–3). In practice, however, the chance of getting away with the deception does not seem good enough to free the would-be perpetrator from the constraints of deterrence logic (Waltz, 1981, 27–8).

Multipolarity also undermines the utility of parity and so makes arms control and disarmament agreement more complicated (Treverton, 1980, pp. 42–4). And the simple fact of more fingers on more nuclear triggers raises the probability of war, whether intended or accidental (Intrilligator and Brito, 1979, pp. 11–15). There is also the issue of the transition from bipolarity to multipolarity, with the potential for war arising from moves by existing powers to stop rivals from joining their club.

On the 'easy' side, there are two points of note. The first is that multipolarity destroys the zero-sum character of bipolar deterrence. By doing so it both reduces the likely intensity of hostility in deterrence relations, and makes it impossible for any actor to calculate the outcome in an attack on any other. Both effects lower the incentives to resort to aggression. In a multipolar system, the elaborate LNW scenarios of 'difficult' bipolar deterrence become impossible to calculate because three or more actors destroy the credibility of long chains of 'if-then' logic. The probability that the principal beneficiaries from any war would be those powers abstaining from the fight also seems likely to reduce incentives for aggression (Intrilligator and Brito, 1979, pp. 6–10; Rosecrance, 1972, pp. 6–9; 1973, p. 286). The second point concerns the reduced need for extended deterrence in a multipolar system. It should by now be clear that ED has been a major source of difficulty in deterrence policy, and therefore any development that reduces the need for it can be seen as a gain. This issue will be taken up in detail in section 12.3.4 below.

The question of multipolar systems raises the broader issue of nuclear proliferation, with its threat of descending tiers of middle and small nuclear powers. Such powers would not rank as 'poles' in the strict sense used above, but their possession of nuclear weapons none the less raises important questions for deterrence logic. Opinion differs sharply as to whether deterrence logic would work between minor nuclear powers like, say, India and Pakistan. A few argue for the essential universality of nuclear deterrence logic (Waltz, 1981). Others take the view that the less developed political and technological conditions in many potential small nuclear powers would make proliferation a recipe for local nuclear wars (Dror, 1980, pp. 49–50; Dunn, 1982, ch. 4). If the positive view is correct, then nuclear proliferation would contribute to world order by spreading the war prevention imperative to regions now prone to periodic conflict. If the negative view is correct, then proliferation might raise the risk of escalation from peripheral wars into the central nuclear balance.

The spread of minor nuclear powers could impinge on central nuclear deterrence in a variety of ways other than spillover effects from their impact on relations within the periphery. The existence of minor powers could encourage the major powers to hold very large nuclear arsenals so as to differentiate themselves from the lower ranks. It could also encourage the major powers to adopt policies of strategic defence (SD) (Brennan, 1972, pp. 13–28; Hoag, 1972, pp. 41–8). SD would add distance between the status of major and minor nuclear powers, and would protect the major powers against threats of catalytic actions from minor ones. But any resort to SD would complicate deterrence relations between the superpowers. SD would also erode the position of medium nuclear powers like Britain, France and China, whose nuclear forces are intended to deter superpowers (Freedman, 1980a, pp. 50–2). It would encourage them either to get out of the game, or to bid for full status by developing larger and more sophisticated nuclear forces, an effect already registered by the existing medium nuclear powers in relation to SDI. Medium-sized nuclear forces can complicate arms control between the superpowers in the same way as multipolarity. This effect is evident from the impact of European and Chinese nuclear forces on superpower strategic nuclear arms control negotiations.

## 12.3.2 **Technology**

As already revealed by the emphasis on nuclear weapons in Chapter 11, technological factors are central to deterrence. Deterrence logic can stem either from defensive or offensive capability, the former leading to deterrence by denial, the latter to deterrence by retaliation. Nuclear weapons give a great edge to the offensive because their huge destructive powers can only be blunted by a virtually perfect defence. Notwithstanding current enthusiasm for SD, perfect defence, or anything like it, is highly improbable for the foreseeable future. Consequently, the focus here will be on the logic of deterrence by retaliation, not ignoring the fact that even partially effective defensive technology can have an important impact on deterrence policy.

Technological factors can affect the ease or difficulty of deterrence in many ways. The basic requirement for 'easy' deterrence is the huge capacity for destruction provided by nuclear weapons. Indeed, it is that capacity which provides the central, stable condition on which the primacy of deterrence theory in strategic thinking rests. But although a surplus capacity of destructive power is essential for easy deterrence, it also creates a difficulty. The weapons that threaten obliteration by retaliation are often not dissimilar to those needed to threaten a first strike against the retaliatory forces of the other side. If the technology exists to make large-scale attacks against hardened targets, then deterrence becomes difficult because the existence of MAD is constantly open to question.

So far, the maintenance of a secure second strike has been

managed fairly easily, even though the acquisition of hard target counterforce capabilities by the United States and the Soviet Union has required technological sophistication and large force deployments on both sides to sustain secure second strike requirements. One of the main rationales for maintaining a 'triad' of strategic forces – ICBMs, long-range bombers, and ballistic missile submarines – is precisely to guard against the possibility that one's opponent will develop the capability to destroy pre-emptively any single 'leg' of the triad. Hardened and diversified targets are much more difficult to attack reliably than soft and uniform ones. The current 'star wars' enthusiasm seems more likely to reinforce the secure second strike by adding to the protection of land-based missile forces than to undermine it by threatening the penetration capability of nuclear weapons against soft countervalue targets. The possibility of neutralizing an opponent's secure second strike by attacking it thus shows no signs of triumphing over available measures of protection, even though the security of land-based ICBMs is much lower than it was during the 1960s and 1970s.

The possibility of degrading assured destruction by mounting a comprehensive defence against nuclear attack seems unlikely ever to be realized. The best systems under discussion are hugely expensive, are themselves vulnerable to attack, cannot guarantee anything approaching perfect defence even against ballistic missiles alone, and cannot meet all the various other ways in which nuclear warheads can be delivered to their targets. As Glaser argues, even a perfect strategic defence would not provide security. Its perfection could never be tested adequately enough to convince. Constant doubts would exist as to whether one's opponent had developed new means for penetrating what was previously impenetrable (Glaser, 1984).

The pressure of technological innovation is a general difficulty for deterrence since it requires continuous reassessment of forces. Sometimes developments add to the difficulty of maintaining deterrence, as MIRV did by tipping the ratio of missiles needed to attack, versus missiles destroyed by attack, in favour of the attacking force. But sometimes they make deterrence easier, as both improved surveillance systems and virtually undetectable missile-carrying submarines have done. To a substantial extent this pressure is unstoppable because it stems from the technological imperative described in Chapter 8. Its intensity can also vary very considerably according to whether the powers in a deterrence relationship challenge, or acquiesce in, each other's secure second strike capability.

In theory, the technological requirements of MAD could be kept relatively simple if all parties agreed not to challenge each other's secure second strike capabilities. In practice, the two superpowers have challenged each other at least partially, and this has made the technological requirements of MAD much more demanding. Both have deployed, and look like continuing to improve, hard target counterforce capability against the other side's land-based missiles and control systems. In response, both have had to develop expensive alternatives to hardened silo-basing for ICBMs, most notably in the form of mobile missile systems. Both have also made efforts to threaten the other's strategic missile-carrying submarines (SSBN) by improving their capabilities for underwater detection. For technological and geographical reasons, the West has been more successful in this enterprise than has the Soviet Union, though neither can threaten the other's SSBN to anything like the same extent as is true for fixed-silo ICBMs (Daniel, 1986). Domestic pressures favouring such 'damage limiting' capabilities to attack the opponent's strategic forces are hard to deny, even though their principal impact is simply to raise the size of the forces necessary to sustain MAD. The SDI commitment represents a major escalation in this process of challenge, but no defensive escape from the reality of MAD looks possible for a very long time, if ever.

MAD is available either by the easy route of acquiescence and agreement, or by the difficult route of challenge and response. So far, the superpowers have chosen the difficult route, though for a time during the 1960s the United States gave verbal support to the easy one. The fact that they have chosen to do things the hard way should not disguise the essential robustness of MAD as a condition. Even if they reject MAD as a doctrine, and so choose the difficult route, the superpowers work to sustain it as a reality because of the powerful commitment each has to maintain its own AD capability against the other. Because MAD is essentially robust, technological pressure is not such a threat to the 'easy' logic as it might at first appear to be. The price paid for choosing the difficult route, however, is the intense arms dynamic between the superpowers described in Chapter 9.

Where technology does cause serious problems for deterrence is in relation to accidental war. Although MAD is virtually inescapable, a highly competitive approach to it by the nuclear powers may force them into postures that raise the probability of uncontrolled escalation during a crisis. A state facing substantial counterforce threats, and/or threats to 'decapitate' its command system, may, for example, respond by putting its forces under launch-on-warning (LoW) instructions. LoW raises the danger of military logic taking over from political control during a crisis, or even to purely accidental war resulting from errors in the warning system triggering nuclear forces. Technology shrinks the time available for decision, and necessitates the automation of many stages of alert (Bracken, 1983). Especially where both sides are challenging the secure second strike of the other, technological factors can become an independent source of tension and instability in the relationship. The dangers of intense technological competition in deterrence, when viewed against the unbreakable logic of MAD, underline the case for taking the easy rather than the difficult route to the achievement of MAD. Doing so, however, may be blocked by domestic political aversion, as in the Soviet Union, to the idea of acquiescing in vulnerability to one's opponent's assured destruction capability. The 'easy' path may also be blocked, as for the United States, by extended deterrence commitments requiring capability additional to simple AD (see 12.3.4).

### 12.3.3  Geography

The key geographical variable is whether the states in a deterrence relationship are adjacent to, or remote from, each other. Remoteness makes deterrence easier, while adjacency makes it more difficult.

The logic of MAD remains simple, provided first that the two states are remote from each other, and second that their political objectives in deterrence are confined to preventing attacks on themselves (core deterrence). The United States and the Soviet Union meet the first of these criteria, but not, at present, the second. When both conditions are met, neither state can invade the other in the conventional sense of the term, and therefore all that has to be deterred is nuclear attack. So long as each side maintains a secure second strike, deterrence will be stable.

When the states in a deterrence relationship are adjacent, like the Soviet Union and China, then the logic of MAD is vulnerable to the threat of conventional attacks. This problem can be defined in terms of the *threshold* of deterrence. Under conditions of MAD, the mutual nuclear threats restrain each other effectively. But since each side's nuclear threat is balanced by the other's, neither can use nuclear threats to deter aggressive actions which are below a magnitude sufficient to justify a risk of nuclear war. Under MAD both sides are strongly motivated to avoid nuclear war, since neither has any hope of winning without risking its own destruction. Consequently, neither can comfortably use nuclear threats to deter limited conventional attacks across their mutual border. Nuclear threats would not be credible because the risk of applying them greatly outweighs the threat they are aimed against. The general fear of war arising under MAD means that each side is self-deterred from resorting to nuclear weapons for anything except the most grave and massive threats. Under conditions of MAD, the threshold of deterrence is high, and so does not cover the lower level threats and 'salami tactics' (taking one thin slice at a time) which are part of the problem faced by adjacent states.

To meet this problem, as Michael Howard has argued, it is necessary to deploy defensive forces sufficient to deny an adjacent opponent the option of low-level aggression (Howard, 1973, pp. 261–5). These forces do not have to match the opponent's in size and strength. Their role is to deny the opponent the freedom to use low level force, and in that sense they can be seen as deterrence-by-denial forces covering the lower end of the spectrum of threats. That denial role blends into a tripwire role at the point where the opponent would need to make such a large conventional attack to have any hope of success that the scale of his threat would be sufficient to give credibility to counterthreats of nuclear retaliation. The defensive forces thus serve as an escalation mechanism to bring nuclear deterrence into play.

As with MAD, there are easy and difficult paths to achieving adequate denial. If both sides take a competitive attitude towards their border deployments, then the force requirements will be large. If they can agree on an acceptable balance, or if they simply match each other at low levels, then the requirements may be modest. A particularly vexed question arising in relation to denial forces is whether or not they should include shorter-range nuclear weapons for use on the battlefield. Such weapons enforce the dispersal of opposing forces, and thereby greatly complicate the making of conventional attacks. In so doing, they increase the strength of deterrence by denial, but actual use of them breaches the nuclear threshold, may risk premature escalation, and raises all the problems of LNW strategies. That risk may undermine their credibility for the same reason that secure second strike forces are not credible against lower levels of threat.

This problem of thresholds, and the need for denial forces, obviously applies to Western Europe and the Soviet Union as well as to China. But in the case of Europe, the issue is more than just geographical, for it relates also to the range of political objectives that states pursue using deterrence.

### 12.3.4 The Deterrer's Political Objectives: Core versus Extended Deterrence

The problem of scope is inherent to deterrence policy: what range of political objectives is deterrence supposed to cover? So far the discussion in this chapter has mostly assumed a situation in which countries simply sought to prevent attacks on themselves, that is, core deterrence. Once a condition of MAD is reached, if one or both countries seek to extend the cover of deterrence to third countries, then deterrence becomes much more difficult to achieve.

The problem for extended deterrence (ED) is similar to that for the geographical problem of deterrence between adjacent states: when deterrence is mutual, neither side is in a strong position to use threats of nuclear retaliation against the other on secondary or minor issues. Because of this threshold problem, the most convincing way to achieve ED is by mounting an adequate denial capability against the threatening aggressor. Unlike the case with adjacent deterrence, this denial capability really needs to be a match for the opponent's offensive power. The crucial difference between the two cases hinges on the priority attached to the political objectives of deterrence by the deterrer. With adjacent deterrence, the deterrer is acting in pursuit of its own security. There can be no doubt that this is the highest political objective possible for a state. Therefore the threat to resort to nuclear retaliation in the face of a major conventional defeat is credible.

In the case of ED, this reasoning does not hold. The security of an ally or client, no matter how important, must always rank lower than the security of the deterrer itself. Even if the ally or client is a major bulwark to the security of the deterrer, the fact remains that under conditions of MAD, the deterrer cannot threaten nuclear retaliation for ED without simultaneously placing its own core security at profound risk of nuclear devastation. Consequently, ED can only be made fully believable under MAD by the use of adequate denial forces. If such forces can be mounted, then ED is not problematic, though it may be technically and financially demanding. The difference between adjacent and extended deterrence is illustrated by comparing China and Western Europe. There is little discussion of credibility as a problem for China's deterrence policy, whereas credibility is the central issue in the debates about Europe.

If adequate denial forces are not available, but ED is pursued anyway, then so long as MAD persists, deterrence policy will labour under the fundamental and unavoidable contradictions between the goal of ED and the goal of core deterrence. This situation has some strong parallels with the *ex ante*, *ex post* problem (see 12.3.1). In both cases, the problem hinges on the logical weakness of the deterrer's threat in relation to his own self-interest in survival. Will the deterrer carry out his threat if the deterree makes a limited attack despite it? Is there a significant chance that the deterree will gamble on the self-deterrence of the deterrer in the post-attack situation? Does the necessity for an irrational (that is, self-damaging) response by the deterrer undermine the initial threat and therefore void the whole logic of ED? The discussion that follows explores the case of ED without adequate denial forces. It will be assumed throughout, unless otherwise stated, that ED is being attempted against a background of MAD between the primary deterrer and deterree.

This case is given salience by the fact that it describes the perennial problems of NATO. When the United States first extended deterrence to Western Europe it could do so easily. The Soviet Union did not then have the ability to strike North America and therefore MAD did not obtain. But by the 1960s the Soviets had acquired assured destruction against the United States, and so what began as an easy commitment for the Americans turned into an increasingly difficult one. The option of deploying adequate denial forces has often been mooted, but neither the Europeans nor the Americans are willing to match the high levels of conventional force maintained by the Soviet Union. Consequently, the Americans have been obliged to maintain their commitment by seeking to elaborate the range of their nuclear threats beyond the requirements of AD. The dual objective of these additional threats is to lower the threshold of deterrence while at the same time avoiding, or at least mitigating substantially, the contradiction between the goals of core and extended deterrence. In other words, the United States has tried to provide a nuclear umbrella for Europe which would make up for the deficiencies in NATO denial forces, while not putting the United States in the position of having to take a nearly certain risk of its own destruction in order to save its allies.

The attempt to extend deterrence without adequate denial capability goes right to the heart of the logic which differentiates the 'easy' and 'difficult' schools. Once AD is achieved, there is little scope for supporting ED by increasing the level of possible cost faced by the deterree. The problem raised by ED does not stem from the magnitude of the threat, but from the lower probability that it will be carried out. Attempts to bolster the credibility of ED therefore depend on the deterrer taking measures to raise that probability. This approach puts ED firmly into the framework of the 'difficult' school, which is also concerned with keeping probabilities high. Within the logic of the 'difficult' school, ED represents perhaps the single most problematic type of deterrence. Some argue that ED cannot be achieved if the deterrer is vulnerable to nuclear attack, and that the United States should abandon the attempt (Ravenal, 1982, pp. 36–43). Others argue that ED can be made to work, the essential factors being first, strong economic and political ties between the primary deterrer and the countries to which it is extending deterrence, and second, the existence of strong local denial forces (Huth and Russett, 1984).

Opinion within the 'easy' school is split. Some argue that the very high value of Western Europe to American security virtually eliminates any contradiction between core and extended objectives. In this view, the ED on which NATO rests is therefore credible even within the context of MAD (Schilling, 1981, pp. 44–6; Waltz, 1981, pp. 18–20). American policy, however, has responded to the growth of Soviet strategic power by seeing ED as increasingly difficult (Cordesman, 1982). Even the 'easy' protagonists make some concession to the 'difficult' logic by acknowledging that effective ED requires some nuclear forces additional to those for secure second strike (Art and Waltz, 1971, p. 20; Jervis, 1984, pp. 169–70). These forces are needed to make nuclear threats credible, and thereby compensate for the inevitable contradiction between extended and core deterrence objectives.

There is no escape from the dilemma that, if it came to the choice, the United States might prefer a situation in which the Soviet Union controlled Western Europe and the United States was undamaged, to one in which all three areas had suffered massive nuclear bombardment. Because that choice is intrinsic to the logic of

ED, worries about the credibility of ED threats cannot be escaped. Even those favouring the 'easy' view require a modest probability to be attached to threats. The concern about ED is that the deterrer's own fear of escalation may reduce the probability of retaliation to near zero. As Luttwak observes, when ED is based on the threat of escalation, the scope for coercive diplomacy by the deterree is defined by the deterrer's fear of escalation (Luttwak, 1980a, pp. 32–3). Extended deterrence requires the pursuit of the 'difficult' logic of raising the probabilities of retaliation by enlarging both the types and the numbers of nuclear weapons held by the deterrer.

But the pursuit of ED by attempts to raise risks quickly runs into the self-sustaining and self-defeating logic which characterizes the 'difficult' school in general. In particular, ED generates powerful tendencies towards arms racing and excessively complex rational calculations which dwarf those arising from the *ex ante*, *ex post* dilemma. In practice, the commitment to ED and the influence of the 'difficult' school on the mainstream of deterrence theory, have reinforced each other's influence on the evolution of American nuclear doctrine.

The next two sections will take up two points, both fairly well understood in the literature, which illustrate the self-sustaining and self-defeating characteristics which arise when ED is pursued down the path of 'difficult' logic. The first point is that the logic of threats for ED becomes so complex and technologically demanding that the LNW scenarios which result are not credible as projections of possible realities. The second, arising from this, is the disaffection of the countries for which ED is supposed to provide security.

### 12.3.4.1 *Excessive complexity in logic and technology*
In order to maintain high levels of risk for ED, deterrent threats at the local level must be tied into a general threat to escalate to strategic nuclear exchange. To keep probability, and therefore credibility, high, retaliation options must exist in a continuous spectrum ranging from the point at which denial options fail on the one end, to general strategic exchange on the other. The rationality of controlled escalation requires that deterrent threats can be offered at all levels of action. A broad spectrum of threats has two effects. It prevents one's opponent from getting away with salami tactics, and it connects the overarching threat of strategic nuclear exchange to the objective of ED without necessitating the high risk to the deterrer of immediate escalation to mutual strategic bombardment.

In other words ED, under these conditions, requires the ability to fight both limited conventional wars (as part of denial strategies at the lowest levels of response), and limited nuclear wars (blending from denial strategies into graduated retaliatory responses). The technical and the rational requirements of LNW are extremely demanding. In order to conduct LNW, both sides must have very large inventories of accurate and retargetable warheads, and extremely good and durable command, control, communications and intelligence (C3I) facilities. Both sides must reject any inclination towards strategies of pre-emption (attacking to prevent an imminent attack on yourself), launch-on-warning (LoW) (attacking when your warning systems indicate that an attack against you has been launched), or launch-under-attack (attacking when the opponent's attack on you actually begins to arrive) in the context of core deterrence. Any of these options would undermine the notion of controlled escalation on which the deterrent effect of the limited options rests. If no control is possible, then the additional forces required for limited options simply add to a weight of weaponry already more than adequate for AD. The logic of credibility in ED can also be used to justify the acquisition of strategic defence capabilities by the deterrer (Lodal, 1980).

Serious doubts exist about both the technical and the political ability to conduct limited nuclear conflict. C3I is notoriously difficult to harden against nuclear weapon effects, and any breakdown in political control over nuclear forces would make limited conflict impossible (Bracken, 1983; Russett, 1983b, pp. 156–9; Snow, 1979, p. 466). Attacks against the decision-making and control centres of one's opponent ('decapitation' or 'counter-combatant' attacks) will automatically degrade his ability to conduct limited conflict (Russett, 1983b, pp. 148–53; Williams, 1983, p. 4). Even if control and decision centres are not attacked, it is by no means certain that behaviour could be controlled to the level of fine calculation required by LNW scenarios. When weapons have already begun to fly, and both damage and perceptions of threat and risk are rising rapidly, the logic of complex rational behaviour is at its least credible (Steinbrunner, 1976, pp. 239–45; Snyder, 1978, pp. 345–65). If the arguments about a 'nuclear winter' are correct, the whole notion of limited nuclear war is rendered useless because of the inability to contain the massive environmental side-effects of multiple nuclear detonations (Nye, 1986; Sagan, 1983–4).

In addition, the force requirements for ED exacerbate the problem of arms racing. Not only do the additional forces undermine attempts to achieve parity, but also the counterforce capabilities required for limited nuclear options raise the spectre of disarming first strikes. Any threat to the survivability of strategic forces will raise tensions. It will also create pressures to resort to the pre-emptive, LoW, and launch-under-attack options which undermine the assumptions on which limited nuclear options are based. Declarations by the country acquiring counterforce options that it intends to limit their use, and that no first strike threat is contemplated, are unlikely to provide significant reassurance to those responsible for national security in the rival power. The relentless pressures towards arms racing created by both the number and the character of forces additional to secure second strike required for ED, would be massively reinforced if ED logic led to the deployment of strategic defence capabilities. Such capabilities not only challenge the other side's AD, but also increase his perception of first strike threats against him.

### 12.3.4.2 *The disaffection of allies*
When deterrence relations between the superpowers were unbalanced in favour of the West, the allies of the United States enjoyed ED at little risk to themselves. As nuclear bipolarity has become real, however, they have found their security increasingly squeezed by the impact of parity on ED.

The Western European countries occupy a paradoxical position in relation to deterrence between the superpowers. They do not themselves have the power or the will to attack either superpower, and so are not themselves primary subjects of deterrence by others. Because of their location they depend for their security on the general effectiveness of deterrence between the superpowers. They also depend on the particular effectiveness of ED. They need the American guarantee to supplement the inadequate denial and retaliation capability which is the best they have been prepared to mount against the Soviet Union on their own account. The arrival of parity put the Western Europeans into the difficult position in which all the possible measures to strengthen ED had adverse security consequences for the Europeans. As one writer has noted, there are no happy solutions to the European security problem (Lodal, 1980, pp. 171–2).

Attempts to strengthen deterrence by denial not only strained political and economic resources, but also raised the prospect of limited war in Europe. The very idea of limited war seemed to weaken the absolute assurance that unacceptable damage would be inflicted on the Soviet Union. It therefore weakened the war-preventing logic of deterrence policy. The fear was that excessive pursuit of deterrence by denial would detach ED from core deterrence, and so tempt the Soviet leaders to try for limited gains. Subsequent attempts to reattach ED to core deterrence by enhancing America's limited nuclear options to a level sufficient for major theatre use, raised even greater problems. Although the United States provided the resources, and the emphasis returned to deterrence by retaliation, the Western Europeans found themselves embroiled in the wrong end of an escalation policy which could start on their territory. Now the danger was that controlled escalation would destroy Europe, even if it succeeded in stopping the war before the superpowers became strategically engaged. Even the move by the United States towards strategic defence has upset the Europeans. Although SD should, within the logic of ED, enhance the credibility of American guarantees by returning the United States to the low vulnerability it enjoyed during the 1950s, Europeans have worried about it as a sign that the United States could be detaching its own security from that of Europe.

These scenarios for strengthening ED under conditions of parity suffer from excessive logical complexity. By the strict rules of deterrence calculation, they are sound. Yet because the scenarios themselves involve warfighting as part of deterrence, they encourage the view that war has become more likely. Given European conditions and experience, any such view is extremely difficult to sell to the general public as a sensible and acceptable security policy. Doubts about the viability of both the logic and the technology necessary for ED also undermine faith in these remedies. Europeans perceive little difference to themselves whether a nuclear war is limited or total. Consequently, they tend to prefer a threat of total war which keeps the probability of *any* war to a minimum. A threat of limited war seems merely to lower the level of threatened costs to the Soviet Union, and thereby to increase the possibility of conflict. As more than one writer has noted, another problem of ED is that it takes more deterrence to reassure allies than it does to deter enemies (Howard, 1973, pp. 261–2; Ravenal, 1982, pp. 35–6).

Despite their deserved image of ingratitude, these European worries spring from the basic logic of deterrence. The commitment to keep potential costs infinite is the most important factor in effective deterrence. Any policy which even appears to lower potential costs by emphasizing measured stages of response, undermines the fundamental assumption that what makes deterrence effective is the dominating effects of possibly infinite costs on the mind of the would-be aggressor.

Under these conditions, it becomes hard to convince the public that limited nuclear options will increase the effectiveness of ED and thereby lower the over-all probability of war. From a European perspective, the means necessary to sustain ED have begun to generate more sense of threat than of security. Whatever the logical merits of limited nuclear options, they can never provide a security policy with which Western Europeans can feel comfortable. Because of the nature of their logic, limited nuclear options will always excite suspicions that Europe might become the victim of a superpower war in which the superpowers themselves were largely spared.

The European case indicates a structural problem in the attempt to extend deterrence under conditions of real parity. Under such conditions, the logic of the 'difficult' school becomes so convoluted and complex that it stretches the boundaries of its own assumptions about both technology and human behaviour beyond the point of belief. The expansion of nuclear options was intended to cure the low credibility of ED perceived by many to arise from the 'easy' prescription of minimum deterrence. Ironically, it reproduces the problem it was intended to solve. ED simply replaces threats of massive retaliation which were not credible because they were not rational, with threats of carefully controlled nuclear exchanges which are not credible because their rationality outruns the capability of the human and technological systems on which their implementation rests. The 'difficult' rational approach to ED thus undermines the political basis of security policy in the areas to be protected.

Extended deterrence without adequate denial forces therefore makes deterrence much more difficult than it would be if the political objective was simply core deterrence. By its nature, ED will almost always raise the credibility problem of the difference in the deterrer's attitude towards primary and secondary objectives. To tackle that problem the 'difficult' logic has to be pursued in order to raise risks to the deterree. The means by which this is done, however, work powerfully to enhance those technological variables which have already been identified as making deterrence more difficult (see section 12.3.2). It is this mechanism that makes the 'difficult' logic self-reinforcing, and the attempt to apply it to ED self-defeating.

The problem of ED also connects to other intervening variables that affect the ease or difficulty of deterrence. As noted in section 12.3.1, an increase in the number of fully-fledged nuclear powers is likely to reduce the need for ED. If Western Europe provided its own nuclear deterrence, then the intractable credibility problems of ED would be replaced by the considerably less demanding problems of adjacency. In any system, the need for ED will decline as more centres of power provide their own deterrence. The likelihood of demand for ED can thus be seen as a disadvantage of bipolarity. ED in the context of bipolarity is additionally disadvantageous because it reinforces the tendency towards 'baroque' logic which is already a feature of bipolar systems.

ED is sensitive to variables in technological and political relations for obvious reasons. If technology facilitates credible limited nuclear options, then ED is easier than if it doesn't. If political relations are tense and hostile, then ED will be more difficult than if they are governed by détente. ED is also sensitive to geographical variables. If the country receiving ED is adjacent to the deterree, and remote from the deterrer, then ED will be more difficult. This is the case with Western Europe. If the country receiving ED is adjacent to the deterrer, and remote from the deterree, then ED will be easier. Canada is in this position, as is Eastern Europe. If the country receiving ED is either remote from both, like Australia, and to a lesser extent Japan, or adjacent to both, like Mongolia between the Soviet Union and China, then ED will be affected to a middling degree as compared with the other two cases.

## 12.3.5  Political Relations

The variable of political relations concerns the level of tension between the states in a deterrence relationship. Tension can be fed by hostility and fear, both of which are normal background features of life in the international anarchy. Tension can be independent of deterrence, and therefore a factor feeding into deterrence logic. It can also result from features of deterrence policy, so creating the danger of self-reinforcing conditions in which the pursuit of deterrence adds to the tensions that make it necessary. As argued above, the level of motivation of the deterree is central to deterrence logic. Since tension is an expression of the would-be aggressor's motivation, high levels of tension will tend to make deterrence more difficult, and lower levels will tend to make it easier.

Tension as an independent variable can stem from a variety of factors causing relations between states to be hostile. States may have historical animosities between them, like Greece and Turkey; they may have territorial disputes, like Somalia and Ethiopia; they may be committed to mutually exclusive ideologies like the United States and the Soviet Union; or they may be engaged in a power rivalry, like Argentina and Brazil. Deterrence will be more difficult when these tensions are high, because each party will tend to see the basic motivation of the other as strong. Under such conditions, the 'easy' logic of low concern about probabilities becomes harder to accept. Pressure is created on the deterrer to offset the high motivation of the deterree by raising the probability that retaliation will occur. Where deterrence is mutual, this resort to the 'difficult' logic is self-reinforcing. Each side sees the other's offsetting moves as confirmation of its aggressive intentions. Under these conditions an open-ended deterrence arms race becomes likely.

Tension can also be created directly by fear of the other side's military capability, apart from, or in addition to, whatever hostilities already inform the relationship. Here the logic of deterrence blends into that of the arms dynamic. Raising the probability of retaliation requires deployment of counterforce capabilities and doctrines of limited nuclear war. These capabilities push strongly towards open-ended arms racing, which itself becomes a source of tension, and possibly even a root of hostility. Once that happens, the 'difficult' logic is well on the way to becoming self-sustaining.

Several other variables bear on the level of tension. It can be argued that bipolarity increases tension by focusing hostilities into a rigid, zero-sum framework. Multipolarity tends to make political relations more flexible, and hostility less concentrated. Configurations of technology can facilitate or mitigate fear. Much deterrence technology is aggressive and threatening by definition, since the whole logic of deterrence by retaliation depends on the dominance of offensive weapons. Some technologies even threaten deterrence itself, such as those that enable counterforce attacks to be made on hardened missile silos and strategic missile submarines. When such technologies are ascendant over those which protect secure second strike forces, then technology increases tensions within the deterrence relationship. Political objectives like ED will also tend to raise tensions for the reasons argued above.

### 12.3.6 Conclusions on Intervening Variables

These five sets of intervening variables can occur in numerous combinations. In many of these, pressures towards making deterrence easier will be cancelled out by others making it more difficult, and the net effect will be small. In others, however, the effects will line up, possibly in a mutually reinforcing pattern, to produce strong pressures towards making deterrence either easier or more difficult.

For example, it could be argued that a combination like the following would add considerably to the difficulty of deterrence:

- bipolarity, because it reinforces hostility, raises the demand for ED, and facilitates the baroque logic of the 'difficult' school;
- counterforce technology outruns protective measures for secure second strike forces, thereby increasing tension through fear of first strikes, and counterforce technology is pursued competitively by both sides;
- the states in a deterrence relationship are adjacent, and so need denial capabilities as well as retaliatory ones;
- one or more of the states has ED objectives, and the country receiving ED is adjacent to the deterree but remote from the deterrer;
- political relations are hostile, and each side perceives the other as having high basic motivations towards aggression.

Conversely, it could be argued that a combination like the one below would make deterrence considerably easier:

- multipolarity, because it diffuses hostility, reduces the need for ED, and undermines the credibility of baroque deterrence logic;
- secure second strike forces are not threatened by first strike forces, and technology policy is governed by concern for stability;
- the states in the deterrence relationship are remote, and therefore need only retaliatory forces;
- all states in the deterrence relationship are pursuing only core deterrence objectives;
- political relationships are governed by the principles of détente and peaceful coexistence.

The difference between these two scenarios defines the political latitude for action to make deterrence easier. Although some of the variables, most notably geography, cannot be altered, most of the others are at least partly amenable to politically directed change. To have any long-term chance of success, change aimed at making deterrence easier must be accompanied both by unilateral measures of self-restraint by states, and by measures of international co-ordination and co-operation. These measures are the subject of Part IV. They can be either in terms of the military doctrines and deployments of states, or in terms of their political objectives.

## 12.4  DETERRENCE LOGIC AND DETERRENCE POLICY

The spectrum of deterrence logic that runs from 'easy' to 'difficult' is accompanied by a spectrum of deterrence policies that runs from minimum to maximum in terms of the level and type of forces seen as necessary to implement it.

Minimum deterrence policy rests on the 'easy' logic that the effectiveness of deterrence depends primarily on the deterrer maintaining a threat of very high costs. Its principal emphasis is therefore on providing a secure second strike force of sufficient size to make threats of AD credible. This force must be large enough to wreak unacceptable damage on the deterree after both suffering losses in the best counterforce first strike available to the deterree, and accounting for the inevitable percentage of malfunctions which result in warheads failing to destroy their assigned targets. If the deterree has deployed strategic defences, then the minimum force must also take likely attrition rates into account (Singer, 1962, p. 52). The classic estimate of the minimum force which must actually arrive on target to inflict unacceptable damage on the Soviet Union, as noted above, is 400 megaton-equivalent delivered warheads (Enthoven and Smith, 1971, pp. 207–10). The size of the force required to achieve that delivery may vary considerably, according partly to the operating efficiency of the deterrer's weapons, but most to the losses that the deterree could inflict on the force by first strike and strategic defence measures. Minimum deterrence policies are therefore only distinct from maximum ones when the parties to a deterrence relationship do not drive up the size of deterrence forces by contesting each other's AD capabilities. If AD is not contested, then the size of the forces necessary to implement it is defined by the absolute, and therefore finite, criteria of the mission, and not by the open-ended criteria of comparisons with the force size of the opponent.

The main arguments supporting minimum deterrence policy are as follows:

- it harnesses the war-preventing potential of nuclear weapons in the international anarchy at the lowest possible level of cost and risk;
- it defines a ceiling of sufficiency for nuclear forces, and thereby greatly reduces the pressures for arms racing;
- it reduces the intensity of the security dilemma by confining threats based on offensive weapons to a purely reactive role. The commitment to mount only a second strike allows a policy of no first use to be adopted;
- it avoids the excessively complex and ultimately unconvincing deterrence logic of the 'difficult' school;
- it requires the parties to deterrence to recognize that their securities are interdependent, and encourages them to think about security in holistic and co-operative terms, as well as nationalistic ones.

Maximum deterrence policy rests on the 'difficult' logic that the effectiveness of deterrence depends on keeping both the size, and the probability, of the possible cost to the deterree as large as possible. Its principal emphasis is therefore on operational nuclear forces. These forces need to be capable of fighting, and in some sense winning, nuclear wars across a spectrum of contingencies ranging from warning shots and small-scale conflicts at one end, to full-scale theatre nuclear wars and central wars at the other (Gray, 1980, 1984; Gray and Payne, 1980). The force requirement is therefore large. Because its effectiveness depends on how it compares with opposing forces, it is also open-ended. In addition to secure second strike forces, a maximum deterrence posture requires a wide range of counterforce, strategic defence, and theatre nuclear forces. As Gray and Payne argue it, the essential logic of the maximum deterrence policy is that 'there can be no such thing as an adequate deterrent posture unrelated to probable wartime effectiveness' (Gray and Payne, 1980, pp. 19–20).

The main arguments supporting maximum deterrence policy are as follows:

- it allows national security policy to be self-reliant, and minimizes

the necessity to entrust one's security to the behaviour of one's opponent;
- it allows status quo powers to seek an edge in military strength in order to offset the possibly greater aggressive tendencies of revisionist opponents;
- it allows a major power to pursue the defence of its interests through ED even under conditions of MAD;
— it solves the *ex ante*, *ex post* dilemma;
- it avoids the necessity to accept military and political stalemate, and therefore allows the goal of victory to be used for its traditional political and military purposes.

There are, of course, many intermediate options between maximum and minimum policies. These try to combine the different logics of the two extremes in such a way as to maximize the advantages, and minimize the disadvantages, of both. The desire to find intermediate options can result from pressures on policies at either end of the spectrum. Maximum deterrence is vulnerable to pressure primarily on the grounds of the high costs and tensions created by arms racing. The budgetary reaction against the Reagan Administration's arms build-up in the United States illustrates these pressures in action. Such pressures are more likely to be aimed at whittling deterrence forces down to some intermediate level, rather than at moving all the way to minimum deterrence. Minimum deterrence can become vulnerable to pressures for forces beyond secure second strike requirements on a number of grounds. If ED is a policy objective under conditions of MAD, then, as the American experience since the 1960s illustrates, the logic of flexible response will inexorably increase force levels away from minimum deterrence. Even without an ED commitment, minimum deterrence becomes politically vulnerable if it is not reciprocated by the other parties in the deterrence relationship. A one-sided commitment to minimum deterrence is highly vulnerable to domestic nationalist pressures if the other side seems to think that more extensive nuclear forces confer an advantage in foreign policy. And as already suggested, minimum deterrence effectively decays into an intermediate option if either side seeks to contest the other's AD capability.

The danger of intermediate options is that nearly all of them unleash the self-reinforcing logic of the 'difficult' school. Once minimum deterrence is abandoned, there is no obvious stopping place on the path to maximum policies. Beyond AD, nuclear forces must all be concerned essentially with fighting, or threatening to fight, limited nuclear wars. All warfighting postures are thus a challenge to the other side to match the capability deployed. For this reason, all of the intermediate options share with maximum deterrence policies the propensity to push the arms dynamic towards arms racing. This is especially true if either side defines its security in terms requiring some form of military superiority over its opponent.

Maximum deterrence policy, despite the strong points in its favour, cannot escape undermining not only the stability of deterrence, but also the security that it is aimed at producing. Incessant arms racing maximizes the vulnerability of deterrence to technological change, and constantly challenges the ability of deterrers to maintain a basic secure second strike. It breeds tension not only through arms racing and fears of first strike, but also by the fact that preparations for warfighting, even if justified in deterrence terms, make each actor look aggressive in the eyes of those trying to deter it. Appearances of aggressiveness in the form of broad-spectrum offensive military capability are easily interpreted by opponents as evidence of high basic motivation to resort to force. That interpretation further reinforces the 'difficult' logic, and thus further justifies the maximum policy. The high tensions that result, when added to the context of intensely innovative and competitive nuclear deployments, make accidental war a major hazard of maximum deterrence. This worry about accidental war holds even for those who think that the 'easy' logic is otherwise powerful enough to prevent intentional war at all levels of deployment above assured destruction.

# 13 The Debates about Deterrence

Deterrence is an immensely controversial subject. Fierce debates exist not only between those who think deterrence is a useful policy and those who think it too dangerous, but also amongst its supporters as to how best to bring theory and practice into harmony. In this chapter four areas of debate will be examined. Are deterrence and defence opposites or complements? Is the assumption of rationality a weakness or a strength of deterrence logic? Is deterrence ethically unsound? And does the pursuit of deterrence lead to arms racing? The purpose is to clarify positions and definitions rather than to argue for resolutions.

## 13.1 DETERRENCE VERSUS DEFENCE

As was argued in Chapter 10, the relationship of deterrence and defence hinges on the distinction between the military options of denial and retaliation. The desire to restrict the meaning of deterrence to threats of retaliation can be traced back to the relative simplicities of Golden Age deterrence theory. The logic of MAD arises from the destructive power of nuclear weapons, and represents a form of deterrence that is based on retaliation. Since MAD was the heart of Golden Age theory, and since early thinking about deterrence was very largely in terms of nuclear weapons, the drift towards treating retaliation and deterrence as synonymous made sense. That sense was reinforced by the strong contradiction between the pursuit of MAD as a doctrine, and policies of strategic defence. MAD required that each side forego defence/denial options against countervalue nuclear attack. Only if they did so could MAD doctrine provide the stability of shared vulnerability. The appeal of such a posture was that it set absolute rather than relative force requirements. It offered prospects for restraining the arms dynamic both by unilateral limits on nuclear arsenals, and through arms control agreements on force sizes and structures. In the pure terms of relationships between the superpowers, treating deterrence and

197

defence as alternatives thus made considerable sense. It is still a feature of those writings in the 'easy' school that favour minimum deterrence. The best reasons for continuing to treat deterrence and defence as opposites is that the merger of the two provides an open-ended justification for the accumulation of armaments.

But as was seen in Chapters 11 and 12, deterrence theory has been increasingly subjected to the denial pressures of both the *ex-ante*, *ex-post* problem and extended deterrence (ED). In NATO terms, denial policies are intimately bound up in the logic of deterrence. When deterrence is mutual, and geographical adjacency is a problem, then denial options are necessary to bridge the gap between small-scale aggression and attacks on a scale large enough to make the drastic option of nuclear retaliation credible. Denial options in the form of active and/or passive defences to protect strategic forces from first strikes are also a way of responding to the *ex-ante*, *ex-post* problem. If the deterrer is not vulnerable to counterforce first strikes, then its ED threats become more credible. The whole history of NATO illustrates the impossibility of treating deterrence and defence as alternatives. In practice, denial capabilities have always been an essential part of ED, even when they served only as a 'tripwire' for the retaliatory threat. Under the more demanding conditions of bipolarity, the credibility of ED has come increasingly to rest on a substantial denial capability in Europe backed up by the threat to fight limited nuclear war (LNW) both on the theatre level, and at the level of central war. The logic of flexible response has led to ever more elaborate LNW scenarios in which denial strategies escalate through conventional to theatre and then to strategic nuclear forces. At some point, the escalation of LNW would become indistinguishable from a central war between the superpowers, and it is that threat of a smooth linkage of escalation that is supposed to keep ED credible.

These developments have opened up a host of debates. Some see them as strengthening ED by providing a full spectrum of deterrence threats. Some see them as weakening ED by offering the Soviet Union a theatre war option that might not involve the superpowers in attacks directly on each other. Some see them as raising the danger of uncontrolled escalation, and therefore urge a strengthening of conventional denial forces in order to lower the dependence of ED on nuclear threats (Rogers, 1982). The extreme development of this position is the case that NATO should follow China and the Soviet Union in making a pledge not to use nuclear weapons first

(Bundy *et al.*, 1982; Kaiser *et al.*, 1982). Some of these options will be explored further in Chapter 17. The logic of deterrence by means of conventional military forces can also be found outside the superpower alliances. Countries like Israel, India, and South Africa use the language of deterrence to explain and justify their conventional military policies. Regardless of opinions on these issues, what cannot be denied is that the logic of Flexible Response has opened the door to an ever increasing role for denial in deterrence theory and policy. Along with the *ex ante, ex post* problem, ED has provided a powerful rationale for moving away from the basic MAD formulation. The contemporary debate about deterrence no longer makes sense in terms of a narrow definition in which strategies of deterrence are synonymous with retaliation and an alternative to strategies of defence.

The basic issues in the debate about deterrence and defence underlie two other intense political disagreements about deterrence: that about the pursuit of deterrence through warfighting strategies, and that about the replacement of deterrence by strategic defence.

### 13.1.1 The Issue of Ends and Means in Warfighting Strategies for Deterrence

This debate develops from the fact that warfighting strategies are an extension of denial logic, not only to first priority over retaliation, but also to the use of offensive threats for the purpose of deterrence. The shift of American strategic policy towards threats of warfighting raises basic questions about ends and means in the logic of deterrence. Within the confined framework of military strategy, there are only two possible answers to the question of how to prevent war: threaten your opponent with military defeat, a means which also serves the traditional end of war winning; or threaten him with a cost large enough to outweigh his hoped-for gains.

What made Golden Age deterrence theory initially distinct from traditional strategic thinking was its combination of the war prevention end with the means of deterrence by threat of retaliation. Both elements can be found in earlier strategic thinking, but the advent of nuclear weapons opened up the prospect of a quite new school of thought which raised them both to first priority. Much of the value and excitement of Western deterrence theory has derived from the fact that it was exploring this new combination. Golden Age deterrence theory was thus distinct from traditional strategy in terms of means as well as ends. Its means of retaliatory punishment reinforced its end of war prevention because, under conditions of MAD, they led to a situation in which victory was indistinguishable from defeat, and 'winning' was therefore not a useful concept.

Yet as we have seen, in the two decades since the end of the Golden Age, warfighting strategies have steadily reoccupied centre stage. Retaliation strategies have drifted into the background because of Soviet rejection of MAD as doctrine, and because of contradictions in the logic of MAD as it applied to American policy problems. Mutual paralysis of retaliatory threats was not adequate in the eyes of the 'difficult' school either to deter a highly motivated revisionist opponent from first strikes or to maintain ED. The logic of maximum deterrence followed the Soviet model in requiring warfighting options for two reasons: first, as a fallback position in case deterrence failed, and secondly, to buttress deterrence credibility. The possession of warfighting options by the deterrer would ensure that the deterree was not tempted to gamble on the logical dilemmas of ED and mutual deterrence that arose for the deterrer if MAD doctrine failed to prevent aggression.

The resurgence of warfighting strategies as the principal policy for deterrence, held now by both superpowers, raises fundamental philosophical questions about the separability of end and means. The basic choices are illustrated in Table 13.1.

*Table* 13.1    Ends and means in military policy

|  |  | Primary ends | |
| --- | --- | --- | --- |
|  |  | *War winning* | *War prevention* |
| primary means | warfighting | – traditional military strategy | – Soviet strategic doctrine<br>– Third Wave deterrence theory |
|  | punishment | – theoretically possible in a unipolar deterrence system<br>– Massive retaliation | – Golden Age deterrence theory (MAD) |

The key question arises from the suspicion that ends and means cannot be kept separate, and more specifically that there is an unsustainable contradiction between bad means and good ends. Can the end of war prevention be pursued by the means of deterrence through the threat of warfighting, or must adoption of that means inevitably create pressure for a return to the end of war winning?

Golden Age theory escaped this dilemma because MAD doctrine provided a means that made victory indistinguishable from defeat. A strategy based on mutual vulnerability could not be applied to ends of war winning. Third Wave theory, with its emphasis on denial, escalation dominance, and compellence threats, raises the contradiction to full height by explicitly seeking to deter through the threat of military defeat. If that threat is credible, then war winning becomes a feasible alternative objective in a way that it could not be under MAD. In following the warfighting logic of Soviet strategic doctrine, Third Wave theory opens itself to the same criticism of *apparent* aggressiveness that has so often been levelled at the Soviet Union. Where a state's military capability exists in a warfighting mode, other states have no way of determining its intention from its capability. Armed forces configured for warfighting can support either non-aggressive deterrence intentions or aggressive expansionist ones. Such capabilities therefore heighten the security dilemma for other states, forcing them to respond to the visible reality of the capability rather than to the possibly more benign, but hidden, reality of intentions. If warfighting means do lead towards war winning ends, then maximum deterrence policy retains little that would distinguish it from the strategic thinking of the pre-nuclear era.

It is the worry aroused by this potential contradiction between warfighting means and deterrence ends that underlies much of the disillusionment and unease about deterrence that has developed since the late 1970s. Amongst the public, the fear is that warfighting means will overwhelm deterrence ends. Grounds for that fear can be found in the hostile rhetoric of the superpowers, in conspicuous talk about, and preparation for, limited nuclear war, in the enormous arsenals of the superpowers, and in the continued tensions over the improvement and modernization of weapons. The warfighting approach to deterrence also seems too obviously to serve the interests of the military industrial complex in high levels of military procurement. Since deterrence no longer looks unambiguously like a war prevention policy, and no longer has an obvious damping effect on the arms dynamic, it is not surprising that much public opinion now defines deterrence as the problem rather than as the solution.

Academic disillusionment is less focused on the danger of war, though many do share the public *angst*, and more preoccupied with the breakdown of deterrence theory as a coherent system of logic. As Herken states:

> Not since Brodie's proclamation that strategy had hit a dead end . . . has such profound doubt and despair accompanied the subject of nuclear weapons; nor such an apparently fundamental loss of faith in deterrence . . . the concept of mutual assured destruction has found few champions recently. But the confounders of MAD – the war-fighters – have thus far offered no better hope than the tenuous and untested chance that a nuclear war might prove limited and controllable.
>
> (Herken, 1984, p. 25)

The 'difficult' school has successfully carried the case against MAD on the grounds that it contains serious logical flaws in relation to the problems posed by both Soviet and Western security needs. It has had some unlikely allies in this attack in the form of disarmers anxious to prove that minimum deterrence policies cannot be sustained, and must therefore decay into the warfighting policies of the 'difficult' school (Krass, 1985). The 'easy' school has responded with an equally devastating critique of the 'difficult' logic. Jervis, for example, has systematically unravelled the attempt of the warfighters to 'conventionalize' the logic of nuclear deterrence. He argues that warfighting strategies do not escape the escalation dilemmas of MAD, that they defeat deterrence ends by raising the danger that the other side will think they are about to be attacked, and that they rest on false assumptions about both Soviet behaviour and the limits of the technically possible (Jervis, 1984). Taken together, these mutual critiques have reduced the credibility of the whole logical framework of deterrence theory. The contending 'easy' and 'difficult' schools are on much stronger ground when they attack each other than when they argue for their preferred policies. Neither school has succeeded in establishing a broadly acceptable solution to the problems posed by ED.

Despite the apparent chaos in the logic of deterrence theory, many academic strategists draw comfort from what Bundy has called 'existential deterrence' (Bundy, 1984, pp. 8–13) – the notion that 'what now deters is the fear of the overwhelming cost of engaging in large-scale violence' (Jervis, 1984, p. 12). Existential deterrence is reflected in the attitude of those writers who view the military balance as broadly stable despite the many day-to-day alarums that awake public concern (Buzan, 1986; Calvocoressi, 1984, pp. 90–1; Freedman, 1981, p. 399; 1982, p. 54; 1984b, pp. 31–47; Martin, 1980, p. 11). It stems from the logic of the 'easy' school, but depends on MAD only as a description of the situation, and not as doctrine. In this view, nuclear weapons have transformed international political relations as well as military ones. So long as nuclear arsenals exist that are large enough and well-enough protected to make successful first strikes against them uncertain, then the details of nuclear deployments and strategies do not make much difference. If states are more afraid of their opponent's forces than they are reassured by their own, then they will drift towards maximum deterrence policies. Such policies add considerably to the expense and tension of international relations, but because it is the generality of the terror that deters and not the fine details of complex nuclear exchange scenarios, they make only marginal difference to its risks.

While this rather philosophical view may reassure some detached academics, it does not reassure the 'difficult' school. Neither is it likely to comfort the public, who will remain concerned about the risk of war, about the arms race, and about the ethical questions arising from the pursuit of deterrence. So long as there is no consensus on deterrence theory, public unease about deterrence strategies seems bound to remain high. So long as it does, the urge to escape from MAD either by disarmament or by the pursuit of strategic defence will remain politically potent.

### 13.1.2 Defence as Escape from Deterrence: SDI

Understanding the sources of disillusionment with deterrence provides the key to understanding the political appeal of strategic defence (SD) as an alternative. It is almost a truism of strategy that denial is a more desirable approach to security than retaliation (Art, 1980, pp. 5–7; Freedman, 1981, p. 396; Glaser, 1984, pp. 92–3), though a few writers argue that retaliation is better because it more clearly avoids fighting and uncertainty (Halle, 1984, pp. 25, 33; Schelling, 1963, pp. 478–87). Retaliation, in other words, is widely seen as a second-best option. Defence planners resort to it only when technological conditions make denial strategies unworkable. Denial is preferred because it offers the prospect not only of deterring attack, but also of blocking it if deterrence fails. Retaliation produces the less comfortable condition of being vulnerable if deterrence fails, and therefore of having one's security more openly dependent on the good, or at least rational, behaviour of one's rival.

Given that denial is preferred to retaliation, it is not surprising that disillusionment with deterrence has encouraged interest in the development of SD. If deterrence logic no longer inspires confidence, and even seems to raise the likelihood of the war it is designed to avoid, then seeking escape seems not only reasonable but also eminently saleable in the unsophisticated political market-place of public opinion. The problem is that the political appeal of a return to strategies based on denial is much stronger than the technological prospects of achieving such a condition. As explained in Chapter 11, the creation of a strategic defence perfect enough to fulfil President Reagan's hope of escaping from deterrence is extremely unlikely: the necessary technology for it is not yet available; it is certain to be very expensive; and even if vast sums are spent, it may never overcome the formidable advantages of the nuclear offensive. In practice, existential deterrence seems likely to remain the basic ground rule for as long as the superpowers deploy large arsenals of nuclear weapons. The development of partially effective strategic defence systems provides no escape, but simply reinforces the ever more complex logic of maximum deterrence, whose advocates therefore mostly embrace it with enthusiasm.


## 13.2   THE METHOD OF DETERRENCE LOGIC: THE ASSUMPTION OF RATIONALITY

The loss of faith in deterrence stems most obviously from its failure to generate policies that are logically convincing in their own terms. But that failure itself is connected to a longstanding debate about the whole method of thought on which deterrence theory was based. Criticism has focused on the assumption of rationality, which is strongly rooted in all strategic thinking, but which achieved particular notice as a result of the application of game theory to thinking about nuclear deterrence. Game theory was brought into the field during the 1950s and 1960s by people trained in economics (Schelling, 1960). Its use triggered criticism of nuclear strategy for being amoral, narrow, wedded to conflict assumptions, and remote from the realities of decision-making in political life (Bull 1968; Gray, 1982a, ch. 7; Green, 1968; Rapoport, 1960, 1964a).

The attraction of game theory is the same as that of the formal quantitative methods used by Richardson to study arms racing: it enables some logical problems of strategy to be isolated, and studied in a rigorous and thorough fashion (Freedman, 1981, pp. 182–9; Rapoport, 1960, chs 1–14; Russett, 1983b, chs 5 and 6). As a method of study, game theory was useful in revealing the complete logical structure of various basic conflicts. Games often exposed aspects of conflict that might not otherwise have been obvious, for example, how rational behaviour by the players could lead to either mutually advantageous or mutually damaging situations within a conflict. Indeed, this attraction resulted in the widespread use of game theory by peace researchers, a parallel that throws an interesting light on some of the criticisms of the method underlying deterrence theory.

The reason that game theory inspired critical attack reflected the same problem faced by the followers of Richardson, namely the unbridgeable gulf that existed between the highly simplified assumptions and conditions of the games, and the highly complex conditions and uncertainties of nuclear-armed relationships in the real world. In the case of deterrence theory, however, criticism was heightened by the immediate policy relevance of the subject. The scientific study of arms racing was quite removed from the policy-making process, but the study of deterrence was closely connected to both procurement decisions and strategic doctrines. The worry was that a tool of logical clarification would become a general metaphor for reality, and that military policy would therefore be based on a set of assumptions dangerously far removed from actual conditions in the international system.

There was also a reaction against the formal methodological style of game theory. That style seemed to give a scientific, mathematical objectivity to conclusions that were in fact based on highly arguable and value-laden assumptions. Conspicuous clashes between games and reality occurred at several points. The games favoured as models for nuclear rivalry, such as *chicken*, and *the prisoners' dilemma*, assumed two players, immutable zero-sum conflicts (where conflict is the only option, and the losses of either must be the gains of the other), rationally calculated behaviour, and no communication between the players. All of these assumptions were questionable as representations of conditions in the real world. Yet it was the assumption of rationally calculated behaviour, both in game theory, and in strategic logic generally, that created the most persistent doubts about the validity of deterrence theory.

The idea of rationality – that the behaviour of actors is governed by calculation of the gains and losses consequent on alternative courses of action – is central to all strategic thinking. In military strategy the gains and losses come in the relatively concrete terms of the use of force. Strategy is an attempt to predict behaviour, and then to use that prediction as a basis for controlling the behaviour of others to one's own advantage. In military strategy, prediction requires an understanding of how actors will respond to the threat or use of force. Options for controlling the behaviour of others in this way may be quite limited. Much depends on the balance of strengths and vulnerabilities between actors, and on the firmness of their commitment to the issues at stake. As Gray argues, strategists cannot approach the task of prediction empirically, because there are almost no historical case studies relevant to the process of threat and conflict in the nuclear age. Those who wanted to think about deterrence therefore had no option but to derive theory from what he nicely labels 'great chains of reasoning' (Gray, 1982b, pp. 6–7). Such chains could only be constructed by using the assumption of rational actors. Deterrence theory is therefore unavoidably based on chains of 'if-then' propositions which examine the military incentives to attack (the chance of winning at a reasonable cost) in the light of the denial and retaliatory options of the deterrer.

Rational calculation provided the only tool with which strategic thinking could be projected into the unknowns of the nuclear-armed future. It was obviously a gross simplification of the sources of human behaviour, as almost anyone who has been involved in an impassioned argument about trust or fidelity can attest. Nevertheless, the oversimplification could be justified on two grounds other than necessity. First, rational calculation clearly did represent a major determinant of behaviour involving the use of force in international relations. The threat of nuclear war was so huge that it seemed certain to concentrate minds on the calculation of consequences with unprecedented clarity. The size of the nuclear threat also seemed great enough to transcend the differences of culture and values that might otherwise weaken the assumption that rationality was similar in the capitals of all the world's nuclear armed states. The differences between 'soft' cultures like those in the affluent West, that were thought to be rather sensitive to the human and material costs of war, and 'hard' cultures like those in the Soviet Union, and even more so China, that were thought to be rather insensitive, would disappear when the threat was the rapid and almost total vaporization of society.

Secondly, the assumption of rationality was justified because its application revealed genuine problems in the use of deterrence as a policy for national security. The assumption of rational calculation enabled theorists to explore a variety of deterrence scenarios, which in turn enabled them to identify, in advance, points of danger and difficulty for policy-makers. Rational analysis exposed the *ex ante*, *ex post* problem in which decision-makers would be forced to act irrationally in order to fulfil deterrence threats. It highlighted the difficult choices that would arise from using a self-damaging threat (nuclear war) to deter a threat (political defeat) that was of lesser magnitude than the one being used to prevent it (MccGwire, 1983, pp. 17–18; Snyder, 1978, p. 345). And it indicated the problems of conducting deterrence during crisis, where pressures of time, uncertainty of information, heightened fear and suspicion, and worry that one was about to be attacked could create serious dangers of deterrence breaking down.

Attitudes towards rationality fall into three categories. The differences between them underlie many of the major divisions and tensions within the nuclear debate. One view is that the assumption of rationality is so great a distortion from reality that it provides a fundamentally false basis for thinking about nuclear policy. A second view is that the immense threat embodied in nuclear weapons makes the rational model of behaviour valid as a broad approximation of reality, but only inasmuch as a general fear of nuclear war will induce extreme caution into relations among the nuclear powers. A third view is that rationality represents a fairly close approximation of reality, and can therefore be used to predict and condition behaviour in considerable detail. All of these views rest on assumptions about human behaviour, which makes psychology an important element in the study of deterrence (Jervis *et al.*, 1985).

The view that rationality is a false model rests on several layers of doubts. There are doubts as to how fully any situation involving human behaviour can be analysed in terms of the logic of calculations about costs and gains. Within this limit, there are doubts about how far the rationality of leaders goes, either because of temperament, like Idi Amin, or because of illness, like Brezhnev, Churchill and

Roosevelt. Even if they are rational, there are doubts about whether their standards or rationality are the same. Deterrence logic requires that deterrer and deterree share some basic values in order that threats can be appropriate in size and character to offset the attractions of aggression to the deterree. Are Western calculations of costs and risks, with their status quo imperatives, going to be along the same lines as calculations made by revolutionary enthusiasts like the late Mao Zedong, or martyrdom-minded Ayatollahs in Tehran? If differences of value, history, doctrine, and information influence calculations, how can a uniform assumption of rationality be used to predict behaviour? And even if these doubts can be met, there are questions about whether leaders are always in control of events, whether they are rational or not. The detailed behaviour of large collective actors like states can never be perfectly controlled. Events can be moved by accidents, by insubordination, by misunderstanding, by errors or breakdowns in communication, by equipment faults, and by contradictions in the commands that finally reach the lower ranks.

These doubts about control grow under crisis conditions, when pressure of time may deny the option to calculate a rational response. The stronger these doubts are, the more flawed rationality appears to be as a basis for nuclear strategy, since decisions would probably have to be made under crisis conditions. On top of all these problems lies the fact that rational calculation within deterrence logic often leads to requirements for irrational behaviour – Schelling's famous notion of 'the threat that leaves something to chance' (Schelling, 1960, ch. 8). Once deterrence has broken down, would decision-makers actually choose response and/or escalation options that would be likely to condemn their countries to incineration? The fact that they would be faced with such difficult choices seems an invitation to the deterree to call the deterrer's opening bluff. The idea that deterrence must be systematically irrational seems to undo what little security the idea of rationality offered in the first place, especially so given that the whole doctrine need only go badly wrong once in order to trigger a global disaster.

The view that rationality is valid as a broad approximation of reality rests on the levelling effect that nuclear weapons have across cultures. All leaders have extremely high incentives to control the use of nuclear weapons. This view also rests on the assumption that political decision-making is dominated by calculation only of gross risks and payoffs, and that political leaders are therefore insensitive to the more refined levels of rational calculation that so worry the thinkers of the 'difficult' school (Jervis, 1979, pp. 310–12; Steinbrunner, 1976, pp. 237–8). Its emphasis is on the logic of existential deterrence, which returns the prime focus to the deterree, and stresses the strong general inhibition against any moves that might trigger the use of nuclear weapons. The existence of that inhibition seriously discounts the worry about what the deterrer might have to do if his opening bluff was called. Nuclear weapons are seen as having created a fairly simple logical environment in which all nuclear powers have an overriding common interest in avoiding nuclear war.

The view that rationality is a close approximation of reality stems from convictions about both human nature and political process. Evidence for this view in the military field can be found in the long history of carefully prepared deceptions, such as Japan's attack on Pearl Harbor, and the Soviet emplacement of missiles in Cuba. Nuclear weapons contribute to it inasmuch as their tremendous offensive power may tempt a calculating aggressor to seek a crushing and nearly instantaneous victory. In this view, the over-all threat of nuclear war is seen to open opportunities for the use of force as well as setting constraints on it. Because all fear war, the strongly-nerved calculating actor may be able to use limited force to advantage, without triggering all-out war. A willingness to behave 'irrationally' may be rational. This view leads to elaborate strategies based on long chains of 'if-then' propositions which are seen as necessary to deter all the options that a calculating and daring (or reckless) aggressor might find. If the highly rational model is true, then deterrence is not a simple matter, but one requiring detailed strategies of response at every level of possible aggression.

Because rationality is central to strategic logic, the existence of divergent views about it means that there is no set of agreed principles within the deterrence theory. Indeed, these divergent views go a long way towards explaining Gray's lament that American strategy has failed to develop a core of agreed doctrine (Gray, 1982a, ch. 8). Disagreements about rationality underlie the minimum versus maximum debates about how to implement deterrence policy. They also underlie debates between those who favour deterrence as a security policy, and those who see it as part of the problem, and so seek escape.

## 13.3  DETERRENCE AND ETHICS

The debate about deterrence and ethics is based on differing value judgements, and therefore cannot be definitively resolved. It stems from, and blends into, more long-standing debates about the ethics of the use of force, and about the ethics of the state as a form of political organization. Deterrence theory, like most military strategy, is tied to the idea that states are the highest form of political order that we have so far been able to achieve. Defence of the state by military means is therefore justified in ethical terms either as good in itself, or as valid because, even though the state may be flawed, there is no obvious alternative to it capable of providing an equivalent level of order. There is every reason to think that change might be towards chaos. A more cynical view is simply that the vested interests of military organizations are so closely tied to the sponsorship of the state as to be virtually inseparable from it. In defending the state, military organizations are also defending their own resource base, status, and legitimacy. Those people who see states and the state system as the major root of war will therefore oppose deterrence on the grounds that it helps to maintain the structures that are themselves the cause of the problem.

If we leave aside the ethics of the state, we find that the ethics of the use of force hinge much more on the means of deterrence than on its ends. Deterrence as an end is generally not controversial if the state and the state system are accepted as constants within the problem rather than defined as part of what needs to be solved. In terms of ends, deterrence is a war prevention strategy, and thus stands on relatively strong ethical ground. In term of means, however, deterrence raises difficult questions. Are some means fundamentally immoral in themselves? Are some means incompatible with the ends they are supposed to serve because they produce side-effects that are contradictory to the prime end? And are some means inappropriate because they have costs disproportionate to the ends they are supposed to serve? The ethical debates about deterrence thus pick up from strategy questions about the relationship between ends and means discussed above (Winters, 1986).

### 13.3.1  The Ethical Strengths of Deterrence

The ethical position of deterrence is by no means weak. Its baseline is that we live in a dangerous and difficult world. The exigencies of short-term survival are best served by understanding the realities of those conditions that we cannot change quickly. In ethical terms, it can be argued that it is just as sound to accept, and try to deal with, realities that we do not know how to change safely, as it is to pronounce such realities unacceptable and in need of fundamental reform. The realities of a knowledge base in which science undergraduates can draw up workable designs for atomic bombs, and an international anarchy in which war is a constant danger, require immediate responses that do not allow the luxury of awaiting long-term reform. It is no accident that the journal of the IISS (International Institute for Strategic Studies) is called *Survival*, a name that could just as easily serve a radical, anti-nuclear publication. As Gray points out, the realist position makes ethical dilemmas unavoidable, especially those about using 'bad' means like the use of force to pursue 'good' ends like peace (Gray, 1982a, pp. 108–14). In this view it is false to see the realist and idealist positions as mutually exclusive in ethical terms. The ethics of realism are based in the need to deal with the short-term, whether one likes the conditions it offers or not. The ethics of idealism are based on the need to work for change in conditions that one finds unacceptable. There may well be powerful elements of contradiction between them, and the two positions often represent deep differences of opinion about the scope for change. Nevertheless, in one important sense they do represent a division of labour between short-term and long-term perspectives.

Deterrence is firmly on the realist side of this debate. Within that context it displays four distinct ethical virtues. First, it provides a concept for projecting the idea of war prevention as a first priority. The international system was ripened for the idea by the experience of two devastating world wars, but was unable to transform its anarchic political structure into something more coherent. Deterrence is therefore an accurate statement of a desire for peace within the existing reality of an anarchic political system of sovereign states.

Secondly, deterrence takes what would otherwise be the extremely dangerous technological development of nuclear weapons, and uses it to transform perceptions of what armed forces are for. Although the fact that War Departments are now called Defence Departments is often derided, the difference has quite profound moral significance. The identity and function of such Departments has changed. Deterrence has been useful in bringing that change about.

Thirdly, deterrence places a high value on the rule that forces should be used reactively rather than aggressively. By concentrating on the threat of force, rather than on the active use of it, deterrence moves firmly away from a long military tradition of giving first priority to how force can be used to win wars. Deterrence, in other words, encourages the skill of using military means to achieve security without recourse to fighting.

Fourthly, deterrence carries the idea of vulnerability firmly into the heart of military thinking, a place where it was formerly despised. The idea of security through vulnerability underlines more than any previous security concept has done, the point that national securities under modern technological and social conditions must be interdependent. By keeping itself vulnerable but well armed, a state can perform the previously impossible trick of maintaining a strong military position without making others fear that they are about to be attacked. Vulnerability is a strong statement of non-aggressive intentions even though the state remains well enough armed to deal decisively with attack on itself. The vulnerability of society to retaliation drains part of the truth from the old military axiom that the best defence is a good offence, and in so doing does much to weaken the security dilemma. Gains of this sort represent important transformations in strategic thinking. Their moral weight is too often discounted by those whose desire for greater changes blinds them to what has already been achieved. In this view, deterrence represents a kind of moral bridge between realism and idealism which enables both sides to talk seriously about war prevention as the prime goal.

### 13.3.2  The Ethical Weaknesses of Deterrence

Against these advantages there can be no doubt that deterrence does raise hard ethical questions about means. Deterrence has, of course, no defence against the pacifist view that the use of force is wrong for any political purpose. Yet the pacifist view itself raises serious problems about the organization of political life. It has never attracted a wide enough following to occupy the mainstream of opposition, and does not therefore have much political influence.

There are ethical points of view other than pure pacifism that raise doubts about whether deterrence as a means is immoral in itself. The most obvious of these is that the type of military capability necessary for deterrence involves such great destructive power as to put the future of the human species into doubt. This charge cannot be denied. It is true that the effectiveness of deterrence depends on profound terror of the consequences of war. The only response to it is that we cannot get rid of that threat. It is deeply embedded in the expanding body of human knowledge, as well as superficially manifested in the form of nuclear weapons. As a species we have lost the innocence of ignorance. From now on, humankind has to learn to live permanently with the knowledge that it possesses the ability to destroy itself. Since we cannot divest ourselves of the knowledge for self-destruction, we can at least use it to serve the goal of war prevention.

It can also be argued that it is morally wrong to threaten the destruction of millions of human beings even for high values like national security. The making of such threats corrupts the moral standards by which human relations should be conducted, and may so harden minds as to weaken the restraints against monstrous acts of genocide. This argument is especially strong when deterrence threats involve not only the likely incineration of those whose security is ostensibly being preserved, but also the extinction by radiation and climatic catastrophe of many, perhaps all, outside the warring countries, not to mention future generations. The counter to it follows the difficult but significant line of distinguishing between threat and use. Threat is in a morally different class from use if the intention of threat is to avoid use. Some intent to use is implied in the threat, but that is quite different from an unrestrained commitment to use. This counter has power, but is itself vulnerable to the argument that any risk of use, no matter how low the probability, is morally unacceptable when the consequences jeopardize human survival.

One of the more bizarre twists in the ethical debates about deterrence is the use of this argument by advocates of limited war strategies to condemn the moral position of those supporting MAD. The lower level, counterforce-orientated threats of LNW could be seen as more moral than the society-crushing, countervalue threat of MAD, but only if there were no doubts that escalation from LNW could be controlled.

The sustained use of threats of mass destruction is also open to the criticism that it requires the cultivation of hatred in order to sustain the credibility of the threats. The bipolar deterrence system of the United States and the Soviet Union depends on hatred for its domestic political support (MccGwire, 1985, pp. 108–12; Rosecrance, 1972, p. 138; 1973, p. 287). Hatred is also a useful corrective for the weaknesses of rationality in deterrence theory discussed above. If the credibility of deterrence threats depends on irrational action, as in the *ex ante*, *ex post* scenario, then hatred makes such threats more believable. Deterrence can thus be seen as a policy that only restrains war between states at the cost of increasing the frictions between them. The encouragement of hatred can be seen, not only as morally wrong, but also as disfunctional. As argued in Chapter 12, higher levels of hostility make deterrence more difficult to achieve.

A moral case against deterrence can also be made on the less stringent, but still substantial grounds that the means of deterrence are incompatible with its ends. This criticism does not require rejection of the means as immoral in themselves. It rests on the functional case that strong contradictions between means and ends create a morally unacceptable probability that application of the means will produce an unwanted and highly adverse outcome. The principal concerns here are about the relationship between deterrence on the one hand, and arms racing and war on the other. If deterrence encourages hostility, fear of attack, and the competitive accumulation of arms, then it makes more difficult the very problem it is designed to solve. If arms racing is also thought to increase the probability of war, this difficulty becomes even more acute, an issue examined in more detail below. Deterrence can generate its own causes of war directly. Because it requires highly poised forces capable of very fast response to attack, mutual deterrence opens up disturbing possibilities of accidental war. Such accidents could result from a variety of causes, all deeply built into the military systems necessary for deterrence. They include crisis tensions, information errors, misperceptions, and excessively automated warning and command procedures (Bracken, 1983; MccGwire, 1985, pp. 121–4).

Pursuit of this functional critique of deterrence leads to a difficult and interesting logical dilemma about what actions to take in pursuit of war prevention. Deterrence may serve this end by creating such a general terror amongst the great powers as to make them extremely keen to avoid war with each other. Yet in order to lower the probability of war in this way, the means of deterrence make it highly likely that, if war does occur, it will be on a scale and level of violence nothing short of catastrophic. The gain of lowered probability is thus purchased at the cost of much greater destruction if war occurs. Trying to remedy this problem by reducing the level of armaments risks lowering the level of terror, and so increasing the probability of war. Since even a major non-nuclear war with modern weapons would wreak immense destruction, it is not at all clear that increasing the probability of war by reducing its intensity represents a gain. This awkward, and inescapable choice between the probability and intensity of war defines the principal line of tension between deterrence and disarmament.

The least stringent, but still formidable, moral grounds for doubts about deterrence rest on the case that the means are disproportionate to the ends. This logic stems from the theory of the Just War, which goes back as far as the early Christian Church in the declining centuries of the Roman Empire. Its emphasis is on the moral obligation to restrict the use of force to the pursuit of just ends, and to limit and control it so that it is proportional to the ends for which it is being applied (Johnson, 1981, 1984). The Just War case against deterrence rests neither on disapproval of means, nor on the argument that the means may be counterproductive. It rests instead on the disproportionality between the means of threatening nuclear war, and the end of national security. Any use of nuclear weapons would rapidly violate the Just War requirements of proportionality, distinction between civilians and combatants, and minimum use of force. The arguments about nuclear weapons and Just War lead to a debate similar to that outlined above about the immorality of threats, and the difference between threatening to prevent the use of force, and using force directly to achieve political ends.

One can conclude on the basis of these positive and negative points that the ethical debate about deterrence is by no means one-sided. Deterrence represents a marked advance over strategic doctrines unhesitatingly committed to warfighting. The weight of the criticisms does, however, mean that deterrence is not an easy solution, and points strongly towards the need for arms control. Deterrence may be an improvement over the military doctrines and attitudes of the pre-nuclear era, but in its current form it is not a morally attractive solution to the problem of international security for the long term.

## 13.4 DETERRENCE AND THE ARMS DYNAMIC

It is widely felt that deterrence is an important driving force behind the arms dynamic. If the relationship between the superpowers is seen as an arms race, then deterrence is implicated by default, since it has been the guiding doctrine during most of the post-war period. To the extent that arms racing is seen as raising the probability of war, the link between the two poses a direct contradiction with the war-prevention rationale of deterrence. This potential contradiction becomes a complementarity for those inclined to see the war-prevention rationale of deterrence as in retreat before the pressure of warfighting means. In that view, the war dangers from deterrence and arms racing reinforce each other.

The attempt to understand the relationship between deterrence and the arms dynamic is hampered by the fact that there is only one case to examine. Even that case is problematic. It is not complete, and we have to observe from the not very detached position of living within it. Attempts to theorize are therefore limited to Gray's 'great chains of reasoning'. Attempts to study the historical record are limited by the relatively small experience of deterrence that we have so far acquired, and by the many changes in technological conditions even within the short period of nuclear deterrence.

Observation of the record suggests that there are many ways in which pursuit of deterrence can stimulate the arms dynamic. These can be examined using the three models of the arms dynamic from Part II. In terms of the technological imperative, the most important points to make are that deterrence depends on certain types of mass destruction technology being available, and that it is extremely sensitive to technological variables. As was seen in Chapters 11 and 12, technological developments pushed deterrence into prominence in the first place. Without nuclear weapons, deterrence theory would not have become nearly as prominent as it has. Subsequent developments like missile submarines, MIRV, BMD, and precision guidance have been responsible for much of the evolution of deterrence theory, and play a big role in determining whether deterrence is easy or difficult to achieve. Because deterrence is influenced by technological variables, it cannot escape being vulnerable to the continuous pressure of qualitative advance. To some extent the pursuit of deterrence contributes to that pressure. Yet the baseline of movement from civil developments alone is sufficient to generate permanent uncertainty about whatever technological conditions define stability within deterrence. Just as the 1960s security of ICBMs in hardened silos was undermined by MIRV and higher accuracies in the 1970s, so SDI now threatens the capability of missiles to preserve an assured destruction capability. It is almost impossible to imagine likely circumstances in which there will not be a dialectic of challenges and opportunities for deterrence arising out of the advancing frontier of the technologically possible.

The sensitivity of deterrence to technological variables feeds predictably into the domestic structure component of the arms dynamic. If the security of deterrence is vulnerable to technological change, and the process of change is too deeply infused into society to be amenable to much control, then a commitment to deterrence requires that a state also commit itself to staying close to the relevant frontiers of technological advance by institutionalizing the process of military R&D. Failure to do so risks the collapse of one's deterrent capability against an opponent who does. Doing so, however, does not guarantee that security will be achieved. The attempt to keep up has the paradoxical effect of accelerating the pace of advance, so leading to the autism effect of the most advanced state 'arms racing' with itself. The products that result from this pursuit of change may either make deterrence easier, like thermonuclear weapons, better satellite observation systems, and missile carrying submarines, or more difficult, like MIRV and strategic defence. Depending on whether the 'easy' or 'difficult' effects dominate, the impact of deterrence on the domestic structure model could either stimulate or dampen the tendency towards arms racing.

Deterrence supports the development and maintenance of the military-industrial complex by providing it with work. Deterrence policy requires forces in being to back up its threats. When deterrence is mutual, these forces need to be quite large in order not to be too vulnerable to first strikes. They need to be large enough to cope with the demands of the full conflict they are designed to prevent, because in the event of deterrence failing, war will have to be fought with whatever forces exist. The pace of nuclear conflict is unlikely to allow much scope for mobilization along the lines of the First and Second World Wars. To remain credible, deterrence forces also need to keep up with advances in technology. In other words, deterrence requires that the states pursuing it maintain a form of permanent military mobilization. The level of that mobilization is nothing like a full-scale war footing in the traditional sense. But it is quite sufficient to require, and to sustain, permanent military R&D and production establishments, and armed forces, on a substantial scale.

Deterrence also provides a politically acceptable rationale for the military-industrial complex. Since deterrence is about war prevention, it saves the arms industry from the 'merchants of death' image that has always connected its work to war. Deterrence puts the development and manufacture of arms firmly on the side of peace, or at least of military paralysis (Arendt, 1969, p. 4). Deterrence achieves this transformation of image at little cost to the freedom of the arms industry. As Freedman notes, the concept is so vague that it is capable of being used for 'justifying the maintenance of almost any military capability on the grounds that it might be doing good and we could well be worse off without it' (Freedman, 1980a, p. 52). On this basis it is no exaggeration to say that deterrence and the military-industrial complex are closely related. Neither could exist easily, if at all, without the other.

The fact that deterrence gives strong support to the domestic structures of the arms dynamic feeds into its impact on the action-reaction process. As was argued in Chapter 7, domestic structures have, to a considerable extent, usurped the role of traditional action-reaction processes. One would therefore expect that any strong influence on the military-industrial complex would spill over into relations between states, and this does seem to be the case with deterrence.

In analysing the relationship between deterrence and arms racing, some authors go so far as to merge the action-reaction dynamics of arms racing and deterrence into a single process (Kugler *et al.*, 1980). There is plenty of evidence from the superpower case to suggest that such a merger may be appropriate. In other words, many of the action-reaction processes deriving specifically from deterrence considerations do seem to push towards competitive accumulations of arms, especially when conditions or doctrines are such as to make deterrence difficult. On the most basic level, for example, it is clear that the shift from unipolar to bipolar deterrence requires large increases of armaments (Rosecrance, 1975, pp. 4–6). These increases are needed not just because one side needs to catch up, as the Soviet Union did during the 1950s and 1960s. They are also needed because mutual deterrence requires higher force levels on both sides in order to ensure that each can preserve a secure second strike force against the possibility of a counterforce first strike by the other. In this sense, Huntington's argument about the relationship of quantity and quality in arms racing can be inverted: under conditions of mutual deterrence, quantitative accumulations provide stability against both first strikes and the possibility of qualitative breakthroughs by one's opponent (Intrilligator and Brito, 1984, pp. 82–3).

The process of maintaining secure second strike forces under conditions of technological change and challenge from the opponent can easily lead to further military competition, especially where there are fears that the opponent is hostile enough to consider a first strike if opportunity offers (Freedman, 1981, pp. 69–71, 134–65; Gillespie *et al.*, 1979, p. 251; Kugler *et al.*, 1980, pp. 107–9; McGuire, 1968). In cases where either side seeks strategic defence or damage limitation capabilities, the possibilities for arms racing are limitless (Baylis *et al.*, 1975, p. 78). No more perfect formula for action-reaction arms racing could be found than the competition between the desire for strategic defence or damage limitation on the one hand, and the necessity to maintain assured destruction capability as the baseline of deterrent threat on the other. Uncertainties of information about the other side's forces, and even greater uncertainties about motivation, also provide a built-in motor for military competition. Each side will tend to reduce its insecurity by deploying forces based on conservative assumptions about the opposition (Steinbrunner, 1976, pp. 226–9), or by seeking an edge for itself (Gasteyger, 1980, p. 8), policies that can hardly fail to interact in the direction of arms racing.

Deterrence policies that seek warfighting capabilities contain a strong predisposition towards arms racing. This is true regardless of why such capabilities are sought. The two principal reasons for it in the case of the superpowers have been commented on by many writers. The first is the attempt to support Flexible Response by building up denial capabilities for ED. The second is the seeking of limited nuclear nuclear options (LNO) as a response both to the escalation control requirement of ED, and the worry about counterforce first strikes in the context of the *ex ante*, *ex post* problem (Ball, 1983, pp. 19–41; Freedman, 1981, pp. 380–2; Jervis, 1979–80; Martin, 1980, p. 15; Ravenal, 1982, pp. 26, 31; Rosecrance, 1975, pp. 26–7; Segal, 1979, p. 569). Warfighting options for deterrence automatically make the relative balance of forces important by the same logic that moved competition in traditional arms races. Such options consequently move away from the idea that a surplus capacity of destructive power can lead to an absolute sufficiency of force regardless of the level of destructive power possessed by the other side.

As elaborated in Chapter 4, it can also be argued that deterrence stimulates the arms dynamic by encouraging action and reaction in the form of the proliferation of nuclear weapons. This case, as explained in Chapter 12, can be argued both ways.

The formidable record of observed linkages between deterrence and arms racing seems at first to seal the case against deterrence on this issue. The main lines of defence are all in the realm of theory, which may seem to make them less convincing than facts drawn from the actual record of performance. Any tendency to discount the value of theory in this instance should, however, be muted by the shortness and narrowness of our experience with nuclear deterrence. As suggested in Chapter 12, deterrence varies enormously according to the conditions within which it is practised. There are many possible configurations of deterrence of which we have no experience, and it can easily be argued that in many respects the conditions of which we do have experience – particularly bipolarity, the shifting balance of power, and the rapid change in novel technologies – are among the most difficult in the theoretical spectrum.

There are two lines of defence for deterrence in relation to arms racing: the idea of sufficiency; and the argument that the likely alternatives to the present arrangements would be worse than what we now have. The first line is well understood, and stems from the minimum deterrence logic of the 'easy' school. It rests on acceptance of the view that fear of nuclear war is an exceptionally strong general deterrent, and that minimum deterrence postures are therefore sufficient. If this logic is accepted, then a policy of minimum deterrence provides a powerful damper on tendencies to arms race (Jervis, 1979–80, p. 618; Mandelbaum, 1981, ch. 5). Minimum deterrence requires only forces sufficient to inflict AD after they have been attacked themselves. If neither side challenges the other's AD capability, then force levels can be determined by the fairly modest absolute criteria for the AD mission. The incentives to improve and modernize such forces would be low, and the arrangement would give military security without driving an arms race. The reasons why minimum deterrence has failed to appeal to the superpowers are numerous (Krass, 1985, pp. 109–25). The foremost amongst them are the American commitment to ED, and Soviet preference for strategies based on denial and warfighting. Yet the idea of minimum deterrence offers a major long-term objective for arms control and disarmament, and provides strong ground for denying that there is any necessary connection between the pursuit of deterrence and the heating up of the arms dynamic. Some approaches to deterrence will stimulate arms racing; others will dampen it.

The argument that we could easily be worse off in arms racing terms than we now are rests on the assumption that we cannot quickly change the fundamental political and technological characteristics of the system in which we presently live. In other words, the international anarchy will continue to define the political conditions of international relations, and the ability to deliver weapons of enormous destructive power quickly and accurately to any part of the planet will continue to set the military baseline of relationships amongst the great powers. Given those conditions, the possibilities for arms racing fall into a spectrum defined by three broad scenarios.

The first and best scenario would be minimum deterrence with highly damped maintenance of the military status quo in which both sides accept and do not oppose the other's AD capability. This scenario is unlikely for the reasons given above. The second, and second best, scenario is roughly what existed during the 1970s. Both sides accept the reality of MAD, but take warfighting approaches to deterrence which require them to build up large arsenals of offensive weapons. Deterrence is still the order of the day, and the underlying reality of MAD causes the competitive accumulation of arms to reach a tolerable stability at a high level of maintenance of the military status quo. Open-ended arms racing is avoided.

The third, and worst, scenario is the one we may be moving towards in the 1980s, where serious attempts are made to challenge MAD in order to escape to a pure form of denial/defence. In arms racing terms, the attempt to escape from deterrence creates the maximum incentives for an interactive military competition. As argued above, the logic of strategic defence is fundamentally contradictory to that of maintaining AD. Perfect strategic defence could never be tested fully enough to give security, and would always be vulnerable to new offensive technologies (Glaser, 1984). Imperfect strategic defence simply raises the costs of maintaining AD. It also heightens the security dilemma by making first strikes look more plausible under the terms of the 'difficult' school's logic.

On this basis, it can be argued that deterrence is less bad in arms racing terms than the most likely alternative. Any consideration of deterrence and arms racing must also be undertaken with full

awareness that there is no simple relationship between arms racing
and war. If deterrence does stimulate the arms dynamic in some
ways, that does not mean that it necessarily, or even probably,
increases the likelihood of war.


## 13.5 CONCLUSIONS: DETERRENCE AND FOREIGN POLICY

As the discussion above indicates, these four debates feed into each
other at a sufficient number of points to connect them into a single
body of concern about deterrence as a policy for national security.
The intensity of that concern ranges from near hysteria amongst
some of those who see deterrence as the major problem of human
survival, to a disquieting unease within the minds of those otherwise
convinced that deterrence is a necessary and/or good policy for
security. Given the disparity of opinion, grounds for consensus are
hard to find.

Amongst analysts of deterrence, there is quite widespread
agreement that it is dangerous to allow the military side of deterrence
logic to become ascendant over its political side. Sometimes this is
phrased as a plea for more linkage between the fields of Strategic
Studies and International Relations (Bull, 1981, pp. 279–80; Gray,
1982b, ch. 12). In other places it takes the form of the case that
deterrence should be confined to specific areas of state relations,
and that it should not be allowed to usurp the broader function of
foreign policy in relations between states (Bull, 1980; George and
Smoke, 1974, esp. ch. 21; Jervis, 1979, pp. 314–24). In yet other
places the argument is that deterrence itself needs to be analysed
more as the political phenomenon that it actually is, and less as
simply a technical formula for a military balance (Freedman, 1981,
pp. 399–400; Gasteyger, 1980, pp. 7–8; Jervis, 1984, esp. ch. 6;
MccGwire, 1985, 121–4).

The concern here is that deterrence logic and policy have become
too dominated by purely military calculations. The reasons for this
development are varied, but it cannot be denied that a principal one
is the relative concreteness of military factors in comparison with
political ones. It is always easier to measure the military capability
of one's opponent with confidence than it is to gauge his motives
and intentions (Booth, 1979, ch. 7). But without a strong political
input, military calculations of deterrence are in danger, not only of

becoming excessively complex and sterile, but also of dominating the whole spectrum of relations between the states in the deterrence relationship. Deterrence logic cannot be divorced from the political relations between states that provides its *raison d'être*. As was seen in Chapter 12, the strength of the deterree's basic motivation to attack is a vital element in deterrence calculus. If that motivation is seen purely as a function of narrowly calculated military opportunity, rather than being a function of a wider array of factors both political and military, then deterrence logic is almost bound to go astray.

A narrowly military view of deterrence logic will tend to underestimate the political motivation of militarily weak opponents like Vietnam, and overestimate that of militarily strong opponents like the other superpower. When an opponent's military strength is interpreted as evidence of aggressive intentions, deterrence gets pushed down the self-reinforcing path of the 'difficult' school. Such a course raises the danger that deterrence policy will produce an arms race. Purely conflictual military concerns will govern the relationship, steadily squeezing out sensitivity to areas of indifference and harmony in relations between states. Interactions will drift towards being entirely in terms of coercive instruments rather than reflecting a normal diplomatic mix of threats, inducements and attempts to convince. Deterrence policy can therefore be seen as a failure not only if its threats have to be carried out. It also fails if those threats come so to dominate the relationship between deterrer and deterree that they exacerbate and perpetuate the political conflict that they were primarily intended to paralyse. The politics of deterrence are at their worst when the concept is interpreted so as to enhance nationalist attitudes towards security. They are at their best when deterrence logic is interpreted as a statement that security cannot be other than international and interdependent.

# Part IV

# Responses to the Problem of Military Means

# 14 Military Means as a Security Problem

## 14.1 MILITARY MEANS AS A PROBLEM IN THEMSELVES

During the last three decades, deterrence and the arms dynamic have increasingly merged into a single phenomenon. A large and diverse body of opinion views this synthesis as a problem. The main criticism is that modern military means create more, and more serious, difficulties than they solve. Although designed to make states feel more secure, modern military means serve that end only by raising states' fears of each other. Those fears in turn create a widespread public anxiety about a major war that would be a catastrophe for the human species because the military means controlled by states encompass such immense destructive power. The security of states thus depends on means which themselves heighten insecurity in the international system as a whole.

Before the twentieth century, the fear that states inspired in each other was bearable because the prevailing military technology gave them fairly limited powers of destruction. Under those conditions, the national security gains of military power generally outweighed its security dilemma costs. Under modern conditions, however, the interaction between a security dilemma and a fear of war, both enhanced by long-range weapons of mass destruction, makes the balance look much less favourable. The need for national military security is still there, but the available means create powerful contradictions in any acceptable interpretation of national security. In what I have elsewhere called the *defence dilemma*, military means undermine their own rationale by raising the fear of war above the fear of defeat (Buzan, 1983, ch. 6). Because the international system is composed of sovereign states, military means in the hands of others have always been, and still are, a problem. Since the awful, and largely unexpected, slaughter of the First World War, military means have increasingly come to be seen as a problem in themselves.

The first major manifestation of this view was the worry about arms racing after the First World War. With the spread of industrialization, arms racing looked like becoming an autonomous process in which states forced each other to grind out ever more numerous, costly, powerful and sophisticated weapons. They did so whether they wanted to or not, and industrialization therefore added a new factor to the traditional sources of friction and dispute among states. Against this background, the seeking of national security through military strength seemed independently to increase not only the probability that war should have to be fought, but also the scale of violence that any war would unleash.

The arrival of deterrence theory in the 1950s at first seemed a way of resolving the problem of arms racing and war that had haunted the interwar period. By tying the fear of war to the goal of war prevention, deterrence neatly short-circuited the link between arms racing and war. Under deterrence, arms racing was not a naked preparation for war, but a means of serving peace. Within the framework of Golden Age theory, the surplus capacity for destruction of nuclear weapons even seemed to offer a way of closing off the open-ended arms accumulation of traditional arms races. This apparent solution turned out to be short-lived. Deterrence has become a doctrine that not only justifies huge accumulations of nuclear weapons, but by bringing back the threat of warfighting makes the arms dynamic look once more like a harbinger of war. With the modern fusion of deterrence and the arms dynamic, military means seem to have outrun political ends. Human survival hangs on the logic of a theory that commands no agreement amongst its adherents, and on the less than perfect certainties of command and control over the forces of Armageddon.

The view that the arms dynamic of nuclear deterrence is a major independent security problem poses obvious difficulties for Strategic Studies as a field. These difficulties explain why not all of the literature arising from it falls within the boundaries of Strategic Studies. If the arms dynamic and deterrence are defined as the problem, then the main body of strategic thinking – which is about how to use the instruments of force most effectively for political ends – cannot escape being seen as part of that problem. Strategic thinking tends to accept the arms dynamic and the international anarchy as conditions of existence which require a response. Its emphasis is on the problem of military means in the hands of others. By definition, therefore, strategic thinking tends to confine itself to questions of military means in relation to the security ends of states. Within that framework, the arms dynamic and deterrence can certainly be seen as problematic. Yet to define them as the main problem at the very least inverts the normal strategic priorities: military means cease to be solutions to problems, and become themselves the problem that requires solution.

The most worrying criticism is that Strategic Studies helps to legitimize the role of military force in human affairs by perpetuating and institutionalizing the intellectual position that military means can be used effectively to tackle political problems. By concentrating on the traditional view that the problem is military means in the hands of others, strategic thinking helps to sustain the attitude that one's own military means are more a solution than a problem in themselves. The problem with deterrence, for example, is that it accepts technological and political conditions as given, and comes up with a military solution to the military and political problems posed by those conditions. That solution itself generates risks of a sufficient order to raise doubts in some minds about the morality, the logic, and even the sanity of the whole exercise. To the extent that strategic thinking sustains deterrence policies, it can therefore itself be defined as part of what has to be opposed.

Given its traditions and priorities, the field of Strategic Studies cannot be expected to take the lead in promoting this extreme view of military means as a problem. Yet the field does contain a considerable amount of the professional knowledge necessary for thinking about the issue of military means as a problem. The debate, especially its more moderate end, does penetrate the field quite deeply. Strategists are obliged to consider the broader issues of military means as a problem. Such issues directly affect the utility of military means as a solution to the security problems of states. Discussion of arms control, for example, is an integral part of thinking about deterrence, and disarmament is an item on the strategic agenda, even if it is no longer considered a particularly interesting or attractive subject.

## 14.2 DISAGREEMENTS ABOUT THE NATURE AND SERIOUSNESS OF THE PROBLEM

Major disagreements exist about both the extent and the character of the problem posed by military means, and consequently Strategic Studies is not under strong pressure to take a highly critical view of itself. These disagreements can be described along two dimensions. The first is how serious the problem of military means is in itself.

The second is how tractable the problem is in the sense of whether anything can be done about it. On both dimensions opinion ranges along a continuum from high to low, but the important interaction between them can be seen by looking at the extreme ends, crudely represented in a 2 × 2 matrix in Table 14.1.

*Table* 14.1   Opinion on military means as a problem

|  | very serious | not very serious |
|---|---|---|
| tractable |  |  |
| intractable |  |  |

Those who see the problem as very serious are mostly worried about the danger of war. Their worry has two components. The first is that the arms dynamic will increase the probability that war will occur. Arms racing increases tensions, and mutual deterrence creates risks of accidental war and uncontrolled escalation. The second is that if war does occur the consequences will be cataclysmic. As was seen in Chapter 13, the logic of deterrence creates a paradox between these two worries. Measures to reduce the destructiveness of war may well increase the probability that it will occur, and measures to reduce probability may require increasing the threat of destruction if war does occur. In the nuclear age, the worry about the consequences of war has assumed a special status which is almost independent from concerns about degrees of probability. Given the terminal consequences of all-out nuclear war, *any* chance, even one close to zero, that it will occur is sufficient grounds for many people to see the problem as extremely serious. It is because of this fear of consequences that any apparent increase in the probability of war – such as talk of warfighting strategies for deterrence – arouses strong opposition. Since the costs of fighting an all-out nuclear war outweigh almost any conceivable consequences of surrender and defeat, the view that military means are a very serious problem rests primarily on fear of war. Those who take this view usually express themselves in terms that give primacy to the concept of peace.

The view that military means are not, in themselves, a very serious problem rests on the broad logic of existential deterrence. The very dangers that drive some to see military means as the prime problem, strike others as a major creative force against central war in the international system. By this reasoning, the balance of terror is profoundly stable for political reasons. The deep and widespread fear of war prevents war not only at the technical level of rationally calculated costs and risks within specific situations, but also by changing the whole framework within which the major powers relate to each other politically. It is therefore to be welcomed rather than rejected. Although technical issues like crisis instability and accidental war are by no means to be ignored, they do not define the major reality, which is that war as an instrument of policy between the major powers has become almost unthinkable. Under such conditions, worries about the arms race have low salience because the race does not lead towards war. The arms dynamic maintains deterrence in the face of technological change, and so works both to prevent war and to support state objectives of national security through strength.

The question of whether anything can be done about the problem is usually less emotional and more intellectual than that of seriousness. For that reason it is usually a less conspicuous feature of people's attitudes on the problem of military means. Not much information is required to form firm opinions on the question of seriousness, but a firm judgement about tractability requires philosophical sophistication and/or a fairly broad command of technical knowledge about political and technological affairs. As with a failing car, one can easily judge how serious the consequences will be if it doesn't work. One cannot know whether or not the problem can be solved without understanding the technicalities of the fault in relation to how the car works.

The judgement about the seriousness of military means as a problem can be made entirely in military terms, and so encourages the half-truth that military means have become an independent problem. Yet it is not true that the problem of military means can be tackled separately from that of the anarchic international political structure. The fact that modern weapons have become a problem in their own right does not override the more basic issue of military means being a problem because they are in the hands of others. So long as the international political structure remains fragmented into independent states, power will be a factor in relations among those states. Military power, whether potential or in being, will play a major role in security relations amongst them. The fact that military power is in the hands of others links the issue of military technology firmly to that of political structure. In terms of tractability, therefore, military means cannot be considered as an independent problem, but have to be dealt with as a dual military/political one. This linkage between the military and political dimensions of security becomes increasingly unavoidable when one moves away from simply defining what the problem is, and towards proposing what might be done about it.

The view that the problem is tractable rests on the traditional idealist faith in the potential for change and harmony in human affairs. This faith is essentially that if people's attitudes can be changed, then their behaviour will change, and that harmony is an achievable social condition. Much of history can be read as confirming the malleability of human values and relations, whether it be the decline of monarchy, the triumph of anti-slavery, or the twentieth-century shift in attitudes towards the status of women. Since the problem of military means is self-made, it lies within the area of potential human change. The instruments of force are concrete objects. Common sense suggests that it must be within the power of the human species to alter or cease the activities which lead to their production. It must likewise be possible to change the attitudes of fear and mistrust that motivate the accumulation of weapons. Of late, much appeal has been made to the common value of survival as a positive foundation for changing attitudes towards military means (Report of the Independent Commission on Disarmament and Security Issues, 1982; Report of the Secretary General, 1985; Tuchman, 1984, pp. 136–41).

The view that the problem is intractable stems from the realist tradition, which is much less sanguine about the prospects for either change or harmony. Realists see conflict as a more pervasive feature of human relations than harmony, both because of human nature, and because of the deep momentum in the fragmentation of political life. In the realist view, the intractability of military means as a problem rests on the durability of the political and technological conditions, as well as the psychological ones, that underlie it (Buzan, 1984b). The structure of anarchy shows every sign of continuing its self-reinforcing existence as the defining feature of the international political system. States and nationalism are almost universally accepted values, and there is no sign of the ideological consensus, or the political harmony, or the accumulation of power that would be necessary to shift from anarchy to some form of world government. So long as the anarchic structure reigns, states will find it extremely difficult to conduct their relations without the basic security of national armed forces. The technological conditions that underlie the problem of military means also look highly durable. The technological imperative rests on a base of knowledge and industrial capacity that cannot be disentangled from the general process of civil life. Military options are inherent in scientific and industrial societies, and unavoidably impinge on political relations under conditions of anarchy.

On this reasoning, there is no obvious escape from the problem of military means. The problem is defined by deeply-rooted structures of politics and technology. There are not sufficient political resources at hand to change these structures, and it is not even obvious how one might set about creating such resources in anything but the very long term. As with views on the seriousness of the problem, these extremes of views on tractability are connected by a spectrum of mixed opinion. It is quite possible to think that there is some room for movement within the existing structures of politics and technology even if one accepts that the basic structures cannot themselves be changed for the foreseeable future (Buzan, 1984b).

There is no necessary correlation between views on the seriousness of the problem and assessments of its tractability. By looking at the combinations in the four boxes of Table 14.1 one can therefore gain some useful insights into the way people respond to the problem of military means. The combination of 'very serious' and 'tractable' means that the incentives for change are seen as high, and the barriers to it as low. Such a view leads directly to enthusiasm for radical and transformative measures like disarmament. The combination of 'very serious' and 'intractable' is too uncomfortable to attract mass opinion, though some experts find themselves stuck in it. It can radicalize opinion against the political structures that underlie intractability. Or it can be one route to arms control, where the emphasis is on reducing dangers by managing what cannot be changed.

The combination of 'not very serious' and 'tractable' is uncommon. It points towards enthusiasm for minimum deterrence, which capitalizes on both the perceived merits of the military system and the opportunity for significant change away from the heavily-armed deterrence policies of the present. The combination of 'not very serious' and 'intractable' represents orthodox strategic opinion about the efficacy of deterrence and the durability of conflictual international realities. It can point either to a more relaxed support for arms control than those who come to it from the 'very serious' opinion, or to the harder position of the warfighting theorists, who see the problem mainly in terms of miliary means in the hands of others, and who favour deterrence through competitive strength. A myriad of more subtle combinations is, of course, possible as one moves up and down the spectra of opinion separating the two sets of extremes in Table 14.1.

This diversity of opinion on basic issues explains why the debate about the problem of military means is so complicated. It is often a series of parallel monologues rather than a real debate, and arguments between opposed views usually generate more heat than light. Disagreements have to be seen, not only in terms of differing assessments of the problem, but also in terms of differing views on its tractability. As Hoffman has argued, these disagreements have a high political content. National security debates in several different times and places all tended to polarize between a radical anti-militarist view, arguing that the problem of military means was serious and that change was necessary, and a conservative, status quo view, arguing the necessity for self-defence and the difficulty of change in a hostile international environment (Hoffman, 1970). On the radical side, fear of war leads to the demand for peace. On the conservative side, fear of defeat leads to the demand for national security. Either way the analysis quickly engages political as well as strategic attitudes.


## 14.3  MILITARY VERSUS POLITICAL APPROACHES TO THE PROBLEM

If military means are seen as a serious problem requiring action, then the linkage between military and political factors becomes central to the debate about what to do. The destructive nature of modern military technology has made the military security of states increasingly interdependent. In the nuclear age, no state can guarantee its own security by competitively pursuing national military strength. Measures to remedy the problem of military means have to address the reality of this security interdependence. In theory, they can do so either by seeking to change the military means themselves, or by seeking to change the political relations that require states to arm against each other. Proposals for disarmament, arms control and non-provocative defence all take the route of changing military means. In practice, however, the separation of military and political factors implicit in such single-track approaches is hard to sustain. One can see why by examining the longstanding debate about whether the whole problem is best approached by tackling military means or political relations first.

This debate confronts a definitional dilemma. On the one hand, it can be argued that the problem of military means is fundamentally political. The fragmented nature of relations in the international system forces states into the security dilemma. In addition, a host of concrete political disputes about territory, ideology and power oblige states to look after their interests by arming themselves. States will therefore remain armed until either the anarchy is transformed into a more orderly and hierarchical world state, or independent states mature sufficiently to settle their disputes and learn to live more easily with each other. Arms simply reflect genuine political insecurities, and until those are removed, the problem of military means will remain. To begin solving the military problem, one has therefore to set about reforming political relations.

On the other hand, it can be argued that the problem of military means is essentially military. As the phenomenon of arms racing demonstrates, the existence of weapons enhances the threats that states feel from each other. It therefore constitutes an independent factor contributing to the over-all insecurity of the system. Lower levels of weapons would reduce these perceptions of threat without changing relative strengths, and would perhaps enable openings of trust to be made towards resolving political disputes. So long as weapons levels remain high, the threats from them will dominate international relations and prevent moves towards political reconciliation.

These two arguments lock together in a closed circle which lies at the heart of the debate about how to respond to the problem of military means. Arms reduction cannot begin until political relations improve, and political relations cannot improve until arms reductions have lowered tensions: stalemate.

Opinion on how to break into this circle is divided (Baylis *et al.*, 1975, p. 98). Singer argues that arms reductions have to come first because high arms levels lock political conflicts, closing the alternative route (Singer, 1970). The arms-first approach also has the attraction of offering clear incremental options, like York's proposal for starting nuclear disarmament at the bottom by eliminating battlefield nuclear weapons (York, 1984). Opposition to the arms-first approach arises on the grounds that military factors are not a principal determinant of political relations (Bull, 1961, pp. 8–12). To treat them as such risks misguided and self-defeating policies like the American attempt to use arms control as the main vehicle for promoting détente in political relations with the Soviet Union (Luttwak, 1980b, pp. 137–9).

This line of thinking blends into advocacy for tackling political relations first, on the grounds that the historical record of the arms-first approach is dismal, and that existing political structures will continue to block significant arms-first moves (Tuchman, 1984). It is not difficult to imagine tension-easing political arrangements. A global condominium between the superpowers would do the trick, as would an evolution towards a 'mature anarchy' composed of stable, status quo states (Buzan, 1983, ch. 4). Like the more traditional advocacy of world government, however, such ideas are unfortunately much easier to imagine than they are to bring about. None of them has yet broken into, or even dented, the closed circle of the military-political dilemma.

In many respects this debate is futile. Neither of the alternative approaches can break into the closed circle because the logic of each is undone by its connection to the other. Arms agreements will always be vulnerable to shifts in political relations, as witness the history of SALT. Political relations will always be sensitive to arms developments, as in the logic of arms racing. In addition, both approaches run into the fundamental intractability of the factors they address. The arms dynamic and the international anarchy are so durable that neither of them seems a promising area for major change. Proposals that require profound change in either factor almost automatically condemn themselves to impracticality. The resultant paralysis has remained a formidable intellectual block for many decades. Even arms control, which once seemed a way out of it, has succumbed to the same logic that earlier defeated disarmament.

For our purposes, however, the arms-first or politics-first debate is useful for underscoring the dual political/military nature of the problem of military means. Awareness of that dual nature is essential for understanding the next four chapters, which cover the logic of disarmament, arms control and non-provocative defence as responses to the problem. Although disarmament, arms control and non-provocative defence are all initially 'arms-first' type proposals, none of them can be understood without close reference to the political side of the problem.

# 15 Disarmament

Disarmament is the most direct – and in a sense the crudest – response to the problem of military means. Its logic is that since weapons create the problem, the solution is to get rid of them. This logic can be applied to all weapons – general and complete disarmament (GCD) – or to specific categories of weapons deemed to be particularly dangerous, such as nuclear bombs and biological warfare agents. It can be applied unilaterally or multilaterally, and can involve partial or complete elimination of the specified type(s) of weapon. The concept refers both to the process by which military capabilities are reduced, and to the end condition of being disarmed.

The history of disarmament is an odd mixture of failed negotiation and recurrent public interest and enthusiasm. The few achievements like the demilitarization of the United States–Canada border in 1817, the Washington Naval Agreements in the 1920s, and the Biological Warfare Convention of 1972, are separated by long periods of proposal-making, campaigning and negotiation leading nowhere. The enforced disarmament of the losers after both world wars was not reciprocated by the winners, who merely demobilized down from wartime to peacetime military establishments. It did not stick for much more than a decade in either instance, and in the interwar period played a part in precipitating the rearmament of the 1930s. Indeed, in the case of Japan, it was the power responsible for disarming it, the United States, that was pushing it to begin rearming even before the occupation period was over.

Early multilateral moves at The Hague Conferences of 1899 and 1907 succumbed to the growing momentum of the pre-First World War arms race. Widespread enthusiasm for disarmament after the First World War peaked with the fruitless League of Nations Disarmament Conference in 1932, and was overwhelmed by the rising political conflicts of the 1930s. After the Second World War disarmament negotiations in the United Nations were mostly propaganda exercises between the superpowers. By the 1960s, arms control had largely replaced disarmament as the organizing concept for negotiations. Disarmament became largely an aspect of arms control, as in the START proposals of the early 1980s for reductions in the size of strategic arsenals. This ineffectual record is reflected in a pessimistic and critical literature (Baylis *et al.*, 1975, pp. 90–100; Bull, 1970; Galtung, 1984b, ch. 4; Morgenthau, 1978, ch. 23). Despite the record, disarmament still generates an optimistic literature and widespread, if episodic, popular enthusiasm (Falk and Barnet, 1965; Noel-Baker, 1958; Report of the Independent Commission, 1982; Report of the Secretary-General, 1985). To understand this paradox one needs to look closely at the logic of the case for disarmament.

Probably the most common motive for advocating disarmament is the desire to escape from the fear of war. This fear is powerfully conditioned by circumstances. It was very strong after the First World War, and has flourished as a reaction against the maximalist forms of deterrence that have come to dominate superpower policy since the 1970s (Krass, 1985, pp. 107–28). Other motives for it include moral disapproval of the use (and therefore of the instruments) of force, opposition to the militarization of society required by the maintenance of armed forces, and the desire to use the huge resources devoted to weapons for other social purposes. These motives are all enduring, and go some way towards explaining the resilience of enthusiasm for disarmament. The logic that accompanies these motives is much more problematic than the motives themselves. In some ways the logic of disarmament is a powerful response to the problem of military means, but in other ways it is weak. This profoundly mixed strength of disarmament logic applies not only to the military case, but also to the political and economic ones.

## 15.1 THE MILITARY LOGIC

Within the military domain, the strength of disarmament logic is that it confronts directly and simply both the fear of war and many of the problematic elements of the arms dynamic. Whether it does so convincingly, is more open to question. In the twentieth century, popular fear of war is indelibly associated with weapons of ever increasing destructive power. Disarmament offers the simple formula of reducing that fear by removing the weapons with which it is associated. Nuclear disarmament has proved durably popular amongst a large segment of the population in the West on this basis. Permanent cohabitation with the threat of Armaggedon is a situation that many people find unacceptable on a level of feeling that has little to do with the logical niceties that drive the discussion in this book.

The process of disarmament cannot avoid weakening the logic of deterrence, which depends on the existence of strong fears. Disarmament forces a choice between mutually exclusive approaches to war prevention. That choice is extremely difficult to make because we have no way of measuring the effectiveness of either alternative. The removal of fears of prompt damage from war not only weakens deterrence, but also may not prove effective as a restraint on major war. The historical record shows that massive damage can be inflicted with very crude weapons: Rome's destruction of Carthage was not as fast as if nuclear weapons had been used, but it was just as complete. Disarmament cannot get rid of the knowledge and technology that would enable states to rearm. Nor can it remove the many civil technologies that would enable disarmed states to inflict massive damage on each other. Disarmament can delay mass destruction, and can make species suicide more difficult, but it cannot ensure that such things will never occur.

Inasmuch as wars are stimulated by the existence of competing armed forces, disarmament offers a means for attacking some of the basic mechanisms of the arms dynamic. A case can be made that disarmament should force the action-reaction dynamic to operate in reverse. If states arm themselves primarily in response to arms in the hands of others, then reductions of arms should stimulate a reverse cycle. Yet even if the action-reaction assumption is sound in relation to the arms dynamic, it does not follow that its logic works smoothly, or at all, in reverse. Many processes can be worked in both directions, like water to ice and ice to water but many cannot. Wood can be easily burned to ash, but not vice versa. Likewise, a device with a ratchet can be moved easily in one direction but encounters a lock when reverse pressure is applied. The arms dynamic may well be one of these processes that are much more difficult to run in reverse than to run forward. The technological imperative and anarchic political structure that drive it forward are both durable, and the forward drive is locked by the ratchet of institutionalization within the domestic structure of the state. Only economic pressures push the reverse movement, and in the industrialized states military spending is not high enough to make these pressures very strong. Economic pressures must compete against the increased sense of security and power that arise from having a comfortable margin of military strength over one's rivals.

Even within the disarmament process, there are factors that might well tend to sustain the action-reaction dynamic. The most obvious of these is the fear of cheating by other states. Verification procedures can never be perfect, so cheating is always a risk in mutual disarmament. If disarmament only involves partial reductions of state arsenals, then some risk of cheating is tolerable. So long as states retain substantial armed forces, their opponents are not likely to be able to cheat both quickly and substantially enough to achieve military dominance. As disarmament moves towards GCD, however, even small-scale cheating becomes significant, and the security of states becomes more and more dependent on verification measures being made foolproof – a requirement that is almost impossible to achieve in practice.

Awkward technical questions about levels of disarmament also feed into the action-reaction dynamic. How is GCD to be defined in terms of the domestic armed forces that states need for internal purposes? Ideologically repressive states like the Soviet Union and Chile, and states with weak political structures like Pakistan and Turkey, need much higher levels of domestic coercive force than do politically open and stable states like Denmark, Sweden and Japan. These differences might well be militarily significant in relations between neighbouring political rivals, such as between Western Europe and the Soviet bloc, Israel and Syria, Iran and Iraq, and Greece and Turkey. The issue of domestic force levels is one of the factors feeding into the broader problem of how to determine what residual armaments levels would be allowed to states under a disarmament regime, whether partial or GCD. Some form of parity is the obvious answer, but the extreme difficulty of defining it even between two states of similar size and power is illustrated by the endless arms control discussion between the United States and the Soviet Union. Finding acceptable terms of equivalence for a large number of states each of which perceives its security problems in relation to more than one other is almost impossible. Differences of size, power, geography, and internal and external security needs would make for negotiations of unbelievable complexity amongst states still locked into the basic insecurity of an anarchic structure.

Disarmament logic has significant strength as an attack on the domestic structure component of the arms dynamic. In this sense disarmament is not just about getting rid of weapons, it is also about breaking up the domestic structures that institutionalize the arms dynamic. The military logic of disarmament requires both the superficial measure of destroying weapons already in being, and the deeper structural measure of excising the means for, and the interests behind, further military production. The arms dynamic cannot be unlocked, and the action-reaction cycle cannot be stopped, until the power of the military-industrial complex within the state is heavily reduced. Only by demilitarizing society can disarmament even hope to ensure that the removal of arms would be durable, and that it would in fact create the basis for transforming international political relations: but the requirement for demilitarization itself raises profound political questions about the nature of the state and the role of force in the process of government.

Leaving aside the broader question of whether a demilitarized state is a contradiction in terms, dismantling the military-industrial complex is still by itself a formidable task. It involves shrinking the armed forces, and the whole R&D and production infrastructure. Both of these are large, powerful, and long-established components of state and society. To make social and political changes on such a scale in anything but a very slow and incremental fashion would require political resources of almost revolutionary magnitude. It would also require extensive economic and social redeployment of the skills and resources currently dedicated to the arms industry and the armed forces. It is not at all clear that the motives behind disarmament are strong enough to make changes on such a scale possible. Some limited technical thinking has been done about the conversion of the arms industry to civil uses (Kaldor, 1980), but this hardly begins to touch upon the larger question of how the reconstruction of the domestic political economy is to be achieved. Disarmament has to overcome domestic as well as international resistance. It also raises difficult secondary questions about how the political economy should be recreated. Should a large, high-technology industrial sector be preserved for civil purposes like space development and centralized power generation, or should a disarming society take a 'Greener' path, moving away from massive, centralized, high-technology ventures altogether? (Lovins, 1977).

Where the military logic of disarmament is weakest is in terms of the technological imperative aspect of the arms dynamic. Disarmament logic focuses primarily on existing weapons, and secondarily on the organization of military production. That focus is justified by the immediate dangers of war and arms racing arising from those two factors. Yet because they are preoccupied with the concrete realities of military means, advocates of disarmament largely miss the deeper running influence of the technological imperative which is only indirectly of military significance. Although the technological imperative works indirectly, it is none the less powerful enough to create a major layer of doubt about the viability of disarmament even if the problems of dismantling existing weapons and military-industrial complexes could be overcome.

The technological imperative links progress in the civil economy to military strength because the civil and military sectors are united by the common bonds of knowledge and technology. Every industrial society has a latent military potential lying just beneath the surface of its civil economy. In a disarmed world that latent potential would become a much more conspicuous feature of the power relations between states than it is in a world where military power is manifest. Technological progress would continue to offer obvious military options. Imagine, for example, the knowledge and technology for miniature high-power lasers, or for extremely sophisticated autonomous robots. Either of these could be developed for civil uses (fusion power, mining), yet both could quickly be turned to formidable military applications such as defence against air or missile attack, and precision-guided delivery vehicles for weapons. Possession of such options would give powerful leverage to those states at the technological leading edge.

In a disarmed but still anarchic world, all states would continue to relate to each other through their military potential. Under such conditions the balance of power would work, not on the current basis of military capability in being, but in terms of mobilization potential. As before the two world wars, power would be calculated not only on the extent of resources available for mobilization, but also on the speed with which civil capacity could be geared to military use, and on the quality of technology available for conversion to military purposes. Fear of war would still haunt people's minds because the latent military potential in the international anarchy would be obvious, not least in terms of civil technologies like aircraft, poisons and explosives immediately usable for military purposes. There would be some gain in the removal of the prompt threat, but that would be offset by the loss of deterrence effects from forces in being. The arms dynamic would not threaten as a daily reality, but that gain would be offset by the uninviting prospect of a headlong rearmament race should the disarmament regime break down. Such a race would be much harder to control than the relatively leisurely and institutionalized 'walk' between the United

States and the Soviet Union (Intrilligator and Brito, 1984, pp. 76–8, 82).

Disarmament does not, and cannot, deal with the problem posed by the technological imperative. Military and civil technology are too closely linked. Industrialized humanity cannot escape from the problem of military means, even by stripping away its accumulations of weapons and its specifically dedicated military production capabilities. This conclusion confronts us again with the political side of the problem. Weapons and military potential only acquire significance in the context of disputes and rivalries arising from the fragmented political structure of the international system. If there is no purely military escape from the problem of military means, then states remain trapped in the insecurity arising from the anarchic relations among them.

## 15.2 THE ECONOMIC LOGIC

The economic logic of disarmament rests on the idea that resources not consumed for military purposes will be available to meet a variety of pressing human needs. For Third World countries struggling to keep up with the global arms dynamic, these other needs are usually seen in terms of development, and the meeting of basic human requirements in food, shelter, health and education. Disarmament and development are often linked, with the former seen as a way of releasing resources for the latter (Jolly, 1978; Myrdal *et al.*, 1977; Report of the Independent Commission, 1982, ch. 7). General disarmament would not only relieve Third World countries of the direct strain that the maintenance of large military establishments puts on their political economies (Luckham, 1977a and b), but could also increase the levels of development aid from North to South. Within the developed countries, disarmament could release resources for a variety of welfare objectives, so easing the annual allocation battles in which education, health, industrial investment, foreign aid, and other highly valued activities have to fight with military demands for their share of the budget. It would also undo the military domination of scientific and technological R&D, so enabling the intellectual resources of humankind to be turned away from improving the instruments of violence, and towards improving the human condition (Brooks, 1975, pp. 94–5). Since annual global military expenditures consume hundreds of billions of dollars, the apparent economic prize from disarmament is very large both within individual countries and for the international system as a whole.

The size of the resources, the strong appeal of the alternative uses for them, and the simplicity of the economic logic, all contribute to the political attractiveness of disarmament. The economic logic of disarmament applies not only to unilateral and multilateral arms reductions, but also to GCD. The purely economic task of adjusting to a demilitarized economy does not pose insuperable difficulties (Kennedy, 1983, ch. 9). The economic gains from disarmament are nevertheless often not straightforward. Both partial and complete disarmament raise economic counterpressures from those parts of the economy that depend on the military for employment and prosperity. Coping with such interests would be part of the larger political problem discussed above of handling the demilitarization of society. Partial disarmament raises the problem that the resources saved would most probably be transferred to other military uses unless strong pressures to use disarmament savings for other purposes could be created. Limited agreements, such as the scrapping of all chemical weapons, do not affect the over-all position of the military interest in society, and are therefore more likely to result in the resources going to other sectors of the military than to the civil sector. Such agreements may, anyway, not release many resources, given that weapons of mass destruction are often relatively cheap.

With extensive multilateral disarmament or GCD, there is also the cost of the disarmament regime itself to consider. As will be seen in the next section, extensive disarmament requires substantial international inspection and world government, the costs of which would not be trivial. These costs would be especially high if the thorny problem of giving the world government adequate enforcement and dispute settlement powers was solved by creating an international armed force. Although many supporters of disarmament would be happy to use the released resources for world government, it is not clear how much, if anything, would be left over for other purposes.

In the case of nuclear disarmament, the economic logic of disarmament is weak or even adverse. If disarmament is aimed at eliminating only nuclear weapons, on the grounds of their prompt threat to human survival, then the military functions of nuclear weapons have to be replaced by conventional military means. One of the persistent attractions of nuclear weapons is their relative cheapness for many strategic missions, especially those associated with deterrence by retaliation. This attractiveness has, if anything, increased over the years since the Second World War. The cost of ever more sophisticated conventional weapons has risen steeply, and high attrition rates attend their use in war. The logic behind the 1950s slogan of 'a bigger bang for a buck' (or 'more rubble for a rouble') is perhaps stronger now than when it was first coined. Cities can still be threatened with destruction by conventional weapons, as in the Second World War, but the financial cost of achieving such missions would be astronomical. What can be achieved by a handful of nuclear weapons and delivery vehicles would require hundreds or thousands of delivery vehicles and tens or hundreds of thousands of conventional warheads. Against strong defences, attribution rates would be high. The cost-effectiveness of nuclear weapons also applies to deterrence by denial. Contemporary discussions within NATO about decreasing reliance on nuclear weapons almost all point to the need for increased expenditure on conventional forces to achieve deterrence by denial (Rogers, 1982, pp. 1154–6). For nuclear disarmament within the framework of anarchy, the savings seem likely to be less than the additional costs, and therefore the strictly economic case for it is unattractive.

## 15.3 THE POLITICAL LOGIC

The military logic of disarmament is flawed in its own terms because it cannot solve the military implications of the technological imperative. It is also flawed because it does not break the closed circle of the arms-first or politics-first dilemma. At many points the military logic of disarmament leads directly into the international political side of the problem. The need for high levels of verification, the fears of cheating and of rearmament races, the worries about parity and about the military uses of civil technology, and the continuation of the balance of power through mobilization potential, all reflect the basically political problem of insecurity arising from life in the international anarchy. So long as the international system is composed of independent sovereign states faced with the uncertainties and dangers of cohabiting with each other, it is hard to see how disarmament in purely military terms can create security. If one assumes that international political relations will remain much as they are now – that is, anarchic, and filled with disputes and rivalries – then the process of disarmament is extraordinarily difficult even to begin, let alone sustain, and the achievement of it would be disastrously unstable. A disarmed but still anarchic and conflictual international system would generate high incentives to cheat and high suspicions and fears that cheating was going on. It seems most unlikely that such a system could for long avoid a headlong rearmament race (Harvard Nuclear Study Group, 1983, pp. 188–91). The logic of disarmament thus requires major political changes as well as major military ones. It is on this political ground that the disarmament prescription for the problem of military means is weakest.

The political logic of disarmament envisages two possible routes to the requisite political change: either the process of disarmament makes the international anarchy more peaceful without changing its structure; or else disarmament becomes the vehicle by which the international anarchy is transformed into the hierarchical structure of a world state. The first route – the case that disarmament would make anarchy more peaceful – rests on the assumption that arms are the *principal* source of tension in the international system. In this view, most international conflict results from factors like arms racing, militarist influences within states, misperception of military intentions, and crises arising from opposed military potentials. If this view is true, then disarmament would indeed eliminate most sources of tension and could be expected to make the anarchy significantly more peaceful.

A close look at the day-to-day realities of international relations raises grave doubts about whether other sources of conflict can be discounted to the extent required to sustain this view. The political logic of disarmament requires that territorial and political disputes, and power rivalries, be a relatively minor residual source of tension and conflict in the disarmed system. If they are more than minor, then disarmament will unleash its own forms of insecurity and instability described above. Hedley Bull has explored this weakness thoroughly in terms of the disruptive effect of disarmament on the major ordering function that armaments play in the balance of power (Bull, 1961, ch. 2; 1970). Armaments are essential to the security of states in the anarchy. They underpin the balance of power which is the principal ordering mechanism in anarchic systems. As Osgood points out, the role of armaments is paradoxical. They are both the primary instrument of order and the primary threat to security (Osgood and Tucker, 1967, p. 32). The weakness of disarmament is that it addresses only the problem side of Osgood's equation. It ignores the positive function that arms play in the international system. Disarmament logic thus begs the question of whether more security would be lost than gained if arms were removed from the system.

The historical record offers little reason to think that the political sources of conflict are minor, or that they would be much muted by a general lowering of arms levels. Political disputes like those between Iran and Iraq, India and Pakistan, the Soviet Union and the West, Israel and the Arabs, South Africa and the black-ruled states, Greece and Turkey, and North and South Korea have deep roots. These political disputes certainly generate military rivalries, and those rivalries may worsen political relations and make them harder to resolve. Yet there is no cause to think that the political rivalries are caused by the military ones. Disarmament would simply tip the balance in favour of other power resources: countries like Israel and Pakistan would lose their major bulwark against the power of more populous neighbours. The Soviet Union would find itself competing directly with the greater economic and cultural dynamism of the West. Whichever party was disadvantaged by the new terms of power balance would have every incentive to rearm. Disarmament also neglects the problem of states that are politically weak, and in which the armed forces play a major domestic political role. Lebanon, Chad, Kampuchea, Uganda, El Salvador, Ethiopia, Sudan, Pakistan, the Philippines and Afghanistan are among the most conspicuous examples of such states, and for them anything approaching complete disarmament would have serious implications for the maintenance of the state (Buzan, 1987).

The political logic of disarmament thus offers no convincing way of resolving the political problems of insecurity within the framework of the international anarchy. It says little about what is to replace the mediating role of military power in relations between states. At best it offers a hope that the process of disarmament would reduce tensions, but that hope is discounted by the fact that unresolved political disputes would make disarmament itself a source of tension in many cases. By this route, disarmament does not break into the closed circle of the arms-first or politics-first dilemma. It offers no independent way of removing or settling the political disputes and rivalries that generate the demand for weapons in the first place. At best, a measure of disarmament might accompany a period of détente that occurred for other reasons. It cannot create détente, and when détente erodes under the pressure of anarchy, disarmament would also erode.

This criticism is especially applicable to proposals for unilateral disarmament. If political disputes remain unresolved, then a major self-weakening move by one side risks raising the probability of war. It offers an aggressive state the opportunity to exploit weakness. It is an interesting conjecture as to whether war would have been less likely in the late 1930s if Britain, France and the United States had followed a more vigorous rearmament policy than they did. It is hard to argue that unilateral disarmament by any of them would have reduced the probability of war. It is also interesting to note that Lenin shared the view that disarmament logic was weak in relation to the deeper existence of political conflicts. Given his Marxist view of the fundamental realities of class conflict and rivalry between capitalist and socialist states, he could only argue that 'the main defect of the disarmament demand is its evasion of the concrete questions of revolution . . . Disarmament means simply running away from unpleasant reality, not fighting it' (Lenin, 1964, p. 84). So long as the political structure of anarchy remains, disarmament runs the danger of stimulating the very behaviour that it seeks to prevent.

The difficulties posed by the first route of disarmament within anarchy push enquiry towards the logically more coherent second route. Can the disarmament process be used to transform the political structure of the international system away from anarchy? If it is the politics of international anarchy that make disarmament unworkable, then disarmament must be accompanied by a permanent transformation of the international political structure: the fragmentation of anarchy must be replaced by the unity of world government. A world government would resolve political disputes and replace the positive function that armaments currently play in ordering the balance of power.

There is a strong logic connecting disarmament, especially GCD, and world government (Harvard Nuclear Study Group, 1983, pp. 188–91; Singer, 1962, pp. 232–7). One of the core difficulties with disarmament is the problem of cheating that arises as the security of each state comes to depend more on the assumed military impotence of others than on its own military strength. As disarmament proceeds, inspection and verification become increasingly important, as does the question of what is to happen if someone is found cheating. Is GCD to be accompanied by an international enforcement machinery, or are states to be kept faithful to their disarmament undertakings only by the threat of a chaotic rearmament race if cheating is discovered? To ensure the stability of GCD, strong inspection and enforcement machinery seem vital. To overcome the political problems of anarchy, potent dispute settlement provisions would also have to be created. To ensure the acceptability and impartiality of this machinery, it would have to be internationally organized. To administer and control such a politically powerful and central organization would require political arrangements indistinguishable from world government.

Linking disarmament to world government produces a position that is logically much stronger than that of disarmament within anarchy. The disarmament-plus-world-government approach breaks the dilemma of arms first or politics first by tackling both simultaneously. Unfortunately, the logical elegance of this solution is marred only by its complete impracticality. While the functional linkage between GCD and world government is sound in itself, it represents only the logic of a single issue. It lacks anything like the political breadth that would be necessary to activate the momentous shift from a system of sovereign states to one of world government. Establishment of a world state involves basic changes in the way people are governed. It inevitably raises an extensive agenda of basic economc and political questions that would confront a governing body at the global level. It also raises major constitutional and ideological questions about how such a government would be structured, and by what rules it would work.

To establish world government would require either a preponderance of power sufficient to overawe the many deep divisions in the world polity, or an ideological consensus strong enough to make available agreed organizing principles for a global confederation of some sort. Neither of these is anywhere in sight, and global trends do not seem to favour their emergence. Political and economic power are becoming more dispersed. Even the military duopoly of the superpowers does not look durable in the longer term. A similar tendency towards multiplicity is evident in ideological terms. Communism is fragmenting into strong national variants, and Islam is emerging as a political force in parts of the Third World. Only democratic capitalism and one-party socialism are serious contenders for a world ideology, but neither looks to be headed for such a triumph. Both are burdened by a lengthening record of disappointed expectations. Neither commands the freshness or credibility necessary to overcome the immense barriers of history and political culture that stand in the way of world government.

The political logic of disarmament thus runs into a dead end by either of its main routes. Within anarchy, the logic of disarmament is so obviously flawed that except for propaganda purposes, and for limited reductions in the context of arms control, the idea is, as the historical record indicates, a non-starter. The logic of disarmament with world government is much stronger, but the broader conditions necessary for world government are not available. The single issue of disarmament does not by itself have the power to create them.

Despair at this impasse drives some peace opinion into more radical anti-state positions, sometimes labelled 'green'. Since the state is not only at the root of military and political problems, but also blocks the path to the disarmament solution, the only logical route to peace that remains is over the corpse of the state. The macro-approach of subordinating the state to world government is unachievable, and therefore only the green micro-approach of undermining the state by organizing alternatives to it remains. Immediate opportunities present themselves in local politics, where the green approach is manifested in things like towns or boroughs, or even houses declaring themselves nuclear free zones. Transnational counter-state organizations like Greenpeace and Amnesty International also provide potent vehicles for the green approach. Yet while the green approach has generated effective local action and organization for campaigns on specific issues, it lacks any coherent political vision of a peaceful world order without states. World society has a pleasing utopian ring to it. The superficial spread of Western culture and communications systems offer a plausible basis for the idea, but it does not look convincing as a basis for peace in a world filled with political rivalries and hatreds. Moreover, it has not so far escaped the dilemma that political success at the local level creates strong pressure either to build state-like political structures, or else to compete for the levers of power within existing states.

Given that the political logic of disarmament is so flawed, it is a considerable paradox that its political appeal has remained robust. Disarmament issues seldom dominate electoral behaviour, but there is a large enough constituency that favours disarmament to force parties and governments to pay systematic lip service to it as an objective, and to engage in competitive disarmament propaganda with rivals. In order to explain this one can but resort to the cynical aphorism that in politics, the popular appeal of an idea is often inversely proportional to its logical power.

The mass appeal of disarmament is based on at least three qualities. First, it is a simple idea. It is easily grasped, and goes directly to the heart of a problem that causes genuine, justified, and widespread anxiety. The logic that poses disarmament as a solution to the problem of military means is not convincing in depth. Nevertheless, to the many who see the problem, but either do not judge it by the realist criteria of logic and practicality, or do not have the time or the resources to think it through in detail, it does appear to be a clear and unambiguous response. Secondly, disarmament offers a concrete and permanent solution, which is to eliminate the military means that define the problem. Thus as well as being simple, disarmament has the political appeal of being definite and decisive. Again, one can demonstrate the flaws in this apparent solution, but only on a level of detail and sophistication that is unlikely to register much in public political debate. Thirdly, and probably most important, disarmament has a strong moral and emotional appeal. The ideas that peace requires the abandonment of violence in human affairs, that the weapons and threats of mass destruction are immoral and uncivilized, that armaments represent a huge waste of resources urgently needed for human development, and that militarism is culturally retrograde, have an undeniable political force that transcends issues of mere practicality.

Ken Booth points to the essence of the matter with his observation that, 'as long as one's individual conscience does not place non-violence as the highest of all principles, the case for disarmament on political, economic, military and even ethical grounds is not obvious' (Baylis *et al.*, 1975, p. 93). That the political appeal of disarmament is stronger than its logical power is consequently itself part of the problem. It means that much of the public debate is dominated by a solution that would be dangerous if it was implemented. This odd feature of disarmament stands in contrast to the other main proposals for solving the problem of military means. Both arms control and non-provocative defence are logically stronger but politically less appealing than disarmament.

# 16 Arms Control

Like disarmament, arms control is also concerned with the impact of technology on the arms dynamic and deterrence strategies. Although it shares this root, arms control is less ambitious and more sophisticated than disarmament. It differs fundamentally from disarmament in the principles that govern its approach to the problem of military means. The basic response of disarmament is to see weapons as the key issue, and therefore to seek solutions in the reduction and abolition of weapons. The process of disarmament goes directly counter to that of the arms dynamic, and is fundamentally contradictory to the logic of deterrence as a means of preventing war. The ultimate objective of disarmament is to render arms racing and deterrence both unnecessary and impossible.

By contrast, the basic response of arms control is to attempt to manage the arms dynamic, whether unilaterally or by negotiation, in such a way as to restrain arms racing tendencies and to reduce instabilities within a relationship of mutual deterrence. Arms control does not see the arms dynamic, or deterrence, or weapons, as problems in themselves. For the most part, those who advocate arms control do not share the disarmers' faith that these things could be removed even if it was desirable to do so. Arms control sees them in more neutral terms, as things that may serve the interests of both national and international security policy if properly managed, but that may generate serious risks of unwanted conflict and expense if left untended (Freedman, 1984b, pp. 35–7). The problem in arms control terms is the military and political instability that results from each side's fear that the other will achieve military superiority. Instability increases the probability of war. The basic principle of arms control is that states should find ways of reassuring each other that they are not seeking military superiority (Freedman, 1981, ch. 5). Arms racing is therefore a problem because it heightens the competition for superiority. Maintenance of the military status quo at the lowest level compatible with deterrence stability is the objective.

Arms control is thus about the realistic management of political conflict rather than about achieving some grander vision of peace (Blechman, 1980, pp. 118–19). It is about strengthening the operation

252

of the balance of power against the disruptive effects of the arms dynamic, especially arms racing and technological developments tending to make deterrence more difficult (Bull, 1961, pp. 62–4). Arms control may include measures of disarmament, but it does not necessarily prefer them. It may sometimes encourage deployment of preferred (because stabilizing) weapons systems like submarine-based ballistic missiles. Its key word is restraint, rather than reduction (Baylis *et al.*, 1975, pp. 89–90; Bull, 1961, pp. ix–xi). Its repertoire is much more extensive than that of disarmament. It includes such measures as preferred types of weapons and modes of deployment; communications arrangements and codes of conduct between rivals; and the setting of target levels for new weapons systems, which may involve either setting ceilings on deployments or banning deployment altogether.

The history of arms control is quite short. Since it is available from a wide variety of sources, a brief account will suffice here (Baugh, 1984, ch. 6; Baylis *et al.*, 1975, ch. 5; Committee on International Security and Arms Control, 1985; Dahlitz, 1984; Freedman, 1986; SIPRI, 1978; Tuchman, 1984; Zurhellen, 1981). As was seen in Chapter 11, the idea of arms control grew out of Golden Age deterrence theory in the late 1950s. Arms control was a necessary element in the creation and maintenance of MAD. Its role was to make deterrence into a means for turning arms racing tendencies between the superpowers into a mechanism for encouraging the maintenance of the military status quo at levels sufficient for assured destruction. Avoidance of arms racing was necessary if deterrence was to be protected from the disturbing pressures of competitive technological change. Arms control maintained continuity with the older disarmament tradition by picking up its goals of reducing defence costs and lowering the probability of war.

Arms control also developed as an alternative to disarmament. In some senses it was a reaction against the lengthening record of failure of ambitious disarmament schemes to make any impact on reality (Freedman, 1984b, pp. 35–7). The record of disarmament is much longer than that of arms control, and has its origins in resistance to arms racing in the pre-nuclear period, but disarmament fared badly in the nuclear era. Nuclear weapons could not be disinvented. With the emergence of deterrence theory, disarmament found itself in a losing struggle to sustain its position as the premier alternative approach to war prevention. Deterrence made the military approach to war prevention (if you want peace, prepare for war) much more credible than it had been in the pre-nuclear age. Disarmament suffered because its own principle could not avoid directly contradicting the logic of deterrence. Arms control, by contrast, was in harmony with deterrence. Although its basic principles are appropriate for non-nuclear military relationships, in practice most thinking about arms control has been in the nuclear domain. On the grounds that it provided a way of making small first steps that might, if successful, pave the way for disarmament later, arms control was able to attract some of those who supported disarmament (Blechman, 1980, pp. 112–18).

The heyday of arms control was in the two decades from the late 1950s to the late 1970s, a period with an obvious parallel to that of Golden Age deterrence theory as a whole. In the late 1950s, the basic ideas of arms control were worked out as part of Golden Age theory. The first application came with the Partial Test Ban Treaty of 1963 and, for the following decade and a half, arms control was closely associated with détente between the superpowers. The other highlights of arms control were the Hotline Agreement (1963), the Agreement on the Peaceful Uses of Outer Space (1967), the Non-proliferation Treaty (1968), the Seabed Arms Control Treaty (1971), and the Strategic Arms Limitation Talks (SALT I and II) running from 1969 to 1979. The climate induced by SALT produced several agreements setting limits on deployments of strategic weapons, extending the 1963 Test Ban arrangements, limiting the deployment of anti-ballistic missile (ABM) systems, controlling the provocative behaviour of naval forces, and banning biological weapons.

Nevertheless, by the late 1970s arms control was in deep trouble (Blechman, 1980). Political relations between the superpowers were deteriorating over competition in the Third World, negotiations on strategic arms limitation were bogged down in complexity, and the 'difficult' school of deterrence, which was both unsympathetic to arms control and hostile to the Soviet Union, was in the ascendant in American politics. Arms control had failed to stem the growth of nuclear arsenals; it had not led to a reduction of rivalry between the superpowers; and it lacked ideas about how to cope with problematic new technologies like cruise missiles. From the perspective of the politically dominant hawks in the United States, arms control had led the United States to weaken itself. In their view, American security was in jeopardy because an aggressive Soviet Union was in command of significant military superiority. A vigorous round of arms build-up and, if necessary, arms racing, was therefore required to restore the credibility of American power.

Under these conditions, the political support for arms control in the United States disintegrated. Those whose real interest was disarmament were disillusioned by the continued increases in military arsenals under the arms control regime. Many of those who favoured deterrence were drawn into the 'difficult' school on the strength of the arguments that the Soviet Union had exploited American interest in arms control to advance its own military and political interests (Freedman, 1982, p. 42). By the early 1980s the Reagan Administration was promoting SDI as an alternative to the whole deterrence system. Arms control was largely reduced to a sustained propaganda duel between the superpowers over proposals for negotiations on intermediate-range nuclear forces (INF) and strategic arms reductions (START). There was little evidence of will on either side to engage in serious substantive negotiations. Disarmament opinion in Europe exhausted itself in the fruitless campaign against NATO's deployment of cruise and *Pershing II* missiles. In the United States it mainly devoted itself to campaigning for a freeze on strategic forces in an attempt to stop both the escalation of the military budget and the move towards arms racing with the Soviet Union (Committee on International Security, 1985, ch. 3).

As Freedman observed, 'the essence of arms control theory, that potential enemies can co-operate in the military sphere, has been discredited' (Freedman, 1982, p. 52). Despite its apparent bankruptcy, arms control remained the dominant concept for thinking about the problem of military means. Its eclipse gave some boost to disarmament, but no popular new idea surfaced to provide fresh impetus in the way that arms control did in the late 1950s. Some of those who remained committed to the logic of arms control took refuge in existential deterrence, and the view that the nuclear balance was stable within a wide span of possible superpower behaviours and deployments (Freeman, 1984b). Others argued for a return to a purely technical arms control, unencumbered by the political baggage of détente (Blechman, 1980, pp. 112–25; Freedman, 1982, pp. 53–4; Harvard Nuclear Study Group, 1983, pp. 212–13; Windsor, 1982). In practical terms, arms control thus appeared by the mid-1980s to have reached a similar dead end to disarmament. No matter how sensible and powerful an idea it was in theory, in the real world it not only failed to shape the forces it addressed, but at times seemed to have become their slave. To understand why two such different ideas should share the same fate, one can use the same scheme to investigate the logic of arms control as was used to examine disarmament.

## 16.1  THE MILITARY LOGIC

### 16.1.1  Reasons for Rivals to Co-operate

The military logic of arms control rests on the assumption that, under conditions of MAD, even enemies share a common interest in war avoidance. Given the threat of nuclear war, that common interest was thought to be strong enough to serve as a basis for joint action to manage potentially destabilizing, and therefore mutually disadvantageous, developments in the arms dynamic. The rivals might also develop a secondary interest in reducing the costs of defence expenditure, though the logic of autism explored in Chapter 7 might well override such a development if each wished to cultivate external threats for domestic political reasons. The military logic of arms control initially rested on the further assumption that sharing the *condition* of MAD (that is, being vulnerable whether one wanted to be or not) would force a convergence in superpower military policies towards a *doctrine* of MAD (that is, preferring to be vulnerable as a matter of strategic choice). This distinction between condition and doctrine is vital to understanding the significance of MAD. For the reasons explored in Part III, the expected convergence on doctrine did not occur. That failure greatly limited the possibilities for arms control, but the basic condition of MAD has remained, leaving the common interest in war prevention as the bedrock for arms control. There is no reason why the logic of arms control cannot be applied to conventional rivalries like those in the Third World. Nuclear weapons do, however, make the common interest in survival between rivals much more compelling than the common interests that might be generated by desire to avoid a conventional arms race.

The beauty of arms control was that its military logic seemed to transcend the political rivalries between states that had proved such an obstacle to disarmament. Arms control did not require states to give up either their military strength or their political rivalries. It invited them to consider the incontrovertible realities of their security interdependence within a MAD framework, and to seek actions that would improve their mutual security. Given that neither could escape from MAD, and that neither wanted a nuclear war, there seemed to be a lot of scope for technical co-operation in the management of deterrence. The common interest in war prevention pointed to two key areas for such co-operation: the avoidance and/or management of crises; and managing the arms dynamic in such a way that maintenance of the military status quo did not deteriorate into arms racing.

### 16.1.1.1 *Crisis avoidance and crisis management*

Avoiding or managing crises made sense because it was in crisis conditions that the logic of deterrence was most likely to come unstuck (Brecher, 1979; Craig and George, 1983, ch. 15; Holsti, 1972; Williams, 1976). Both superpowers had experienced the dangers of crisis in their 1962 confrontation over the Soviet deployment of missiles in Cuba. That experience provided an important basis for the decade and a half of détente and arms control that followed it. In a crisis, acute pressure of time makes rationally calculated behaviour difficult at best, and perhaps impossible. The probability of misinformation and misunderstanding rises sharply, and the problem of reliable communication becomes severe. Poorly understood standard operating procedures in the vast military bureaucracies make precise central control over military moves difficult. Such procedures raise the dangers of automatic escalation as each side responds to its detection of moves by the other. In a crisis, mistakes or accidents can more easily have disproportionate effects on the decisions of both sides. The desire to avoid war comes under intense counter-pressure from the compulsion not to lose the confrontation over whatever immediate issue is at stake. In a crisis, the need to preserve face and credibility thus work directly against the over-all constraint of the fear of triggering war.

In a really intense crisis, it is possible to imagine either side deciding to initiate a nuclear attack because it thought it was about to be attacked, even though in reality both sides were still trying to avoid war. Whatever the merits of the action-reaction dynamic in describing arms racing, it was very clear from the experience of 1962 that it operated with a vengeance during crisis. The compressed time-scale and high intensity of crisis might make behaviour extremely difficult to control. The particular problem in crisis management was to ensure that the use of military means did not generate an action-reaction momentum of its own that would quickly outrun the ability of political leaders to maintain the primacy of political logic (George, 1984).

There were many things that the superpowers could and did do to reduce the probabilities of finding themselves in this situation. They could and did improve their ability to communicate with each other quickly. They could and did devise codes of conduct to lower the probability of unwanted clashes resulting from contact between their armed forces. They could and did take steps to discourage the spread of nuclear weapons to minor powers. They could and did agree on confidence-building measures (CBM), like notification of major military movements, as a method of reducing uncertainties about each other's behaviour. The superpowers' record here is not bad, although they could have done more (Landi *et al.*, 1984).

They could, but in the end only did partially, agree to configure their strategic nuclear forces in such a way that neither posed significant threats to each other's capability for AD. Such a configuration would require that neither challenges the secure second strike forces of the other, either by mounting area defences against nuclear strikes, or by deploying missiles accurate enough to make disarming first-strike attacks against the missiles and command centres of the other. The objective of such measures would be to ensure crisis stability in the relationship of the two nuclear arsenals. In other words, strategic forces should be configured so that neither side felt in danger of losing its AD capability under any circumstances. Only with that assurance could each ride out a crisis.

In the event, the superpowers did agree not to deploy anti-ballistic missile systems in the ABM Treaty of 1972. That agreement is currently under pressure from R&D on both sides towards new technologies for strategic defence (SD). By contrast, neither could for long resist emerging technological opportunities for increasing their counterforce capabilities against each other. From the early 1970s onward, increasing accuracies of warheads combined with multiple re-entry vehicles (MIRV) to give both sides expanding counterforce options against the fixed strategic forces of the other. Anti-submarine capabilities were also pursued by both sides, though with much less success, as a means of destroying the other's strategic missile-carrying submarines before they could launch their weapons. Because of these decisions, the crisis stability of strategic forces is considerably less than is desirable, and both sides face pressures to adopt hair-trigger postures like launch-on-warning (LoW) in order to avoid being disarmed in a first strike. This sense of vulnerability to a first strike is one of the prime motives behind moves towards technologies for SD, but such moves only enhance the threat to AD from the other direction. The failure of the superpowers to achieve crisis stability in their nuclear arsenals means that it is more important for them to avoid getting into a crisis than would otherwise be the case. Whether it is a good idea to raise incentives for crisis avoidance by lowering capabilities for crisis management is an interesting question for debate.

### 16.1.1.2 *Managing the arms dynamic*

The second main area for arms control was managing the arms dynamic in order to prevent arms racing. Although less urgent in war-prevention terms than crisis avoidance, containing the arms race was still an important common interest. Under conditions of MAD, competitive accumulations of weapons could not by definition significantly increase the real military capability of each side to damage the other. Such accumulations would, however, adversely affect superpower relations in a variety of ways. Their cost would require the cultivation of hostile enemy images amongst the population of both sides in order to justify it. Open-ended arms racing would increase each side's uncertainty about the first-strike intentions of the other, and about the security of its own second strike forces. That uncertainty would strain the stability of deterrence by making each fear a 'breakout' by the other from the all-restraining condition of MAD.

Arms racing could not escape taking on the features of a political trial of strength in the eyes of others. The importance of the world audience in the over-all ideological rivalry between the superpowers tends to lock the arms racing competition. Arms racing within MAD was thus more fruitless than traditional arms races aimed at usable warfighting capability. Yet it was just as dangerous in the sense of contributing its own momentum to the probability of war. So long as the security interdependence of MAD prevailed, arms racing was unlikely to reduce the probability of war because additional weapons did not add materially to the size of the threat faced by a would-be aggressor. This logic contrasts with that of pre-nuclear conditions like the late 1930s, when an increase in warfighting strength might make a marked difference to the calculations of an aggressor about whether or not to initiate war.

Some of the arms control measures that the superpowers could take to avoid arms racing are similar to the things they needed to do in order to give crisis stability to their strategic forces. These included not challenging each other's AD capability either by mounting strategic defences or by deploying significant counterforce capacity. Either type of deployment would force the other side to increase the number of its own strike weapons in order to ensure that it retained a credible AD capability even if it suffered a surprise attack. In theory, the pressure to maintain a credible secure second strike force could lead to enormous numbers of weapons being deployed. The competition between AD objectives on the one hand, and the damage limitation objectives of strategic defence and counterforce capabilities on the other, is open-ended.

The superpowers' record of restraint in the face of technological opportunities for counterforce and strategic defence has not been good, although they have so far managed to avoid unrestrained arms racing. Where the technology was reliable, as it was for counterforce capability, the tendency has been to develop and deploy it. Strategic defence technology has proved much more problematic in itself. The 1972 restraints were as much an admission of impracticability as a statement of preference, and this is precisely why the ABM Treaty is now in danger. If either superpower decides that strategic defence technology is becoming practicable, then the basis for mutual restraint will be very weak. Other factors tending to make deterrence more difficult, especially extended deterrence, have also contributed to the failure of the superpowers to achieve deterrence at lower levels of armaments.

During the 1970s, the superpowers did have some success controlling the arms dynamic in terms of negotiating parallel restraints on the size and character of their strategic forces. The various ceilings negotiated during the SALT era were high, and did not put much restraint on counterforce capabilities. The ceilings none the less did constitute a framework for maintenance of the military status quo, and served to block pressures for more open-ending arms racing. Parallel restraints enabled the superpowers to avoid rival deployments in certain areas (like space, Antarctica and the seabed), and rival activities in such things as atmospheric testing. They took some of the heat out of pressures on the superpowers to compete in military strength as part of their global ideological rivalry. They also enabled the rivals to negotiate how they would deal with the continuous pressures for force modernization that the technological imperative imposed on them.

## 16.1.2    The Impact of Strategic Doctrine on Arms Control

Although the theoretical scope for the military logic of arms control is considerable, the actual range of measures available is very much determined by the over-all character of the deterrence relationship. The ideal conditions for arms control are where *both* sides hold MAD as a doctrine, and thus share minimum deterrence as an objective. Arms control then becomes the means for achieving maintenance of the military status quo at relatively low levels, and both sides share subsidiary objectives such as lowering defence costs, and damping down the domestic structure inputs into the technological imperative. The early proponents of arms control clearly had this scenario in mind. The fact that events did not follow this route, and that the scope for arms control was therefore much narrower than the ideal, perhaps explains the accumulation of frustrated expectations that helped to break up the arms control coalition in the late 1970s.

If mutual deterrence is pushed down the path of the 'difficult' logic by conditions like ED commitments, or the desire for SD, or high levels of hostility, then the scope for arms control diminishes. When both sides are committed to maximum deterrence policies, as appeared increasingly to be the case during the 1980s, then their pursuit of warfighting options greatly narrows the possible areas for arms control. Some room for manoeuvre remains in relation to crisis management and war avoidance, and parallel restraints on the arms dynamic. But under conditions of maximum deterrence the corrosive effect of counterforce and SD options is almost impossible to stop because the doctrine requires that such capabilities be deployed. Even under maximum deterrence, however, the continued reality of MAD as a condition leaves a limited, but important, role for arms control to play. The willingness to negotiate the maintenance of a commitment to crisis control and possibly some confidence-building measures (CBM), and the observance of parallel restraints like arms ceilings, all provide a baseline of reassurance about the fundamental character of the relationship. Refusal to observe these minimum conditions signals abandonment of the basic commitment in arms control not to seek military superiority. Arms control under conditions of maximum deterrence may thus amount to little more than continuing to talk, and to keeping high levels of maintenance of the military status quo from drifting into arms racing.

The condition where the two sides do not share the same doctrine of deterrence is almost certainly the most difficult for arms control. When doctrines do not match, large opportunities for misunderstanding arise, and grounds for agreement are limited. Opportunities for misunderstanding by one side, and manipulation by the other, are particularly acute if one side is under a sustained misapprehension about the strategic doctrine of the other and therefore underestimates the real differences (Gray, 1982b, pp. 129–33). This scenario describes the situation between the United States and the Soviet Union during the 1960s and 1970s, an apparent paradox since those two decades saw arms control at its height. The paradox is explained by the starting superiority of the United States, which enabled it to carry the costs of arms control from a position of strength. As its superiority eroded, however, the differences in doctrine became more apparent, leading to rising tensions and a strong reaction in the United States against arms control. That reaction has put both sides on the equal footing of maximum deterrence doctrines, which may, after the dust of reaction has settled, provide a more stable, if much less ambitious, basis for a return to the arms control process.

As a rule, then, the more difficult deterrence is thought to be, the more problematic arms control becomes. Those conditions that make deterrence more difficult will therefore also complicate the process of arms control. This vulnerability of arms control to different conditions of doctrine serves to amplify a range of other difficulties with its military logic that arise from its attempt to seek technological solutions to the problem of military means. Many of these difficulties are similar to the problems of disarmament, though usually less severe.

### 16.1.3   Dilemmas of the Technological Approach

Unlike disarmament, arms control makes no attempt to stop the arms dynamic. This position is taken on the pragmatic grounds that however desirable such a solution might be, it is impossible to achieve within the existing political framework which is itself durable. Arms control therefore makes no pretence to be a permanent single solution to the problem of military means. What it offers is a continuous process of management as a way of responding to political and technological change. This essentially piecemeal and reactive stance means that arms control always confronts a changing and complicated menu of issues. That menu itself changes continuously in response to advances in technology. Sometimes the changes will favour arms control, such as the vast improvement in surveillance and information-gathering technology that enables each superpower to monitor closely the military activities of the other. Other changes make arms control more difficult by increasing the ease with which strategic weapons can be concealed (mobile ICBMs, cruise missiles), or by increasing the uncertainties about the actual capability of a given weapon (MIRV, dual-capability systems that can and do carry either nuclear or conventional warheads).

### 16.1.3.1   *The inviolability of innovation*
Because arms control cannot stop the process of innovation, it is particularly vulnerable to adverse technological developments. This means that its achievements are always fragile and frequently transitory. The most striking recent illustration of this vulnerability is the conflict between SDI and the 1972 ABM Treaty. New technological opportunities threaten to bring down what is arguably the most significant achievement of arms control to date (Drell *et al.*, 1984).

Several factors prevent arms control from reaching into the R&D process to anticipate such developments. First, the process of R&D does not lend itself to clear predictions of future military technology. Even where a development can be anticipated, its implications for strategic stability might be very mixed, making the arms control implications hard to evaluate. This was the case with MIRV which maintained the credibility of secure second strike forces against SD only at the cost of increasing capability for counterforce first strikes. It is also the case with proposals for a comprehensive nuclear test ban (CTB). Even pro-arms control opinion is divided on whether such a measure is desirable. Is it useful as a restraint on further development of warheads by the nuclear powers, and on proliferation by non-nuclear powers? Or is it mistaken because it would block desirable improvements in strategic forces, and erode confidence in existing stockpiles? (Edmonds, 1984; Howard, 1985, p. 10; Hussain, 1981).

Secondly, secrecy about the R&D process is a matter of national security. In the case of the Soviet Union especially, this secrecy blocks the path to anticipatory arms control. And thirdly, the West in general, and the United States in particular, are committed to technological innovation as a key element in their military strength against the Soviet Union. They would therefore be reluctant to restrict their R&D options. The unstoppable momentum of technology also makes the idea of a freeze a weak approach to arms control. A freeze is such a blunt instrument that it stops desirable technological developments as well as undesirable ones, and fixes imbalances as well as balances. In addition, it faces the same problem as disarmament in relation to the technological imperative. Under a freeze, a known and growing military potential in the civil economy would create a looming threat of breakout from the agreement by whichever side decided to exploit it first.

### 16.1.3.2   *The limits of verification*

Like disarmament, arms control confronts the issue of verification, though not in such an extreme form as that posed by GCD. For arms control, verification is more a matter of reassurance about the good faith of one's rival than the alternative basis for national security that it becomes under GCD. Nevertheless, when relations are hostile, only high certainties of compliance will reassure. These may be impossible to achieve without levels of inspection so intrusive as to be politically unacceptable. Inadequate inspection makes arms control vulnerable to suspicions of cheating. Such suspicions arise easily between rivals, and can be encouraged for political purposes. As the debate about compliance in the United States illustrates, they can quickly poison the whole process of arms control (Jasani and Barnaby, 1984, pp. 5–20; Voas, 1986). Some things, such as ICBM silos, aircraft, and submarines, are relatively easy to inspect adequately by national technical means (NTM) of verification like satellites. Others are not, such as mobile ICBM, cruise missiles, and the details of MIRV warheads. As the negotiators of SALT discovered, easily inspectable things may be an inadequate and quickly exhausted basis for arms control. The achievement of limits on them may actually encourage development of less easily inspected technologies (Luttwak, 1980b, pp. 126–7).

### 16.1.3.3   *The complexities of parity*

Again like disarmament, the military logic of arms control runs into the problem of parity. On this issue, the roles are reversed, and it is arms control that raises the most acute difficulties. The military logic of arms control leads towards parity as the obvious basis for agreement between rival powers. The condition of MAD is itself a kind of parity in terms of equal vulnerability. Measures like parallel restraints and force ceilings lead to numerical parity as the easiest and fairest objective to pursue. The idea of parity is strongest in a situation of two powers both espousing MAD as doctrine. In such a case, each would accept the logic that there was no advantage to military superiority under conditions of MAD. Parity at force levels sufficient for AD would be politically acceptable. Parity could be defined in terms of capability for AD, which in the case of the two superpowers would result in roughly equivalent strategic forces for minimum deterrence. Since neither would threaten the secure second strike capability of the other, calculations of parity would not be complicated by worries about the attrition effects of counterforce first strikes.

As one moves away from this ideal towards conditions in which deterrence gets more difficult, the defining of parity becomes increasingly problematic. Moves towards maximum deterrence policies bring in counterforce and SD capabilities. These in turn require larger secure second strike forces. The whole concept of parity thus becomes more difficult because of the possibility that one side will gain advantage by striking first against the deterrent forces of the other. Even if strategic forces are equal in size and quality to begin with, an advantage to striking first makes them uneven in practice. When the factor of counterforce first strike is significant, competing strategic forces can never be made equal. Each side will seek to insure against being the victim of a first strike by maintaining an edge in the size and quality of its forces.

The greater diversity of forces required for maximum deterrence enhances the qualitative complexities of force comparison. This problem arises because of differences between states in such factors as their choices about preferred weapons; the military requirements resulting from their doctrines, military traditions and geostrategic conditions; and their technological capabilities. The Soviet Union, for example, prefers large, land-based ICBMs to sea-based missiles for reasons of geography (restricted access to open oceans), and military and political tradition (army traditions and desire for close control). The United States is more comfortable with the bulk of its strategic warheads at sea, not least because both its submarine and anti-submarine warfare/weapons (ASW) technologies are better than those of the Soviet Union. No two states will ever have identical armed forces. The more closely definitions of parity approach such a requirement, the greater the number of obstacles there will be to reaching agreement.

The SALT process fell into this trap. By interpreting parity in terms of detailed similarity of forces, the superpowers put themselves on an increasingly complicated, difficult, and counterproductive track. Parity in those terms not only made arms control extremely complicated to negotiate, but also created a wealth of potential for minor violations and so called 'grey area' activities which might or might not be infringements of agreements. As political relations between the superpowers deteriorated, the demand for detail increased, as did suspicion on both sides that the other was gaining advantage from the agreed configurations. The collapse of SALT was not unconnected to the rising difficulties of pursuing detailed equivalence. Advocates of renewed arms control efforts consequently stress the need for a redefinition of parity in terms of concepts like 'balanced asymmetries' in which the two sides would agree to trade off areas of preference in their force structures rather than try to find a uniform mould across the board (Brown and Davis, 1984; Freedman, 1986).

This problem of dissimilar forces becomes more acute when arms control is concerned with conventional forces. Without the levelling effect of the surplus capacity of destruction available with nuclear weapons, the definition of parity depends on a myriad of qualitative factors ranging from technology through training to morale. Every detail is important because it has implications for warfighting capability. As the experience of the Middle East Wars of 1967 and 1973 shows, mere comparisons of weapons lists indicate little.

Other factors that make deterrence more difficult also complicate parity. Having more than two powers in the relationship works in both directions for deterrence, but is wholly negative for parity. Two powers have at least a theoretical possibility of agreeing terms of equality, but amongst three or more powers parity is almost impossible to formulate. Each power must reckon on the possibility of a combined attack from more than one other, and so cannot easily agree arms control terms in relation to any other power alone. If any one tries to match the strength of all of the others, then it will appear superior to any one of them. This problem is illustrated most clearly by the Soviet Union, which faces China as well as the West. Although Chinese strategic forces are still small, the Soviet reaction to them is already large enough to complicate arms control with NATO, particularly in terms of INF.

Extended deterrence complicates parity for similar reasons to multipolarity. The military logic of parity requires that neither side have an advantage. Yet maintaining the credibility of ED under conditions of parity creates strong pressure to have some advantage.

The 'easy' logic of deterrence argues that ED may be effective even without superiority. The response of NATO to superpower arms control based on parity shows that such reasoning does little to reassure allies, regardless of whether it works on opponents. To the recipients of ED, parity between their guarantor and their opponent looks as if they have been 'decoupled' from core deterrence and made into ripe candidates for a self-contained theatre war on their territory.

Even if parity can be achieved against these difficulties it is not necessarily a comfortable position to be in. Under conditions of mutual minimum deterrence parity is acceptable because large, and therefore easily detectable, changes would be required before either side could wield a military advantage. The required changes would involve major deployments of counterforce capability or strategic defence. Under the more strained conditions further across the spectrum towards maximum deterrence, however, parity is comparatively unstable. One side may only have to add marginally to its existing counterforce or SD capabilities to make the other worry about being vulnerable to a first strike. Because the opposed forces are geared for warfighting, relatively small changes can shift the balance from one of equals to one of superior and inferior. Status instability of that kind is fragile, and may make agreement on a definition of parity impossible to achieve. The problem of status instability is even more marked for parity between conventional forces. The warfighting implications of a shift from equal to inferior under conventional conditions may have much more immediate consequences than in situations where the over-all constraint of existential nuclear deterrence applies.

For all these reasons, parity is not the simple and equitable basic formula for arms control that it appears at first to be. Its logic, like that of deterrence, is strongest in the ideal world of Golden Age theory where both sides seek minimum deterrence. The real world, unfortunately, has never generated those conditions. In the logic of the more difficult deterrence that dominates superpower policy, parity is hard to define in acceptable operational terms. As the Americans discovered during the 1970s, it is not necessarily comfortable, or stable, or even desirable, once attained.

### 16.1.3.4 *Resource diversion*
A further problem with the military logic of arms control is that the whole process simply diverts resources from one area of military

activity to another (Brooks, 1975, p. 75; Gray, 1974, p. 209). This is the same problem as arises for partial disarmament. If restrictions are placed on specified types of weapon, such as the banning of orbital weapons, the low ceilings on ABM systems, or even the high SALT ceilings on long-range ballistic missiles, then the resources that would have gone into those weapons will simply flow to unimpeded lines of development like cruise missiles and the R&D for SDI. On this basis, arms control may shape the arms dynamic, but does little or nothing to diminish its size or pace. At worst, arms control may complicate its own future by releasing resources towards developments like cruise missiles that will themselves be difficult to observe, and so to restrict, once they reach production.

### 16.1.3.5 *Falling victim to the arms dynamic*
Two other ways in which arms control can defeat its own purposes are first, by creating demand for weapons which would otherwise not have been acquired, and secondly, by serving as a rationale for new developments to use as 'bargaining chips' in arms control negotiations.

Arms control can most easily create a demand for weapons when parity is being pursued in terms of the detailed similarity of forces discussed above. That pursuit leads to each side assessing its strength against that of the other on the basis of comparisons in each separate category of weapons – ICBMs, submarine-launched ballistic missiles (SLBMs), tactical or theatre nuclear weapons (TNWs), tanks, aircraft, troop numbers, and so forth. This process is reinforced by the perception that third parties will also assess the relative military prowess of the superpowers in this way. Such calculations lead to perceptions of weakness on the basis of an imbalance within any significant category, rather than to comparisons in terms of over-all military capability. Pressure to correct specific imbalances strengthens the domestic bargaining position of those who want to acquire the weapons in question, but whose case might otherwise not be strong enough to prevail in the fierce competition for a share of the military budget. Thus the domestic pressures in the United States favouring large, multi-warheaded ICBMs, an anti-satellite (ASAT) system, and chemical weapons, become stronger because the Soviet Union has them. The Soviet Union seems to have experienced a parallel process in relation to cruise missiles and enhanced radiation warheads. Sometimes there are good strategic reasons for acquiring parallel weapons systems, as in the case of

SSBN and mobile ICBMs. The danger is that arms control will lead to some acquisitions merely for the sake of appearances arising from an excessively rigid interpretation of parity.

The issue of 'bargaining chips' is probably more serious than that of mirror imaging of forces. Because arms control is about the management of conflict rather than its resolution, the process of arms control easily gets absorbed into the over-all framework of rivalry. Negotiations become a forum in which the rivals display their strengths, both to each other and to their audience in the rest of the world. There is often as much propaganda as substance in their proposals. Concessions are easily seen as a sign of weakness (in terms of inability or lack of will to compete in the arms dynamic) rather than as expressions of a desire to achieve joint gains.

Because of this competitive element, and also because the outcomes of negotiations affect national policy, arms control becomes an important element in the domestic political debate. Great play can be made of the need to negotiate from a position of strength, and to avoid sending one's diplomats naked into the bargaining chamber. By this process arms control becomes a means for justifying new weapons programmes in order to put the country in a strong position to bargain. Unless one's negotiators have plenty of 'chips' with which to play, there is a danger that they will be forced into a weaker position by a rival who has more to give away. This kind of thinking has played a conspicuous role in American policy-making, notably over the long debates about the *MX* missile. The notion of the bargaining chip is an all-purpose legitimizing device for almost any weapon system in such a competitive context. The problem is that the use of arms control logic in this way easily generates more weapons than control. Once initiated, major weapons projects acquire domestic momentum and become difficult, though not impossible, to stop. Arms control negotiations are often slow, and may not keep up with either the pace or the scale of new weapons innovations. Arms control can thus defeat its own purposes by this route, actually stimulating the arms dynamic rather than dampening it.

As with the military logic of disarmament, many of the problems arising in the military logic of arms control lead quickly to the political side of the over-all problem of military means. Verification, parity, resource diversion and bargaining chips all pose problems in their own right. The significance and intensity of those problems varies directly with the degree of tension and hostility in political relations. It is clear that the initial assumption of arms control that MAD created common interests strong enough to transcend rivalry is at best a half truth. Common interests do exist, but they are easily overwhelmed by bad political relations. Pursuit of them under conditions of hostility can prove self-defeating by leading to mistrust, feelings of betrayal, and increased armaments. At the extreme, they can lead to reactions of arms racing like that triggered in the United States in the late 1970s.

## 16.2   THE ECONOMIC LOGIC

The rationales for arms control are primarily military and political. Its logic is aimed at security goals, and the prospect of economic gains does not play as big a part as it does for disarmament. One seldom sees, for example, the linking between arms control and development that one sees between disarmament and development. The reason for the relatively low profile of economic logic in arms control is clear: since no major assault on the arms dynamic is envisaged, no major release of resources from military to other uses is likely to result. The source of savings from disarmament is obvious, because a shrinkage in the size of the military establishment must quite quickly result in annual expenditure savings even if scrapping weapons does not in itself generate surplus revenue. If any savings result from arms control they are much less visible because they tend to be reductions in hypothetical future expenditures rather than cuts in present ones.

Managing the arms dynamic by such arms control means as deployment ceilings and restrictions on types of weapons may result in savings on what would have been spent in the absence of such restraints. In other words, by defining agreed terms for maintenance of the military status quo, arms control can keep military expenditures from rising to the higher levels necessary to sustain open-ended arms racing. These savings are by no means unattractive, and are part of the propaganda of arms control. Yet they are marginal compared to what disarmers offer, and they do not make much impact on the day-to-day reality of large expenditures for military purposes. In the ideal arms control conditions of mutual minimum deterrence, savings would perhaps be large enough and visible enough to make a difference. As conditions move towards maximum deterrence, the narrower scope for arms control leaves little prospect for savings, and little hope for transferring R&D resources out of the military sector into the civil one. Managing the arms dynamic releases states neither from the pressure of the technological imperative, nor from the associated security need not to fall too far behind the leading edge of qualitative advance.

## 16.3   THE POLITICAL LOGIC

In theory, the political logic of arms control should be one of its strong points. Arms control avoids the main political pitfalls of disarmament by accepting the political structure of the international system as a given fact and seeking to work within its constraints. It even seems to offer a way around the arms-first or politics-first dilemma by opening up clear grounds for joint gain between rivals. Unlike disarmament, with arms control rival states could pursue some security interests jointly without having to give up either their own armed forces or the political positions underlying the rivalry. Optimists reasonably hoped that the low sacrifices and significant security gains offered by arms control might serve as a way of beginning to build habits of trust and co-operation between rivals. Arms control could start with incremental agreements. It might build steadily into an increasingly broad range of co-operation that would eventually begin to mute the political rivalry, and perhaps even lead to disarmament. Like disarmament, the logic of arms control is 'arms-first', but arms control is a more subtle version of the approach than disarmament. There was thus real hope that it might break into the closed circle of the arms-first or politics-first dilemma.

In the event, however, the linkage of arms control to expectations of improved political relations proved to be a greater burden than the arms control process could bear. During the heyday of arms control between 1963 and 1979, the process became deeply entangled with political détente between the superpowers. In the West, arms control became virtually the idiom for détente. Continued arms control agreements were a necessary condition for the maintenance of restrained political relations. This linkage worked for a while, in part because arms control was new, and the early agreements were relatively easy to formulate. The United States still felt superior, not yet having confronted the shock of real equivalence.

By the mid-1970s arms control was getting more difficult. All the easy agreements had been made. Military doctrines were shifting towards maximum deterrence, and new technologies like MIRV and cruise missiles posed thorny problems for arms control. Political relations between the superpowers were deteriorating. In part this deterioration was over rivalries in the Third World. In part it was because of the quite severe problems of status instability that arose in the United States as a result of the advance of the Soviet Union to military equality. When the collapse came in the late 1970s, it was dramatic. The failure of arms control and the erosion of détente amplified each other so that both broke down simultaneously. After that breakdown, there could only be a period of hostility and intensified arms dynamic.

Many analysts now consider the American linking of arms control and détente to have been a mistake (Blechman, 1980, pp. 106–12; Luttwak, 1980b, pp. 137–9). The calls referred to above for a return to a more strictly technical arms control are based on this analysis. The mistake was the classically American one of seeking technological solutions to political problems. The Soviets give primacy to politics as part of their ideology. They were in no doubt that arms control depended on détente rather than the other way around (Blechman, 1980, pp. 106–12). Arms control could not carry détente, and with hindsight should not have been expected to. But this analysis returns us squarely to the arms-first or politics-first dilemma. If arms control is confined to the technical pursuit of joint security interests between unfriendly rivals unwillingly locked into MAD, then not much can be expected of it. Hostility not only limits the potential for arms control directly, but also generates moves towards maximum deterrence policies which further reduce the scope for arms control. If arms control is to make a significant impact on the problem of military means, then it would appear to require a modicum of détente as a precondition.

This position was taken by Hedley Bull before arms control had any track record (Bull, 1961, ch. 3). Others have returned to it on the basis of bitter experience (Freedman, 1982, pp. 52–5; Howard, 1985, p. 7). As Michael Howard puts it, 'arms control becomes possible only when the underlying power balance has been mutually agreed' (Howard, 1983, p. 21). Unless the rivals have some common views about their security interdependence, no firm basis for arms control exists. One of the clearest examples of such a common view transcending rivalry between the superpowers has been their early and long-standing opposition to horizontal nuclear proliferation.

Acknowledging the need for political agreement as a precondition for arms control still, however, begs the question of how to begin; how to stimulate improved relations. If even the promising arms control variant of the arms-first approach does not work, how can one break into the circle of the arms-first or politics-first dilemma? In failing to solve that problem, arms control has been blocked by the same obstacle as disarmament. About all that can be said – and it is not an insignificant point – is that if détente exists, the logic of arms control is likely to prove much more attractive and feasible than that of disarmament. If détente does not exist, neither disarmament nor arms control will prevail against the arms dynamic.

This advantage of arms control is, however, balanced by its serious defects in terms of political appeal. Disarmament is politically attractive despite its logical weakness because it is a simple concept, engages deep emotional and moral feelings, and offers a direct and permanent solution to a widely feared problem. Arms control has almost none of these assets. As the preceding discussion indicates, arms control is not a simple idea. Its basic principle is quite subtle compared to disarmament. Its operational logic quickly becomes very complex and dependent on technical knowledge. Arms control does not offer a definite or permanent solution to the problem of military means, but only an endless sequence of fragile and transitory management measures. Arms control has little in the way of the direct emotional and moral appeal of disarmament. It is not clearly opposed to either weapons or militarism, and so it cannot tap the sentiments of pacifism more than indirectly. Neither can it offer much of a lure in terms of released economic resources. At best it has a certain functional morality, in that when it works it can claim to be reducing the probability of war. As the events of the late 1970s illustrate, however, when results cease to flow, the idea itself has nothing but cold logic to sustain it. Cold logic is no foundation for durable mass support.

Arms control is vulnerable to political attack from anti-militarist opinion because of the ease with which its military logic can be co-opted into the process of the arms dynamic. Arms control accepts the arms dynamic and tries to manage it. Management, however, can easily become complicity (Howard, 1985, p. 6). As outlined above, there are many ways – bargaining chips, resource diversions, the pursuit of force symmetry, status instability – in which the process of arms control can actually stimulate hostility and the competitive accumulation of armaments. The record of arms control provides grounds for suspicion that the concept is more useful for putting a polite face on the arms race, and for manipulating public opinion, then it is for achieving restraint (Freedman, 1982, p. 41). This is especially true under conditions of maximum deterrence, where the scope for arms control is small, and the need for weapons is large. Under those conditions, the logic of bargaining chips is powerful, and arms control is unlikely to escape exploitation and cynicism.

From the side of nationalist opinion, arms control is vulnerable to attack on the grounds that it requires co-operation with opponents. It therefore makes national security dependent on the good faith of rivals. Such faith can easily be attacked as naïve when the opponents hold antithetical ideologies, and see each other as structurally aggressive and undemocratic. Suspicions that one's opponent has somehow gained advantage from agreements on restraint are easy to raise, as illustrated by American worries over Soviet assaults on the 'spirit' of the SALT agreements by such actions as the MIRVing of heavy ICBMs. So are accusations of cheating and bad faith in observation of agreements as discussed above.

Some arms control measures are vulnerable to exploitation by a calculating aggressor, so the risk is real enough to be exploited by those who view opponents with extreme hostility. Either CBM arrangements for notification of military exercises, or crisis control arrangements for communication, for example, could be used by an aggressor to delay suspicions about an attack that was in fact carefully planned (Hart, 1984; Landi *et al.*, 1984, pp. 201–2). By carefully planning a deception which exploited co-operative arms control measures, an aggressor might hope to gain enough days or hours to make a significant difference to the prospects for a successful attack. Worries of this sort are harder to ignore when hostility is high. Arms control is therefore always vulnerable from this direction when the rival power is perceived as aggressively revisionist. Gray's sustained critique of arms control reflects this view (Gray, 1976, ch. 6; 1982b, pp. 129–33, 160–6).

The political strength of disarmament is that although it may be damned as impossible, or even counterproductive, it never loses its moral rectitude and the basic directness and simplicity of its appeal. Arms control is politically fragile by comparison. Its key political strength is as compromise ground between normally opposed disarmament and defence interests (Blechman, 1980, pp. 112–18; Freedman, 1982, p. 42). Yet if it fails, arms control has no durable moral base. It can be condemned not only as counterproductive, but also, and more damagingly, as deceptive. For all that, arms control is a less dangerous policy than disarmament because it does not envisage military and political change on the ambitious scale required by GCD. If it works, it contributes to lowering the probability of war. If it fails it is unlikely to create either the massive crises of national security or the catastrophic system instability which are the attendant risks of disarmament. At worst the failure of arms control means a return to the market-place of the military balance of power governed only by the logic of deterrence.

One is left with the disturbing conclusion that neither of the major responses to the problem of military means can overcome the central dilemma of arms-first or politics-first. Adding to that problem is the fact that the most ambitious scheme, and therefore the most dangerous if applied, possesses the strongest political appeal. The safer and less radical approach lacks a firm basis for durable political support.

# 17 Non-Provocative Defence

The idea of non-provocative defence re-emerged into the strategic debate during the early 1980s. It is based on a distinction between offensive and defensive military capabilities, a notion that goes back to the disarmament conferences of the pre-nuclear era. It identifies offensive weapons, and the fear of being attacked that such weapons stimulate, as the core of the problem of military means. It does not share the disarmament view that weapons *per se* are the problem. It is closer to the arms control view that the problem is instabilities in the configuration of opposed military forces, but it rejects arms control's acceptance of the logic that security can be found in the mutual paralysis of opposed offensive forces.

Interest in non-provocative defence has developed within an area of overlap between the fields of Strategic Studies and Peace Research. The concept thus offers an important opportunity to combine the intellectual forces of two fields that do not normally see their activities as being harmonious except in the neutral area of data collection and publication. From the Peace Research side, the idea is discussed under the awkward and non-self-evident label of 'transarmament' (Fischer, 1984; Galtung, 1984a and 1984b; Sharp, 1985). Transarmament refers to the process of shift away from mutually threatening forms of military security, and towards a condition of non-provocative or defensive defence. Although some interpret transarmament as a shift to civilian defence (Sharp, 1985, p. 67), the mainstream is prepared to accept the military terms of strategic debate. This acceptance is an important move. It surrenders the broad utopian idealism of disarmament, but retains strongly the narrower idealism that the existing military system needs to be changed extensively. It accepts the basic realist premise that, as Galtung puts it, 'we live in a dangerous world . . . there is a need for some kind of defence' (Galtung, 1984a, p. 138), but does so in the normative context of the pursuit of peace.

From the Strategic Studies side, interest in non-provocative defence has built on what was previously a peripheral theoretical interest pioneered by Adam Roberts in strategies for territorial

276

defence (Roberts, 1976). This idea for long occupied the intellectual no man's land between the two fields, and so is also a source for transarmament. The more widespread recent interest amongst strategists has grown out of the European dilemma within extended deterrence, and particularly the desire to push back the use of nuclear threats by increasing capabilities for conventional denial. Much of the debate about improving conventional defence is firmly within the mainstream strategic tradition of warfighting. Some of it, however, reflects a wish to exploit a perceived shift of technological advantage to the defence in order to re-orientate European military strategy towards non-provocative conventional defence (Pierre, 1986; Windass, 1985). Here the aim is to acknowledge the reality of security interdependence, and to pursue common security in terms of the mutual 'right not to be overwhelmed by the military forces of the other' (Windass, 1985, p. 120).

The spectrum of non-provocative defence thus ranges from an idealist extreme, where the focus is on civilian defence, through the many-layered strategy of territorial defence and transarmament, to a concentration on non-provocative conventional denial options within the context of NATO. The civilian defence options are close to disarmament, while the debates about conventional denial options for NATO blend into the logic of arms control and deterrence. Non-provocative defence thus fits clearly into a pattern of responses to the problem of military means that is the subject of this group of chapters. It occupies the space in the spectrum of response between disarmament and arms control. It is more radical than arms control because it rejects the idea that security can be achieved using offensive military capabilities, but it is less radical than disarmament because it does not reject the utility of military means in the pursuit of security. It can be seen as a reaction to the failure of disarmament and arms control to make much impact on the arms dynamic. It also represents a refusal to accept nuclear deterrence as a safe and reasonable way of assuring national security.

In general terms, the ideal of non-provocative defence is 'defensive defence'. This means making the country hard to attack, expensive to invade, and difficult to occupy. It means having strong denial forces which are not themselves suitable for long-range offensive action, and preparing defences in depth, such as taking measures to destroy assets of value to the invader, like transportation routes, before he can use them. Defensive defence means that one's military capability should be confined as much as possible to one's own territory. Such a configuration enables potential aggressors to be threatened only if they attack. It does not pose offensive threats to other countries. The objective of defensive defence is to dampen the destructive operation of both the arms dynamic and the security dilemma as much as possible, while still retaining the security benefits of a strong national defence. In terms of the discussion about deterrence and defence in Chapter 10, the principles of non-provocative defence make it incompatible with deterrence by retaliation, but very much seek to build on the logic deterrence by denial (Galtung, 1984a, pp. 132–5).

Because the re-emergence of non-provocative defence as a concept in strategic debate is recent, it is not yet burdened with the unfavourable historical record of disarmament and arms control. Some of its components do, however, have histories worthy of note. The distinction between offensive and defensive military capability has been debated for much of this century, and a few countries have tried to implement defensive defence as a national security policy.

The distinction between offensive and defensive military capability was raised in Chapter 2. Although it is clear in theory, it has proved notoriously difficult to define in practice. Almost any weapon can be applied for defensive and offensive purposes, although a few, like long-range strategic bombers and missiles, are almost unambiguously offensive. Mobile weapons like tanks are just as suitable for offence as for defence, and even apparently defensive capabilities like fixed fortifications, mines, fighter aircraft and anti-aircraft missiles can be used to support offensive actions. The most striking contemporary manifestation of this problem is SDI. Taken by itself, SDI fits into the non-provocative defence logic of defensive defence. The objective of escaping from MAD by putting up a defence against missiles, and of replacing mutual paralysis of threats of retaliation with the mutual paralysis of impenetrable defensive screens, is undeniably a high technology version of defensive defence. The problem is that if an effective strategic defence is at any point combined with offensive capability, then defence becomes a powerful complement to offence. Strategic defence would increase incentives for first strikes by offering the attacker the possibility of blocking his victim's threat of retaliatory response. The inescapable analogy here is the combination of offensive and defensive capability represented by the sword and the shield. Because of this ambiguity, the notion of purely defensive military capability as an achievable goal needs to be treated with caution.

The practice of defensive defence as a national security policy has some noteworthy history in the record of European neutrals like Sweden, Switzerland, Austria, and Yugoslavia (Fischer, 1982; Johnson, 1973; Roberts, 1976/1986), and in the distinctive post-1945 record of Japan (Momoi, 1981; Satoh, 1982). Sweden and Switzerland both have long-standing policies of neutrality in which the principle of defensive defence plays an important role. Both pursue self-reliant military strategies based on making the country difficult and unrewarding to occupy. Both have had long-term success in staying out of the major hostilities that have raged around them, and neither spends amounts dissimilar to their NATO neighbours on defence in terms of GNP per capita (*Military Balance*, 1984–5, p. 140). The record of Austria and Yugoslavia is much shorter, but within the confines of their post-war experience, both can claim that policies with a large element of defensive defence have successfully supported their national security requirements.

The Japanese case is rather different. Japan is not neutral, but a major ally of the United States. Its commitment to defensive defence arose from the post-war disarmament imposed on it by the United States, and enshrined in Article 9 of the American-inspired 'peace' constitution. Article 9 theoretically forbids Japan from maintaining war potential or using force in its foreign relations. But over the years this absolute prohibition has been steadily reinterpreted as allowing military self-defence. Because Japan is an island state, it has much less of a problem distinguishing between offensive and defensive military capabilities than would be the case for countries with neighbours adjacent on land. Japan has only to deny itself long-range air, missile and naval (other than ASW) capability in order to sustain a credible defensive defence posture. Its defence spending is much less per capita than that of other large Western states. The significance of the Japanese case is considerably muddled by the fact of its open dependence on the American alliance to provide not only nuclear deterrence, but also a major reinforcement component for denial capability. Although it can also be argued that the European neutrals get a substantial free ride on the defence capabilities of NATO, Japan's dependence is so marked and so direct, that its validity as a useful model for non-provocative defence must be doubted.

Despite this rather thin historical record, the logic of non-provocative defence can be examined on the same basis as disarmament and arms control.

## 17.1   THE MILITARY LOGIC

Like arms control, the military logic of non-provocative defence is quite clear about the direction that military policy should take. Unlike disarmament, it lacks a stable model of what its end state looks like. One can easily envisage a considerable range of end conditions that might qualify as defensive defence, and continuous change in technological variables would require such end states to be continuously reassessed. It is not obvious where the boundaries around the idea should be located, especially towards the arms control end of the spectrum, where there is some area of overlap.

On the purest interpretation, a state pursuing non-provocative defence should offer virtually no military threat outside its boundaries while none the less maintaining stiff powers of resistance within them. As Galtung (1984a, pp. 127–32) and Fischer (1984, chs 9, 10, 12, 13) argue, such a policy needs to be based on a range of strategies. Some of these would be political, to do with raising the costs and lowering the incentives for other states to attack. Some would be non-military, along the lines of civilian resistance to occupation (Roberts, 1967; Sharp, 1985). Some would be para-military, in the form of broadly-based militia organizations. And some would be regular military, in terms of professional armed forces designed to undertake specific skilled tasks such as coastal, border, and air defence, demolition, and training. Specialist armed forces would be required to take advantage of advanced technology for defence, such as the many varieties of short-range precision-guided munitions (PGM) that can be used against attacking aircraft, ships, armoured vehicles and even missiles. Much that would go into a defensive defence policy draws from earlier literatures on the strategy of territorial defence (Roberts, 1976/1986).

Galtung argues that nuclear weapons can have no place in defensive defence policies because they are too self-damaging as well as too threatening. It is a moot point whether these anti-nuclear sentiments come more from the strict logic of non-provocative defence or more from the pro-disarmament and anti-nuclear opinion that informs Peace Research. The purist image of non-provocative defence is therefore one with a high level of mass participation in defence policy, creating a defence that extends not only throughout the whole territory of the state, but also throughout its society. Conventional military resistance to attack would begin at the border with static defences like mines, tank traps, fixed fortifications, and professional armed forces (Windass, 1985, ch. 3), and continue through militia resistance and civilian resistance even in the face of a militarily successful occupation.

Towards the arms control end of the non-provocative defence spectrum, the military logic of non-provocative defence overlaps with that of arms control. For example, the current debate in NATO about using increased conventional forces to move away from early reliance on tactical nuclear weapons (TNW), and so reduce some of the problems of ED, fits fairly clearly into the process of moving towards defensive defence. Yet even if that process was taken far enough to enable NATO to adopt a policy of no first use of nuclear weapons, as some advocate (Bundy *et al.*, 1982), what resulted would not necessarily be accepted as defensive defence. Some developments in this context go against the logic of non-provocative defence even though they represent an improvement over nuclear weapons in terms of the degree to which they stimulate the other side's fear of being attacked. An example is the use of new and existing conventional technologies to replace TNW as a means of making strikes against 'follow-on forces' and other military targets quite deep inside the territory of the Warsaw Pact. Much better in non-provocative defence terms would be a shift towards a fortified border backed by defence in depth. This strategic option, however, confronts strong German political resistance, either to hardening the boundary between the two Germanies or to using German territory as the 'depth' for a defensive battleground. Quite where the boundary between non-provocative defence and arms control is under these circumstances is uncertain.

Within this range of possibilities the military logic of non-provocative defence is designed to have its main impact on the action-reaction part of the arms dynamic. Non-provocative defence is aimed primarily at reducing the fear of states that they will be attacked. It does so by lowering the offensive potential of military capabilities that are designed for defence. Non-provocative defence requires complete rejection of the traditional military axiom that 'the best defence is a good offence'. A fully transarmed state should pose virtually no military threat to any state that has no military designs against it. Not only does it deny itself the military means for aggression, but in taking the trouble to design its military forces with such care, it makes a clear political statement that it has no aggressive intentions. In a system where all states pursued defensive defence, the security dilemma would virtually cease to operate. The objective of making all states militarily secure without raising threats to others would be fulfilled. Such a system would be well on the way to achieving disarmament, since no state would have high military requirements for its own security. The logical strength of non-provocative defence in relation to the security dilemma contrasts markedly with disarmament and arms control both of which fail to deal with this key problem convincingly.

Non-provocative defence is aimed at restructuring, but not eliminating, the domestic structure component of the arms dynamic. States pursuing non-provocative defence would still need weapons and armed forces. Since self-reliance is a central theme of non-provocative defence, there might even be some increase in military production in states that now import their weapons. High technology weapons would still be important where they supported defensive missions. Non-provocative defence does not follow disarmament in seeking to resist or ignore the technological imperative. Instead, like arms control, but much more thoroughly, it would try to steer and exploit the technological imperative in pursuit of defensive strength. Arms industries would be turned away from the construction of massive offensive arsenals, and their simpler elements would be dispersed in order to support maximum autonomy for local militias in the supply and servicing of their basic weapons.

In military terms, the main difficulties with non-provocative defence arise in mixed systems, where some states have adopted it, but others still retain traditionally structured armed forces. One of the great advantages of non-provocative defence is that it can be implemented unilaterally. Willing states can take the lead, bypassing the ponderous multilateral negotiations that have so often blocked progress towards disarmament and arms control. Unilateral implementation means that states with defensive defence must coexist with offensively armed neighbours. That condition opens up four problems: first, that such states are vulnerable to bombardment; secondly, that they cannot easily form alliances (Galtung, 1984a, pp. 135–8); thirdly, that they will have little or no capability to defend security interests like shipping routes that may be remote from their national territory; and fourthly, that they cannot use offensive options either to deter attack, or as part of a strategy for expelling an invader. By definition, a state pursuing defensive defence has to accept that if the policy fails as a deterrent, all of the collateral damage of war would occur on its own territory.

Even a state thoroughly equipped for defensive defence could not prevent a nuclear bombardment on itself, though it could mute the effects by extensive civil and SD measures. On a purist interpretation, such a state might even have difficulty dealing with a conventional cross-border bombardment. Acquisition of means for either retaliation or preventive attacks on the bombarding forces would violate the basic principles of defensive defence and reopen the security dilemma. To the extent that the policy of defensive defence is vulnerable to bombardment, the security of states adopting it is dependent on the good behaviour of their neighbours. Such vulnerability may be seen as unacceptable. It may also be seen as an acceptable alternative to the chances of war that exist anyway between offensively armed states, especially if they are nuclear armed. The state adopting defensive defence might calculate that it gains more security from lowering its threat to others (by reducing their incentive to attack) than it loses from the possibility of cold-blooded action by others.

A policy of non-provocative defence, particularly in its transarmament form, makes alliances difficult for two reasons: first, that the principle of self-reliance is inherently contradictory to alliances, and secondly, that a military capability confined to the national territory greatly reduces the scope for mutual military support. Advocates of transarmament tend to take the view that the policy is incompatible with alliances (Fischer, 1984, ch. 11; Galtung, 1984a, pp. 135–8). Those discussing non-provocative defence options in the context of NATO, however, have no difficulty envisaging co-ordinated alliance strategies along defence lines (Windass, 1985). A principle of collective self-reliance could be applied to a group of adjacent transarmed states, the combination of which would produce an enlarged and possibly more coherent area of denial to confront an aggressor. Transarmers wish to avoid any hint of offence that combinations of states might represent to others. Forgoing alliance requires fuller mobilization of one's own resources for defence. It runs the risk of presenting an aggressor with a series of small, if hard, targets that can be picked off one at a time. As with the threat of bombardment, the loss of alliance options opens a breach in the military logic of non-provocative defence if the problem is a highly aggressive opponent. If potential opponents are judged to be basically status quo and not inclined to aggression, then these problems with transarmament are much less significant.

The problem of geographically remote security interests arises most obviously in the case of states that are dependent on trade for economic welfare in general, or on a specific resource like oil or food in particular. Japan, for example, has a keen interest in keeping open the sea straits through and around Indonesia, without which its energy supplies and trade routes would be put at risk. The Soviet Union similarly needs to ensure that its trade can pass through the Turkish Straits and the exits from the Baltic and Mediterranean Seas, and the Sea of Japan. A state pursuing defensive defence would be hard put to deploy military capability relevant to these tasks without violating the principle that its military capability should not be able to threaten other states on their own territory. This problem points to a larger political one, taken up below, which is that non-provocative defence prevents the states adopting it from using military power in the larger pursuit of international order.

The renunciation of offensive options is a problem because it reduces the threats available to support deterrence, and narrows the military choices available to the defender. A highly motivated aggressor might be attracted by a strategy that imposes most of the collateral costs of war on its victim, while leaving itself free of the threat of retaliation. Those responsible for creating and sustaining a policy of defensive defence might also have cause to regret the loss of counteroffensive options. Both the Second World War and the Korean War contain major examples of the use of counteroffensive options to restore the position of the defending side. The loss of offensive capabilities in support of defensive goals has to be weighed against the expected reduction in military threats, and the general damping down of the security dilemma, that would follow the adoption of a non-provocative defence policy.

Abandoning the logic of offensive defence is thus both difficult and potentially costly. It is difficult because the boundary between offensive and defensive weapons is hard to define. It is potentially costly because the loss of offensive options for defence imposes some serious limitations and vulnerabilities on security policy. The crux of debate about the military logic of non-provocative defence is whether these costs are offset by the gain of escape from the security dilemma.

## 17.2   THE ECONOMIC LOGIC

Like arms control, the economic logic of non-provocative defence is weak. Non-provocative defence policies offer a major shift in the character of military strength, but not savings from either the immediate reductions of disarmament or the longer-term lower levels of arms control. For reasons similar to the adverse economic logic of nuclear disarmament, fully-fledged non-provocative defence policies may cost more than the policies they replace. Although the cost of major offensive systems would no longer weigh on the economy, much that replaced them would be expensive. Extensive civil defence measures, coastal and border fortifications, and high technology defensive weapons all require large resource commitments. Non-provocative defence does not offer escape from the technological imperative. This fact, plus the possible commitment to self-reliance in transarmament, requires the maintenance of an arms industry with its own R&D component. The logic of non-provocative defence is primarily military and political. Its concern is to achieve a form of military security that is not self-defeating because of its security dilemma effects. Its priority is towards these goals rather than towards resource savings for alternative social purposes.

## 17.3 THE POLITICAL LOGIC

As with disarmament and arms control, the military logic of non-provocative defence connects strongly to its political logic. For non-provocative defence, however, these links do not raise such serious contradictions as they do for the other two concepts. Non-provocative defence is potentially the most successful of the three approaches in opening a way into the arms-first or politics-first dilemma. It offers the possibility of taking the arms-first route towards reducing tensions without either making oneself excessively vulnerable, or requiring agreement with other states. By damping down the security dilemma, it creates the most promising military conditions imaginable for the resolution of political tensions. It does not require the political transformations of disarmament, and it avoids the dependence of arms control on the prior existence of détente. Because non-provocative defence can be pursued unilaterally, it is politically flexible. It allows any state to take a lead, and so bypasses the problem of adjusting to the pace of the slowest that confronts approaches whose military and political logic depends on multilateral implementation.

Despite this strength, however, non-provocative defence also poses some serious political problems. The most obvious of these applies especially to transarmament, which is that the policy presupposes politically cohesive states in which the government rules primarily by consent rather than by force, and in which domestic security concerns are nor a major component of national security (hereafter, *strong states*) (Buzan, 1983, ch. 2; 1987, ch. 1). Without that precondition, it would be almost impossible to implement the non-military and para-military elements of territorial defence. Where the state is weak in the sense that the government depends substantially on the use or' threat of force to maintain control over a large proportion of its own citizens, a strategy of dispersing weapons and militia training throughout the population would be an invitation to civil war. A population that is bitterly divided politically cannot be expected to offer united social and political resistance to an outside power. In a strong state, the dispersal of military power might be seen as an advantageous bulwark against excessive military or other élite control of politics, but many weak states can only maintain themselves as political entities by holding central control over military power. It is no accident that the idea of transarmament originates in the strong states of northern Europe. Although non-provocative defence in many ways commends itself to the external military security problems of the Third World, only a small minority of the states there have the internal political cohesion necessary to apply it.

Non-provocative defence also poses political problems, though of a wholly different character, for the great powers in the international system. The history of defensive defence policies is mostly that of small states. The requirement for high levels of domestic political cohesion also favours the smaller societies where such cohesion is easier to achieve. Non-provocative defence for great powers raises basic questions about the foundations of order in the international system. As indicated above, a defensively-armed state possesses little military reach. It therefore cannot exercise military power in support of international order outside its own immediate area. If pursued by a great power, such a policy would amount to isolationism, and the abandonment of any global role in the shaping of the international order. The adoption of non-provocative defence by the United States, for example, would pull the props from under the whole security system that now rests on American military power. Whether one views such a development as politically desirable or not, there can be no doubt that it would unleash major forces of change, many of them violent. If other great powers did not follow suit, then opportunities for aggression by them could be created similar to those during the 1930s, when the United States and the Soviet Union both occupied withdrawn and marginal roles in the international security system.

Non-provocative defence by major powers thus has implications for the foundations of international order that are quite different from the issues raised by non-provocative defence for minor powers. This does not mean that non-provocative defence is applicable only to minor powers. It does mean that the pursuit of unilateral non-provocative defence policies by great powers has broad political consequences that need to be thought through. A system in which all the great powers had adopted defensive defence policies might begin to look like a 'mature anarchy' and be highly desirable (Buzan, 1983, pp. 96–101). As with disarmament and arms control, however, where contending great powers pursue different defence doctrines, the possibilities for instability multiply. In this sense, non-provocative defence confronts the same problem as disarmament, arms control, and minimum deterrence: how to achieve uniformity of doctrine amongst rival powers?

In terms of its political appeal, non-provocative defence has not been put to the test like disarmament and arms control. Speculation on its political potential produces a mixed bag of factors. Like arms control, it has the disadvantage of being complicated, of offering no permanent solution and no major cost savings, and of requiring continued engagement with the arms dynamic. It can appeal to disarmament sentiments through its rejection of nuclear weapons. Paradoxically, the transarmament prescription cannot easily appeal to anti-militarist sentiments because of its requirement for mass participation in national defence. The political impact of this requirement for mass participation cuts both ways. On the one hand, it might be seen as militarizing the whole of society (Galtung, 1984a, pp. 135–8). Even though the form of militarization would be decentralized, democratic, and demonstrably defensive, it would still alienate opinion deriving from pacifist sentiments. On the other hand, the idea of national service taps some of the moral and emotional forces – though of course not the same ones – that give political strength to both disarmament and militant nationalism.

The significance of non-provocative defence for the 'green' body of opinion discussed in Chapter 15 is ambiguous. Non-provocative defence, especially transarmament, might appear to favour the anti-state and pro-local autonomy analysis of the greens by decentralizing military power. Yet it only does so within the framework of the state, and therefore accepts the state system that the greens see as being the core of the problem. It is not obvious whether the logic of non-provocative defence could convince green opinion that the state system could be made to work as a force against war.

Under the right circumstances, non-provocative defence might well generate a firm political consensus. It offers a pragmatic synthesis of the idealist vision of escape from the security dilemma, with the realist vision of a world in which old antagonisms and new opportunisms require states to defend their political values with military means. Such a synthesis requires a politically sophisticated population to embrace it, as does a security policy based on the logic of defensive defence. For that reason, and also because of the problems it raises for great powers, weak states, and states facing aggressive neighbours, non-provocative defence is unfortunately not likely to find more than limited application within the foreseeable future.

# 18 Summary and Conclusions

Parts I to III sketched what might be called the natural dialectic between armaments and the military security of states. The anarchic political structure of the international system was the constant background condition that both set the historical context for this discussion and provided its political framework. Against that background the evolution and diffusion of military technology were outlined; the arms dynamic that resulted from this development was defined and explored; and the contemporary expression of the whole process in the strategy of deterrence was explained in some detail.

When viewed as a whole, the literature of Strategic Studies displays a persistent uncertainty about what constitutes the central problem in its subject matter. From one perspective, the problem was the security of states in the anarchy. The issue was how to adjust military strategy to meet that end in an environment dominated by continuous and often quite radical technological and political change. From another perspective, the problem was increasingly the whole system of military rivalry itself. In this context the issue was how to ensure human survival in an environment dominated by immense powers of destruction. The opposition was not other states, but a system seemingly possessed of an autonomous momentum of its own that was beyond the range of the only political structures capable of addressing it. These two problems cannot be separated because their causes and their solutions are intertwined. The concept of deterrence offers the possibility of a strategic solution to both: in other words a solution in terms of military means. Yet deterrence itself raises enough doubts to support the view that a good part of the problem *is* military means. Solutions in terms of such means would simply recreate the problem in new forms.

Part IV has examined this idea of military means as a problem in itself, and looked at the range of responses to it. From the discussion in the preceding three chapters it is clear that none of the main responses is by itself likely to remove or solve the problem within the foreseeable future. All of them have serious logical flaws. Those in which the logical flaws are least serious are also the least ambitious and/or have weak political foundations.

Somewhat firmer political and logical ground can be found by combining approaches that cannot be made to work by themselves. A strategy based on territorial defence plus minimum nuclear deterrence, for example, would contain elements of disarmament (disbanding offensive conventional forces and counterforce nuclear ones), non-provocative defence (unilateral action, preparing defensive defence in depth), and arms control (embracing the logic of MAD as doctrine, seeking agreements to restrain force levels and types). Such a strategy would inevitably raise contradictions of basic principles. The element of minimum deterrence would clash with the renunciation of offensive capability central to non-provocative defence, and the pursuit of military solutions would clash with the ultimate principle of disarmament. These clashes could be muted by emphasizing the purely reactive nature of minimum deterrence forces – although fundamentally offensive in character, nuclear forces that are purely countervalue in capability offer their possessor no incentives to make first strikes. The principle that offensive forces should be configured in purely reactive modes goes some way to reconciling offensive capability with defensive intentions. The gain from such a combination would be the resolution of some key logical flaws in the individual approaches. Territorial defence plus minimum deterrence would reduce the vulnerability of non-provocative defence to bombardment, and address the difficulty that salami tactics pose for minimum deterrence. It is not impossible to imagine a strategy along these lines being attractive to stable, powerful and deeply status quo societies. Japan, or a more integrated Western Europe, might adopt it if they found themselves moving away from their present levels of defence dependence on the United States. Its more general adoption would raise problems not only about nuclear proliferation, but also about the role of great powers in shaping and maintaining international order.

What makes the problem of military means so intractable is the immovability of the two conditions on which it rests: the anarchic political structure of the international system; and the relentlessly expanding human knowledge that drives the technological imperative (Buzan, 1984b). So long as both of these conditions exist, any attempt to resolve the problem will confront the dilemma that military means are not only a problem in themselves, but also a problem in the hands of others. These two aspects of the problem are inseparable, and it is their combination that makes resolution so difficult. The intellectual response of disarmament to this dilemma is to try to escape from it by measures radical enough to break through the constraining conditions. That of arms control and non-provocative defence is to try to think it through in strategic terms, the former working closely within the logic of nuclear deterrence, the latter half within it and half outside and against it. Despite their quite opposite approaches to strategy, both arms control and disarmament run into the same logical dead end of requiring international political conditions that they cannot in themselves create. Except for the great powers, the logic of non-provocative defence is stronger on the international political front, but requires domestic political conditions that are difficult to meet in more than a few countries.

Although all three responses confront basic political problems, the differences between them in their relationship to strategic thinking create striking differences in their political appeal. Because arms control and non-provocative defence accept the conceptual framework of strategy, they sink or swim according to their degree of success within it. Disarmament remains perennially buoyant regardless of its practical failure in terms of strategic logic because it is also a way of rejecting the strategic framework as a whole. When the attempt to think through the strategic impasse in its own terms fails, disarmament is always there as a moral redoubt from which to point out that the dangers posed by the modern military system are unacceptable. In this role, disarmament has to be judged more as a way of making a political statement than as a serious proposal for what is to be done.

In every major approach, there is always a point at which political logic begins to dominate the problems of military means. This occurs whether the problem is military means in the hands of others, as in the arms dynamic and deterrence, or military means in themselves, as in disarmament, arms control and non-provocative defence. Collectively, those points define part of the boundary between Strategic Studies and International Relations. This boundary is in fact more an area of overlap than a strict dividing line. The political structure of anarchy and the accumulation of military power by states interact in a pattern of mutual reinforcement. The arms dynamic cannot be understood apart from the structure of anarchy, and the nature of political relations within anarchy cannot be understood apart from the role that the threat and use of force plays in them.

One of the difficulties in thinking about the problem of military means is the need to work across this academic boundary. The search for solutions, whether within or outside the strategic framework, cannot confine itself to the relatively tidy world of military factors. It must inevitably engage itself with the much broader, more complex, and messier world of international politics. This insight explains why authors as diverse in opinion as Colin Gray and Hedley Bull insist that there needs to be closer contact between Strategic Studies and International Relations (Bull, 1981, pp. 279–80; Gray, 1982b, ch. 12). Extending one's vision into the political dimension unfortunately often wins intellectual gain only at the cost of practical loss. Arms control and disarmament look much more convincing as solutions when considered only in terms of military logic than they do in the full context of international politics. The broader view gives a more complete and accurate picture of the problem, but it also exposes the massive impediments that block all existing hopes for quick solutions.

In the absence of comprehensive solutions we are left living in the *laissez-faire* 'market' of the balance of power. In this system states bid the military price of national security up or down according to the intensity with which they compete or co-operate with each other. The market image for the balance of power is appropriate. Many independent and incremental decisions interact to determine the level of military power necessary to ensure national security, just as they determine the market value of goods in the economy. Both systems have built-in regulators, or 'invisible hands', that work to prevent open-ended escalations, but these mechanisms are not always reliable, and both systems also harbour disruptive forces strong enough to overcome them. Unregulated markets of both types are therefore subject to periods of disorder: war in the one case and depression in the other.

In both cases, regulatory intervention in the market is a difficult strategy to play. This difficulty is increased when no single centre of controlling political authority is large enough to encompass the market, and regulation must therefore be pursued within the fragmented political structure of anarchy. The free play of market forces limits the extent to which any single actor can take unilateral actions without placing its security or its welfare at risk. Unilateral disarmament or arms control measures, if unreciprocated, weaken the state's ability to resist aggressive pressures. Even non-provocative defence, which attempts to maximize the scope for constructive unilateral action, cannot escape the eventual need for reciprocation or co-operation.

Because large numbers of interacting factors drive the dynamic of the market, regulation requires control over a complex, flexible, and unpredictable set of conditions. If regulation is too static, then the market will adapt around it to nullify its effect. This happened to OPEC in the mid-1980s in terms of the supply and price of oil. Intervention creates distortion in the market. Maintaining the desired effect of an intervention usually leads to the need for more intervention in order to cope with market responses to the distortion. In the housing market, for example, rent controls can be used as an intervention intended to give security and fair prices to renters. In practice, however, their use quickly leads to a drying up of properties for rent, and so to the demand for the larger intervention of public housing. Likewise, disarmament leads to increasing requirements for world government, and arms control leads to the pursuit of broader and more elusive goals like parity and détente.

Neither regulation nor *laissez-faire* are foolproof ways to avoid difficulty and danger. *Laissez-faire* is by definition easier to implement, and may win on that basis alone. Yet there is still an important question of choice that hinges on the balance of costs and dangers between the two alternatives. Regulation risks not only failure, which is merely a return to *laissez-faire*, but also backlash and counterproductive effect. Public housing achieved fair rents, but only at the cost of creating large public slums, of inflicting architectural nightmares on working-class communities ill-equipped to cope with them, of creating extensive rigidities in the labour market by making it hard for people in public housing to move, and of distorting local electoral politics by creating a pool of voters directly dependent on local government. It is a moot point whether the gains of regulation in this market justify its costs.

The same problem can be seen in the international security 'market'. The collapse of arms control in the late 1970s not only returned the situation to *laissez faire*, but actually added fuel to the deterioration of relations that caused it. Even though arms control never achieved more than marginal effects on the arms dynamic, its breakdown unleashed an intense catch-up round of arms racing and political hostility. The costs of that reaction in terms of the danger of war have to be weighed against the gains of the heyday period of arms control and détente between 1963 and 1979, when the risk of war was presumably lowered. There are no accurate measures for the variations in the probability of war that resulted from the rise and fall of arms control. It is by no means obvious that the over-all balance tips in favour of the regulatory effort. The same could be said of the non-proliferation regime, though the case here is hypothetical. So long as the regime lasts, it has every appearance of being a useful restraint. If it ever cracks, the rush to acquire nuclear weapons may lead to a period of considerable instability that would not have occurred in such a concentrated way without the attempt to regulate. The case of disarmament is also hypothetical, but the implications are even clearer than for arms control. If an extensive disarmament regime broke down because of inadequate verification and suspicions of cheating, the resultant period of rearmament racing would be extremely dangerous. Even if the logic of regulation measures led to world government, there would be new dangers of global tyranny, global civil war, and global mismanagement.

If regulation leads to dangers of failure, backlash and unanticipated negative side-effects, *laissez-faire* is a surrender to market dynamics that have a long record of periodic collapse. The attempt to regulate at least acknowledges that security is now interdependent, and that the problem of modern military means creates real common dangers. The narrow pursuit of national security as a first priority discounts these new facts, and appears to open the way to dangerous and self-defeating escalations of the arms dynamic. Despite its dangers, *laissez-faire* shares with disarmament the advantage of a long-standing political appeal. The idea of national security through armed strength is simple, direct, and taps the emotional sentiments of nationalism. It can still command a political majority in most countries, including the United States. Perhaps only in Western Europe and Japan, where earlier wars resulting from it led to exhaustion, huge destruction, loss of world power, and in many cases defeat and occupation, is there a deep popular resistance to the lure of national military power. The domestic political appeal of national power is one reason why an unregulated system pushes constantly against the restraints of resource limitations and fear that work to prevent the slide to war. Although a *laissez-faire* system is likely to operate more evenly, in the sense of avoiding the backlash caused by the failure of a regulatory distortion, it does not, on past record, offer long-term hope for stability.

The merits of regulation versus *laissez-faire* in the international security 'market' are an interesting topic for debate. There are strong cases to be made for and against both sides. The reality of the situation, however, is that *laissez-faire* dominates. It does so because, under conditions of anarchy, it is easier than regulation, and because the problems attendant on the main proposals for regulation make them unconvincing alternatives. These circumstances seem likely to remain in force for many decades at least. They raise the vital question of whether the traditional record of *laissez-faire* is of any relevance in judging its present and future. If it is, then we are in the 'very serious and intractable' box of Table 14.1, with the problem of military means threatening to obliterate human civilization. Yet it is those military means themselves that offer the prime reason for rejecting the view that the past record of the balance of power is a guide to its future. By placing the issue of human survival at the centre of military affairs, the destructive power of modern military means has made security interdependence more obvious and more compelling than ever before. Has this development transformed the pattern of relations under a *laissez-faire* balance of power, or does the balance still operate in the old way but with a vastly higher risk of catastrophe attached to its periodic breakdowns?

Opinion on this question is divided. There is virtually no disagreement that nuclear weapons have greatly raised the dangers attendant on *any* war fought amongst the great powers, but there is considerable difference on the significance of that fact. Some people see the impact of nuclear weapons on the international system as transformational. The essence of the transformational view rests on the impact that a greatly amplified fear of war has on the behaviour of states (Jervis, 1984, pp. 12–15; Tuchman, 1984, p. 136). The transformational view therefore has obvious connections to the logic of existential deterrence. The strongest form of this view is that the very high fear of war constitutes a virtually absolute block on the resort to war amongst the great powers. There is a weaker view that acknowledges the central role of fear, does not see it as sufficient to make war impossible, but does see it as injecting a common interest in survival into the international system. That common interest itself is seen as providing a new political basis for more co-operative behaviour within the framework of anarchy (Report of the Independent Commission, 1982; Tuchman, 1984, p. 140).

The opposite view acknowledges that nuclear weapons have added a significant element of fear into international relations, but does not see this element as transformational. Hedley Bull argued this point on the grounds that military factors of any sort have a limited impact on international relations, and that there was no reason to think that nuclear weapons had changed the basic operation of the balance of power (Bull, 1961, pp. 8–12, 46). Others see the war-preventing aspect of nuclear weapons as offset by the dangers of war that nuclear weapons themselves introduce, and so conclude against the transformation thesis (Gilpin, 1972; 1981, pp. 213–19). Views on the impact of military technology on international relations are mixed, with some arguing that it is historically just one factor amongst many (Brodie, 1976), and others giving it a more central role (Halle, 1984, pp. 3–5, 75–92, 103–16; Pearton, 1982, pp. 254–8).

This difference of opinion on the impact of nuclear weapons on international relations cannot be resolved empirically. In part it appears to stem from the same difficulty posed by the level of analysis problem that was surveyed in Chapter 9. Does one seek explanations for the phenomena of international relations at the level of individuals? Or in the nature of states? Or in the structure of the international system as a whole?

Those who argue for transformation are finding their explanations at the levels of individuals and states, which is where the factor of fear operates most strongly. Nuclear weapons have transformed the environment within which individuals and states behave by attaching a massive element of fear to behaviours leading towards war amongst the major powers. Those behaviours did not previously arouse fear as a dominant emotional and rational response on anything like the same scale, though the growth of fear can clearly be traced back to the experience of the First World War in Europe. The transformation thesis rests on the view that pervasive terror of the consequences of war causes changes in the whole spectrum of ways in which states relate to each other. In addition to the restraints posed by the rational calculations of deterrence logic, populations in the nuclear powers can no longer be roused to enthusiasm for central wars, and politicians in those powers cannot safely raise the probability of war as a means of strengthening their domestic position. Attitudes of social Darwinism, in which top nations assert dominance by fighting wars, are simply not politically supportable in the nuclear age. Great powers still compete with each other militarily, but they do so within a framework of deterrence, and with no desire or intention to go to war.

Those who argue against transformation find their explanations more on the level of the political structure of the international system, which has not been changed by nuclear weapons. The international anarchy is still firmly in place, with all its historical baggage of dividedness and animosity. States still relate to each other through the mechanism of the balance of power, and great powers still compete with each other for dominance over the ordering of global economic and political relations. Military power is still essential to the security of states. Competitive accumulations of military power still generate arms racing and the security dilemma. In other words, both ambition and miscalculation are still available as paths to war. Nuclear weapons have introduced some constraints into this system, as well as some opportunities, but they have not altered its basic political structure, which is where the problem of war has its roots.

Because these analyses are on different levels, there is no clear ground for choice between them. Both are right in their own terms, leaving us with a difficult assessment about which one dominates the behaviour of states. If the transformationalists are right, then the known hazards of living in a *laissez-faire* security system may well be less than those raised by attempts to implement ambitious, but fundamentally flawed schemes for intervention like disarmament. Such schemes require political resources within and between states that do not exist, and that cannot obviously or easily be created. Experiments with less ambitious interventions like arms control and non-provocative defence can do little harm and perhaps considerable good.

In this perspective, it is nuclear weapons themselves that are the key element in maintaining an international security system which is virtually free from the danger of intentional major wars among the great powers. Because of the nuclear constraints on war, it is not all that difficult for great powers to preserve their military security. The beauty of nuclear weapons in this respect is that they work within the rather limited framework of political resources that is currently available in the international system. Only because of nuclear weapons does fear restrain the resort to war. Only because of nuclear weapons does the interdependence of security become so obvious that national security and international security can be pursued simultaneously. And only because of nuclear weapons can survival serve as the basis for a new politics of common security among states. In the full transformationalist view, nuclear weapons are the essential foundation on which international security can be built in a system with a durable anarchic political structure.

If the transformationalists are wrong, then the risks of living in a *laissez-faire* security system are high, and great powers will find it difficult to guarantee their military security. One's responses to this situation can take either of two highly contrasting routes. One can take the view that national security needs to be pursued at all costs, since it is only military power that offer any hope of security at all. This is the route of many in the 'difficult' school of deterrence. Or one can take the view that there is a great need to find workable forms of intervention, and perhaps even to risk the hazards of intervention concepts with known flaws, on the grounds that those flaws are less worrying than the dangers attendant upon *laissez-faire*. In this view, national security and international security are more opposites than complements, and nuclear weapons are a central problem because of the ever-present risk that they will be used. The destructive capacity of military technology has outgrown the political system it was intended to serve, but in doing so it has not generated the means to reconfigure world politics. The danger is that a widening gap between sophisticated and fast-developing technological systems, and primitive, slow-developing political ones, will trigger disaster. In a curious way, therefore, the hawks and the disarmers share a basic analysis of the situation, even though they draw entirely opposite conclusions about what response is most appropriate.

Strategic Studies embraces these controversies. Because strategic logic encompasses both *laissez-faire* and interventionist approaches, much of the debate takes place in strategic terms. Some of its practitioners take clear positions one way or the other. Many accept that there are no clear answers and that both sides of the case have merit. The impact of the transformation question on the field is enormous, and explains why strategic thinking is so preoccupied with nuclear weapons. There are some strategic verities that cross the divide between the pre-nuclear and nuclear ages (Gray, 1977), and for the majority of the world's countries stategic problems still come primarily in the traditional terms of warfighting with conventional weapons. Yet there can be no doubt that nuclear weapons have radically changed the emphasis of strategic thinking regardless of what impact they have or have not had on the international system. Concepts like deterrence and arms control have largely evolved because of nuclear weapons. They have substantially absorbed or redefined more long-standing concepts like arms racing and disarmament. Even non-provocative defence is a response to the problem of nuclear weapons. The fascination with whether nuclear weapons have in fact transformed the conditions of strategy and international relations is both understandable and appropriate. It explains why so much of strategic thinking is focused on the nuclear powers, and why nuclear proliferation attracts such disproportionate attention within the wider subject of the spread of military capability.

Strategic Studies cannot provide absolute answers to the broad questions raised here. It can, and has, made major contributions to the debate about them. It is easy, and in some senses appropriate, to criticize strategic thinking for being part of the problem of military means, especially when strategic concepts begin to shape the reality that they purport merely to describe. Such criticism, however, itself runs the danger of generating an unhelpful extreme position, and it cannot escape the realities that generate the strategic approach. What needs to be recognized is that strategic thinking is a part, and only a part, of the necessary response to living with the conditions of anarchy and the arms dynamic. The other part of the response lies in the broader study of the political and economic dynamics of the international system. If the over-all problem is conflict and war, then many of the causes, and much of the cure, must lie in the political economy of the international system.

Military factors, in other words, are not the only ones that determine the conditions of international relations. Political developments such as a move from a bipolar to a multipolar structure of great power relations, or the evolution of a superpower consensus on some basic principles of system management, would re-orientate the strategic environment. Some such developments would mute the strategic problem by damping down its political causes, while others would exacerbate it. Likewise, the development of a world economy which makes the welfare, or lack of it, of each country ever more obviously dependent on that of others, also has large implications for the stragic environment. As economic interdependence grows, it not only adds to the cost of war, but also provides instruments of leverage other than force with which states can try to influence each other's behaviour. If the world economy became less integrated and more competitive in a mercantilist sense, then economic causes of conflict would feed into the strategic equation (Buzan, 1984a).

It is true that the durability of the anarchic system of states sets the basic condition for strategic thinking. Anarchy not only provides the framework for the arms dynamic, but also gives the technological imperative its military significance for international relations. It is also true that the impediments to fundamental reform of the international political structure are immense. Nevertheless, the basic condition of anarchy encompasses a huge range of political possibilities (Buzan, 1984b). Although anarchies may be primitive and conflictual, they may also be well-developed, mature, and stable. There is consequently as much scope in the political economy side of international relations as there is in its strategic side for addressing the problems of war and peace. These larger problems simply cannot be adequately addressed within the constricted framework of a single field. To do so risks distortions of analysis so grave as to generate more misunderstanding than insight. It is for this reason that Strategic Studies and International Relations must not allow their debates to become detached from each other.

At present there are no signs – other than the ever-present possibility of a nuclear war – that any developments will remove, or even greatly alleviate, the problem of strategy. In the meantime – and this meantime is likely to be an extended period – the political pressures of anarchy, and the fruitfulness of technological innovation, will create a demand for strategic thinking. Some of the main threads of that thinking will be extensions of the trends reviewed here. Others will be new, as developments in politics and technology reshape the strategic potential of the system. As we have seen, there is room within the strategic debate for diverse and contending points of view. Strategic thinking lends itself just as easily to the logic of security interdependence as it does to the logic of national power. The emergence of interest in non-provocative defence demonstrates the existence of strategists willing to begin moving down that unorthodox, but important, path.

Strategic thinking needs to be informed by a close understanding of the political context in which it is applied. The major strategic concepts all have substantial political content, and it is that content which differentiates strategic concepts like arms racing, deterrence, arms control, disarmament and non-provocative defence, from strictly military concepts like MAD, counterforce, denial, strategic defence, and parity. The principal danger of strategic thinking is that preoccupation with technological issues leads one to start treating broad strategic concepts as if they were narrow military ones. To lose sight of the political domain is to lose sight not only of the purpose of strategy, but also of its limits. One can conclude that there is plenty of strategic thinking left to do, and plenty of good reasons for doing it.

# Bibliography

ALBRECHT, U.; ERNST, D.; LOCK, P. and WULF, H. (1975) 'Militarization, Arms Transfer and Arms Production in Peripheral Countries', *Journal of Peace Research*, XXII, 195–212.

ALLISON, GRAHAM and MORRIS, FREDERIC (1975) 'Armaments and Arms Control: Exploring the Determinants of Military Weapons', *Daedalus*, CIV, 99–129.

ARENDT, HANNAH (1969) *On Violence* (New York: Harcourt Brace & World).

ARNETT, R. L. (1981) 'Soviet Attitudes Towards Nuclear War: Do They Really Think They Can Win?', in JOHN BAYLIS and GERRY SEGAL (eds) *Soviet Strategy* (London: Croom Helm).

ART, ROBERT J. (1980) 'To What Ends Military Power?' *International Security*, IV, 3–35.

ART, ROBERT J. and WALTZ, KENNETH N. (1971) 'Technology, Strategy, and the Uses of Force', in ART and WALTZ (eds) *The Use of Force* (Boston: Little Brown).

AYOOB, MOHAMMED (1980) *Conflict and Intervention in the Third World* (London: Croom Helm).

BALL, DESMOND (1983) *Targeting for Strategic Deterrence*, Adelphi Paper 185 (London: IISS).

BAUGH, WILLIAM H. (1984) *The Politics of the Nuclear Balance* (New York: Longman).

BAYLIS, JOHN (1981) *Anglo-American Defence Relations 1939–80: The Special Relationship* (London: Macmillan).

BAYLIS, JOHN; BOOTH, KEN; GARNETT, JOHN and WILLIAMS, PHIL (1975) *Contemporary Strategy: Theories and Policies* (London: Croom Helm).

BEATON, LEONARD (1966) *Must the Bomb Spread?* (Harmondsworth: Penguin).

BEAUFRE, ANDRE (1965) *An Introduction to Strategy* (London: Faber & Faber).

BELLANY, IAN (1975) 'The Richardson Theory of "Arms Races": Themes and Variations', *British Journal of International Studies*, I, 119–30.

BENOIT, EMILE (1973) *Defence and Economic Growth in Developing Countries* (Lexington: Lexington Books).

BERGHAHN, VOLKER (1973) *Germany and the Approach of War in 1914* (London: Macmillan).

BETTS, R. K. (1979) 'A Diplomatic Bomb for South Africa', *International Security*, IV, 91–115.

BLECHMAN, BARRY (1980) 'Do Negotiated Arms Limitations Have a Future?' *Foreign Affairs*, LIX, 102–25.

BLOMLEY, PETER (1984) 'The Arms Trade and Arms Conversion', in J. O'CONNOR HOWE (ed.) *Armed Peace* (London: Macmillan).

BOOTH, KEN (1979) *Strategy and Ethnocentrism* (London: Croom Helm).
BOUTWELL JEFFREY D.; DOTY, PAUL and TREVERTON, GREGORY F. (eds) (1985) *The Nuclear Confrontation in Europe* (London: Croom Helm).
BRACKEN, PAUL (1983) *The Command and Control of Nuclear Forces* (New Haven: Yale University Press).
BRAMSON, LEON and GEOTHALS, GEORGE W. (eds) (1968) *War: Studies from Psychology, Sociology, Anthropology* (New York: Basic Books).
BRECHER, MICHAEL (ed.) (1979) *Studies in Crisis Behavior* (New Brunswick, N.J.: Transaction Books).
BRENNAN, D. G. (1972) 'Some Remarks on Multipolar Nuclear Strategy', in R. ROSECRANCE (ed.) *The Future of the International Strategic System* (San Francisco: Chandler).
BRODIE, BERNARD (1946) *The Absolute Weapon: Atomic Power and World Order* (New York: Harcourt Brace).
BRODIE, BERNARD (1976) 'Technological Change, Strategic Doctrine, and Political Outcomes', in KLAUS KNORR (ed.) *Historical Dimensions of National Security Problems* (Lawrence: University Press of Kansas).
BRODIE, BERNARD (1978) 'The Development of Nuclear Strategy', *International Security*, II, 65–83.
BRODIE, BERNARD and BRODIE, FAWN M. (1973) *From Crossbow to H-Bomb* (Bloomington: Indiana University Press).
BROOKS, HARVEY (1975) 'The Military Innovation System and the Qualitative Arms Race', *Daedalus*, CIV, 75–98.
BROWN, HAROLD and DAVIS, LYNN E. (1984) 'Nuclear Arms Control: Where do we Stand?' *Survival*, XXVI, 146–55.
BROWN, NEVILLE (1977) *The Future Global Challenge: A Predictive Study of World Security, 1977–1990* (London: Royal United Services Institute).
BROWN, T. A. (1973) 'What is an Arms Race?' *CACFP Seminar Paper 35*.
BRUBAKER, E. R. (1973) 'Economic Models of Arms Races', *Journal of Conflict Resolution*, XVII, 187–205.
BRZOSKA, MICHAEL and OHLSON, THOMAS (1986) *Arms Production in the Third World* (London: Taylor & Francis, for Stockholm International Peace Research Institute).
BULL, HEDLEY (1961) *The Control of the Arms Race* (London: Weidenfeld & Nicolson).
BULL, HEDLEY (1968) 'Strategic Studies and its Critics', *World Politics*, II, 593–605.
BULL, HEDLEY (1970) 'Disarmament and the International System', in JOHN GARNETT (ed.) *Theories of Peace and Security* (London: Macmillan).
BULL, HEDLEY (1977) *The Anarchical Society* (London: Macmillan).
BULL, HEDLEY (1980) 'Future Conditions of Strategic Deterrence', in *The Future of Strategic Deterrence: Part I*, Adelphi Paper 160 (London: IISS).

BULL, HEDLEY (1981) 'Of Means and Ends', in ROBERT O'NEILL and D. M. HORNER (eds), *New Directions in Strategic Thinking* (London: Allen & Unwin).

BULL, HEDLEY (1983) 'European Self-Reliance and the Reform of NATO', *Foreign Affairs*, LXI, 874–92.

BUNDY, MCGEORGE (1984) 'Existential Deterrence and its Consequences', in DOUGLAS MACLEAN (ed.) *The Security Gamble: Deterrence Dilemmas in the Nuclear Age* (Totawa: Rowman & Allanheld).

BUNDY, MCGEORGE; KENNAN, GEORGE F.; MCNAMARA ROBERT S. and SMITH, GERARD K. (1982) 'Nuclear Weapons and the Atlantic Alliance', *Foreign Affairs*, LX, 753–68.

BUPP, I. C. (1981) 'The Actual Growth and Probable Future of the Worldwide Nuclear Industry', *International Organization*, XXXV, 59–76.

BURN, DUNCAN (1978) *Nuclear Power and the Energy Crisis* (London: Macmillan).

BURNS, ARTHUR LEE (1965) 'Must Strategy and Conscience be Disjoined?' *World Politics*, XVII, 687–702.

BURTON, JOHN W. (1972) *World Society* (Cambridge: Cambridge University Press).

BURTON, JOHN (1984) *Global Conflict: The Domestic Sources of International Crisis* (Brighton: Wheatsheaf).

BUSCH, P. A. (1970) 'Mathematical Models of Arms Races', in BRUCE RUSSETT, *What Price Vigilance?* (New Haven: Yale University Press).

BUZAN, BARRY (1981) 'Change and Insecurity: a Critique of Strategic Studies', in BARRY BUZAN and R. J. BARRY JONES (eds) *Change and the Study of International Relations* (London: Frances Pinter).

BUZAN, BARRY (1983) *People, States and Fear: the National Security Problem in International Relations* (Brighton: Harvester).

BUZAN, BARRY (1984a) 'Economic Structure and International Security: the Limits of the Liberal Case', *International Organization*, XXVIII, 597–624.

BUZAN, BARRY (1984b) 'Peace, Power, and Security: Contending Concepts in the Study of International Relations', *Journal of Peace Research*, XXI, 109–25.

BUZAN, BARRY (1986) 'Nuclear Weapons and the Causes of War', Unit 9, Course U235, *Nuclear Weapons: inquiry, analysis and debate* (Milton Keynes: Open University Press).

BUZAN, BARRY (1987) 'People, States and Fear: The National Security Problem in the Third World', in EDWARD AZAR and CHUNG-IN MOON (eds) *Third World National Security: Concepts, Issues and Implications* (Lexington: University of Kentucky Press).

BUZAN, BARRY and RIZVI GOWHER *et al.* (1986) *South Asian Insecurity and the Great Powers* (London: Macmillan).

BYERS, ROD (ed.) (1985) *Deterrence in the 1980s: Crisis and Dilemma* (London: Croom Helm).

CALVOCORESSI, PETER (1984) 'Nuclear Weapons in the Service of Man', *Review of International Studies*, X, 89–101.

CAMILLERI, J. A. (1977) 'The Myth of the Peaceful Atom', *Millennium*, 6:2, 111–27.

CANNIZZO, CINDY (1980) *The Gun Merchants: Politics and Policies of the Major Arms Suppliers* (Oxford: Pergamon).

CAPPELEN, ADNE; GLEDITSCH, NILS PETTER and BJERKHOLT, OLAV (1984) 'Military Spending and Economic Growth in the OECD Countries', *Journal of Peace Research*, XXI, 361–73.

CARR, E. H. (1946, 1981) *The Twenty Years Crisis*, 2nd edn (London: Macmillan).

CHOUCRI, NAZLI and NORTH, ROBERT (1975) *Nations in Conflict: National Growth and International Violence* (San Francisco: Freeman).

CLAUSEWITZ, CARL VON (1968) *On War* (Harmondsworth: Penguin).

COMMITTEE ON INTERNATIONAL SECURITY AND ARMS CONTROL (National Academy of Sciences) (1985) *Nuclear Arms Control: Background and Issues* (Washington: National Academy Press).

CORDESMAN, ANTHONY H. (1982) *Deterrence in the 1980s: American Strategic Forces and Extended Deterrence*, Adelphi Paper 175 (London: IISS).

CRAIG, GORDON A. and GEORGE, ALEXANDER L. (1983) *Force and Statecraft: Diplomatic Problems of Our Time* (Oxford: Oxford University Press).

DAHLITZ, JULIE (1984) *Nuclear Arms Control* (London: Allen & Unwin).

DANIEL, DONALD C. (1986) *Anti-Submarine Warfare and Superpower Strategic Stability* (Basingstoke: Macmillan).

DEDRING, J. (1976) *Recent Advances in Peace and Conflict Research* (Beverly Hills: Sage).

DEUTSCH, KARL W. and SINGER, J. DAVID (1964) 'Multipolar Power Systems and International Stability', *World Politics*, XVI, 390–406.

DIAGRAM GROUP (1980) *Weapons* (London: Macmillan).

DIEHL, PAUL F. (1983) 'Arms Races and Escalation: A Closer Look', *Journal of Peace Research*, XX, 205–12.

DORAN, CHARLES F. (1983) 'War and Power Dynamics: Economic Underpinnings', *International Studies Quarterly*, XXVII, 419–41.

DORIAN, T. F. and SPECTOR, L. S. (1981) 'Covert Nuclear Trade and the International Non-proliferation Regime', *Journal of International Affairs*, XXXV, 29–68.

DRELL, SIDNEY; FARLEY, P. J. and HOLLOWAY, DAVID (1984) 'Preserving the ABM Treaty: A Critique of the Reagan Defence Initiative', *International Security*, IX, 51–91.

DROR, YEHEZKEL (1980) 'Nuclear Weapons in Third World Conflict', in *The Future of Strategic Deterrence: Part II*, Adelphi Paper 161 (London: IISS).

DUNN, LEWIS (1982) *Controlling the Bomb – Nuclear Proliferation in the 1980s* (New Haven: Yale University Press).

EDMONDS, JOHN (1984) 'Proliferation and Test Bans', in J. O'CONNOR HOWE (ed.) *Armed Peace* (London: Macmillan).

ENTHOVEN, ALAIN C. and SMITH, K. WAYNE (1971) *How Much is Enough?* (New York: Harper & Row).

ERMARTH, FRITZ W. (1978) 'Contrasts in American and Soviet Strategic Thought', *International Security*, III, 138–55.

EVANS, CAROL (1986) 'Reappraising Third-World Arms Production', *Survival*, XXVIII, 99–118.

FALK, RICHARD and BARNET, RICHARD (1965) *Security in Disarmament* (Princeton: Princeton University Press).

FELDMAN, SHAI (1982) 'The Bombing of Osirak Revisited', *International Security*, VII, 114–42.

FEWTRELL, DAVID (1983) *The Soviet Economic Crisis: Prospects for the Military and the Consumer*, Adelphi Paper 186 (London: IISS).

FISCHER, DIETRICH (1982) 'Invulnerability Without Threat: The Swiss Concept of General Defence', *Journal of Peace Research*, XIX, 205–25.

FISCHER, DIETRICH (1984) *Preventing War: Towards a Realistic Strategy for Peace in the Nuclear Age* (London: Croom Helm).

FREEDMAN, LAWRENCE (1975) 'Israel's Nuclear Policy', *Survival*, XVII, 114–20.

FREEDMAN, LAWRENCE (1980a) 'The Rationale for Medium-sized Deterrence Forces', in *The Future of Strategic Deterrence: Part I*, Adelphi Paper 160 (London: IISS).

FREEDMAN, LAWRENCE (1980b) *Britain and Nuclear Weapons* (London: Macmillan).

FREEDMAN, LAWRENCE (1981) *The Evolution of Nuclear Strategy* (London: Macmillan).

FREEDMAN, LAWRENCE (1982) 'Arms Control: the Possibility of a Second Coming', in LAWRENCE HAGEN (ed.) *The Crisis in Western Security* (London: Croom Helm).

FREEDMAN, LAWRENCE (1984a) 'Indignation, Influence and Strategic Studies', *International Affairs*, LX, 207–19.

FREEDMAN, LAWRENCE (1984b) 'Strategic Arms Control', in J. O'CONNOR HOWE (ed.) *Armed Peace* (London: Macmillan).

FREEDMAN, LAWRENCE (1986) *Arms Control in Europe*, revised edn (London: Routledge & Kegan Paul).

GALL, N. (1976) 'Atoms for Brazil, Dangers for All', *Foreign Policy*, XXIII, 155–201.

GALTUNG, JOHAN (1964) 'A Structural Theory of Aggression', *Journal of Peace Research*, I, 95–119.

GALTUNG, JOHAN (1984a) 'Transarmament: From Offensive to Defensive Defense', *Journal of Peace Research*, XXI, 127–39.

GALTUNG, JOHAN (1984b) *There Are Alternatives! Four Roads to Peace and Security* (Nottingham: Spokesman).

GARTHOFF, RAYMOND L. (ed.) (1966) *Sino-Soviet Military Relations* (New York: Praeger).

GASTEYGER, CURT (1980) 'The Determinants of Change: Deterrence and the Political Environment', in *The Future of Strategic Deterrence: Part II*, Adelphi Paper 161 (London: IISS).

GEORGE, ALEXANDER L. (1984) 'Crisis Management: The Interaction of Political and Military Considerations', *Survival*, XXVI, 223–34.

GEORGE, ALEXANDER L. and SMOKE, RICHARD (1974) *Deterrence in American Foreign Policy: Theory and Practice* (New York: Columbia University Press).

GILKS, ANNE and SEGAL, GERALD (1985) *China and the Arms Trade* (London: Croom Helm).

GILLESPIE, J. V. *et al.* (1979) 'Deterrence and Arms Races: An Optional Control Systems Model', *Behavioural Science*, XXIV, 250–62.

GILPIN, ROBERT (1972) 'Has Modern Technology Changed International Politics?' in J. N. ROSENAU, V. DAVIS and M. A. EAST (eds) *The Analysis of International Politics* (New York: Free Press).

GILPIN, ROBERT (1975) 'Three Models of the Future', *International Organization*, XXIX, 37–60.

GILPIN, ROBERT (1981) *War and Change in World Politics* (Cambridge: Cambridge University Press).

GIRLING, JOHN L. S. (1980) *American and the Third World: Revolution and Intervention* (London: Routledge & Kegan Paul).

GLASER, CHARLES L. (1984) 'Why Even Good Defenses May be Bad', *International Security*, IX, 92–123.

GOLDSCHMIDT, G. (1977) 'A Historical Survey of Nonproliferation Policies', *International Security*, II, 69–87.

GRAY, COLIN S. 'The Arms Race Phenomenon', *World Politics*, XXIV, 39–79.

GRAY, COLIN S. (1971b) 'Strategists: Some Critical Views of the Profession', *International Journal*, XXVI, 771–90.

GRAY, COLIN S. (1974) 'The Urge to Compete: Rationales for Arms Racing', *World Politics*, XXVI, 207–33.

GRAY, COLIN S. (1976) *The Soviet-American Arms Race* (Westmead: Saxon House).

GRAY, COLIN S. (1977) 'Across the Nuclear Divide: Strategic Studies Past and Present', *International Security*, II, 24–46.

GRAY, COLIN S. (1980) 'Strategic Stability Reconsidered', *Daedalus*, CIX, 135–54.

GRAY, COLIN S. (1982a) *Strategic Studies: A Critical Assessment* (London: Aldwych Press).

GRAY, COLIN S. (1982b) *Strategic Studies and Public Policy: the American Experience* (Lexington: University of Kentucky Press).

GRAY, COLIN S. (1984) *Nuclear Strategy and Strategic Planning* (Philadelphia: Foreign Policy Research Institute).

GRAY, COLIN S. and PAYNE, KEITH (1980) 'Victory is Possible', *Foreign Policy*, XXXIX, 14–27.

GRAY, ROBERT C. (1979) 'Learning from History: Case Studies of the Weapons Acquisition Process', *World Politics*, XXXI, 457–70.

GREEN, PHILIP (1968) *Deadly Logic: The Theory of Nuclear Deterrence* (New York: Schocken).

GREENWOOD, TED *et al.* (1976) *Nuclear Power and Weapons Proliferation*, Adelphi Paper 130 (London: IISS).

GUMMETT, PHILIP (1981) 'From NPT to INFCE', *International Affairs*, LVII, 549–67.

HAAS, MICHAEL (1970) 'International Subsystems: Stability and Polarity', *American Political Science Review*, LXIV, 98–123.

HALLE, LOUIS J. (1984) *The Elements of International Strategy: A Primer for the Nuclear Age*, vol. X; *American Values Projected Abroad* (London: University Press of America).

HALPERIN, MORTON H. (1963) *Limited War in the Nuclear Age* (New York: John Wiley).

HARKAVY, R. E. (1981) 'Pariah States and Nuclear Proliferation', *International Organization*, XXXV, 135–63.

HART, BASIL LIDDELL (1967) *Strategy: The Indirect Approach*, 4th edn (London: Faber & Faber).

HART, DOUGLAS M. (1984) 'Soviet Approaches to Crisis Management: the Military Dimension', *Survival*, XXVI, 214–23.

HARVARD NUCLEAR STUDY GROUP (1983) *Living With Nuclear Weapons* (Cambridge: Harvard University Press).

HERKEN, GREGG (1984) 'The Nuclear Gnostics', in DOUGLAS MACLEAN (ed.) *The Security Gamble: Deterrence Dilemmas in the Nuclear Age* (Totowa: Rowman & Allanheld).

HERWIG, HOLGER H. (1980) *Luxury Fleet: The Imperial German Navy 1888–1918* (London: Allen & Unwin).

HERZ, JOHN H. (1950) 'Idealist Internationalism and the Security Dilemma', *World Politics*, II, 157–80.

HERZ, JOHN H. (1951) *Political Realism and Political Idealism* (Chicago: University of Chicago Press).

HERZ, JOHN H. (1957) 'The Rise and Demise of the Territorial State', *World Politics*, IX, 473–93.

HERZ, JOHN (1959) *International Politics in the Atomic Age* (New York: Columbia University Press).

HERZ, JOHN H. (1969) 'The Territorial State Revisited', in J. N. ROSENAU (ed.) *International Politics and Foreign Policy* (New York: Free Press).

HERZIG, CHRISTOPHER (1983) 'IAEA Safeguards', *International Security*, VII, 195–9.

HINSLEY, F. H. (1963) *Power and the Pursuit of Peace* (Cambridge: Cambridge University Press).

HOAG, MALCOLM W. (1962) 'On Stability in Deterrent Races', in M. A. KAPLAN (ed.) *The Revolution in World Politics* (New York: Wiley).

HOAG, MALCOLM W. (1972) 'Superpower Strategic Postures for a Multipolar World', in R. ROSECRANCE (ed.) *The Future of the International Strategic System* (San Francisco: Chandler).

HOBSON, J. A. (1902, 1938) *Imperialism: A Study* (London: Allen & Unwin).

HOFFMAN, FREDERIK (1970) 'Arms Debates – A "Positional" Interpretation', *Journal of Peace Research*, VII, 219–28.

HOFFMAN, FRED S. (1985) 'The SDI in US Nuclear Strategy', *International Security*, X, 13–24.

HOLIST, W. LADD (1977) 'An Analysis of Arms Processes in the United States and the Soviet Union', *International Studies Quarterly*, XXI, 503–28.

HOLLOWAY, DAVID (1983) *The Soviet Union and the Arms Race* (New

Haven: Yale University Press).

HOLSTI, OLE R. (1972) *Crisis, Escalation and War* (Montreal: McGill-Queen's University Press).

HOWARD, MICHAEL (1970) *Studies in War and Peace* (London: Temple Smith).

HOWARD, MICHAEL (1973) 'The Relevance of Traditional Strategy', *Foreign Affairs*, LI, 253–66.

HOWARD, MICHAEL (1976a) 'The Strategic Approach to International Relations', *British Journal of International Studies*, II, 67–75.

HOWARD, MICHAEL (1976b) *War in European History* (Oxford: Oxford University Press).

HOWARD, MICHAEL (1979) 'The Forgotten Dimensions of Strategy', *Foreign Affairs*, LVII, 975–86.

HOWARD, MICHAEL (1981) *War and the Liberal Conscience* (Oxford: Oxford University Press).

HOWARD, MICHAEL (1983) *The Causes of Wars* (London: Counterpoint).

HOWARD, MICHAEL (1985) *Is Arms Control Really Necessary?* (London: Council for Arms Control).

HUNTINGTON, SAMUEL P. (1958) 'Arms Races: Prerequisites and Results', *Public Policy*, VIII, 1–87.

HUSAIN, AZIM (1982) 'The West, Israel and South Africa: the Strategic Triangle', *Third World Quarterly*, IV, 44–93.

HUSSAIN, FAROOQ (1981) *The Future of Arms Control: Part IV – The Impact of Weapons Test Restrictions*, Adelphi Paper 165 (London: IISS).

HUTCHINGS, RAYMOND (1978) 'Soviet Arms Exports to the Third World: a Pattern and its Implications', *World Today*, 34, 378–89.

HUTH, PAUL and RUSSETT, BRUCE (1984) 'What Makes Deterrence Work? Cases from 1900–1980', *World Politics*, XXXVI, 496–526.

INTERNATIONAL ATOMIC ENERGY AGENCY (IAEA) (1978) *Non-Proliferation and International Safeguards*.

IMBER, MARK F. (1980) 'NPT Safeguards: The Limits of Credibility', *Arms Control*, I, 177–96.

IMBER, MARK F. (1982) 'The Regulation of New Technologies of Military Significance', *Journal of the Institute of Civil Defence*, July–Sept., 1–11.

INTRILLIGATOR, MICHAEL and BRITO, DAGOBERT (1979) *Nuclear Proliferation and the Problem of War* (University of California in Los Angeles: Centre for Arms Control and International Security).

INTRILLIGATOR, MICHAEL and BRITO, DAGOBERT (1984) 'Can Arms Races Lead to the Outbreak of War?' *Journal of Conflict Resolution*, XXVIII, 63–84.

JAHN, E. (1975) 'The Role of the Armaments Complex in Soviet Society', *Journal of Peace Research*, 12, 179–94.

JASANI, BHUPENDRA and BARNABY, FRANK (1984) *Verification Technologies: The Case for Surveillance by Consent* (Leamington Spa: Berg).

JASTROW, ROBERT (1984) 'Reagan vs. the Scientists: Why the President is Right About Missile Defence', *Commentary*, 23–32.

JERVIS, ROBERT (1976) *Perception and Misperception in International Politics* (Princeton: Princeton University Press).

JERVIS, ROBERT (1978) 'Cooperation Under the Security Dilemma', *World Politics*, XXX, 167–214.

JERVIS, ROBERT (1979) 'Deterrence Theory Revisited', *World Politics*, XXXI, 289–324.

JERVIS, ROBERT (1979–80) 'Why Nuclear Superiority Doesn't Matter', *Political Science Quarterly*, XCIV, 617–33.

JERVIS, ROBERT (1984) *The Illogic of American Nuclear Strategy* (Ithaca: Cornell University Press).

JERVIS, ROBERT; LEBOW, RICHARD NED and STEIN, JANICE GROSS (1985) *Psychology and Deterrence* (Baltimore: Johns Hopkins University Press).

JOHNSON, A. R. (1973) 'Yugoslavia's Total National Defence', *Survival*, XV, 54–8.

JOHNSON, JAMES TURNER (1981) *Just War Tradition and the Restraint of War: A Moral and Historical Enquiry* (Princeton: Princeton University Press).

JOHNSON, JAMES TURNER (1984) *Can Modern War be Just?* (New Haven: Yale University Press).

JOLLY, RICHARD (ed.) (1978) *Disarmament and World Development* (Oxford: Pergamon).

JOYNT, C. B. (1964) 'Arms Races and the Problem of Equilibrium', *Yearbook of World Affairs*, 23–40.

JUKES, GEOFFREY (1981) 'Soviet Strategy 1965–1990', in ROBERT O'NEILL and D. M. HORNER (eds) *New Directions in Strategic Thinking* (London: Allen & Unwin).

KAHN, HERMAN (1962) 'The Arms Race and World Order', in M. A. KAPLAN (ed.) *The Revolution in World Politics* (New York: John Wiley).

KAISER, KARL; LEBER, GEORGE; MERTS, ALOIS; SCHULTZE, FRANZ JOSEPH (1982) 'Nuclear Weapons and the Preservation of Peace: A German Response', *Foreign Affairs*, LX, 1157–70.

KALDOR, MARY (1980) 'Disarmament: The Armament Process in Reverse', in E. P. THOMPSON and DAN SMITH (eds) *Protest and Survive* (Harmondsworth: Penguin).

KALDOR, MARY (1982) *The Baroque Arsenal* (London: Andre Deutsch).

KALDOR, MARY (1985) 'The Concept of Common Security', in SIPRI, *Policies for Common Security* (London: Taylor & Francis).

KALDOR, MARY and EIDE, A. (eds) (1979) *The World Military Order* (London: Macmillan).

KAPUR, ASHOK (1980a) 'The Nuclear Spread: a Third World View', *Third World Quarterly*, II, 59–75.

KAPUR, ASHOK (1980b) 'A Nuclearizing Pakistan', *Asian Survey*, XX, 495–516.

KEMP, GEOFFREY (1970a) 'Arms Traffic and Third World Conflicts', *International Conciliation*, DLXXVII.

KEMP, GEOFFREY (1970b) *Classification of Weapons Systems and Force*

*Designs in LDC Environments* (Massachusetts Institute of Technology: Arms Control Project).

KENNEDY, GAVIN (1974) *The Military in the Third World* (London: Duckworth).

KENNEDY, GAVIN (1983) *Defence Economics* (London: Duckworth).

KENNEDY, PAUL (1980) *The Rise of the Anglo-German Antagonism 1860–1914* (London: Allen & Unwin).

KEOHANE, ROBERT (1984) *After Hegemony: Cooperation and Discord in the World Political Economy* (Princeton: Princeton University Press).

KEOHANE, ROBERT and NYE, J. S. (1977) *Power and Interdependence* (Boston: Little, Brown).

KHALIZAD, Z. (1979) 'Pakistan and the Bomb', *Survival*, XXI, 244–50.

KHRUSHCHEV, NIKITA (1961) *On Peaceful Coexistence* (Moscow: Foreign Languages Publishing House).

KHRUSHCHEV, NIKITA (1974) *Khrushchev Remembers: The Last Testament*, vol. 2, trans. and ed. by STROBE TALBOTT (Harmondsworth: Penguin).

KLARE, M. T. (1983) 'The Unnoticed Arms Trade: Exports of Conventional Arms-Making Technology', *International Security*, 8, 68–90.

KODZIC, P. (1975) 'Armaments and Development', in D. CARLTON and C. SCHAERF (eds) *The Dynamics of the Arms Race* (London: Croom Helm).

KOLODZIEJ, EDWARD A. and HARKAVY, ROBERT (1980) 'Developing States and the International Security System', *Journal of International Affairs*, XXXIV, 59–87.

KRASS, A. (1985) 'The Death of Deterrence', in SIPRI, *Policies for Common Security* (London: Taylor & Francis).

KUGLER, JACEK; ORGANZKI, A. F. K. and FOX, DANIEL (1980) 'Deterrence and the Arms Race: The Impotence of Power', *International Security*, IV, 105–38.

KURTH, JAMES R. (1973) 'Why We Buy the Weapons We Do', *Foreign Policy*, XI, 33–56.

LAMBELET, J. C. (1975) 'Do Arms Races Lead to War?' *Journal of Peace Research*, XII, 123–8.

LAMBETH, BENJAMIN (1981) 'How to Think About Soviet Military Doctrine', in JOHN BAYLIS and GERRY SEGAL (eds) *Soviet Strategy* (London: Croom Helm).

LANDES, DAVID S. (1969) *The Unbound Prometheus* (Cambridge: Cambridge University Press).

LANDI, DALE H.; AUGENSTEIN, BRUNO W.; CRAIN, COLLEN M.; HARRIS, WILLIAM R. and JENKINS, BRIAN M. (1984) 'Improving the Means for Intergovernmental Communications in Crisis', *Survival*, XXVI, 200–14.

LANGFORD, DAVID (1979) *War in 2080: The Future of Military Technology* (Newton Abbott: Westbridge Books).

LEISS, AMELIA C. and KEMP, GEOFFREY *et al.* (1970) *Arms Transfers to Less Developed Countries* (Massachusetts Institute of Technology: Arms Control Project, C/70–1).

LELLOUCHE, PIERRE (1981) 'Europe and Her Defense', *Foreign Affairs*, LIX, 813–34.

LENIN, V. I. (1916) *Imperialism, the Highest Stage of Capitalism* (Moscow: Foreign Languages Publishing House).

LENIN, V. I. (1964) 'The Military Programme of the Proletarian Revolution', *Collected Works*, XIII (London: Lawrence & Wishart).

LEVY, JACK S. (1985) 'Theories of General War', *World Politics*, XXXVII, 344–74.

LODAL, JAN M. (1980) 'Deterrence and Nuclear Strategy', *Daedalus*, CIX, 155–75.

LOVINS, B. (1977) *Soft Energy Paths* (Harmondsworth: Penguin).

LOVINS, A. B. (1980) 'Nuclear Power and Nuclear Bombs', *Foreign Affairs*, LVIII, 1137–77.

LUCAS, MICHAEL (1985) 'West Germany: Can Arms Save the Export Giant?' *ADIU Report*, VII, 1–5.

LUCKHAM, ROBIN (1977a) 'Militarism: Arms and the Internationalization of Capital', *IDS Bulletin*, VIII, 38–50.

LUCKHAM, ROBIN (1977b) 'Militarism: Force, Class and International Conflict', *IDS Bulletin*, IX, 19–29.

LUTERBACHER, U. (1975) 'Arms Race Models: Where do we Stand?' *European Journal of Political Research*, III, 199–217.

LUTTWAK, EDWARD (1980a) 'The Problem of Extending Deterrence', in *The Future of Strategic Deterrence: Part I*, Adelphi Paper 160 (London: IISS).

LUTTWAK, EDWARD (1980b) *Strategy and Politics* (New Brunswick: Transaction Books).

MccGWIRE, MICHAEL (1983) 'Peace and War – the Anatomy of an Argument', unpublished typescript, April.

MccGWIRE, MICHAEL (1985) 'Deterrence: the Problem – not the Solution', *SAIS Review*, 5, 105–24.

McGUIRE, MARTIN (1965) *Secrecy and the Arms Race* Cambridge: Harvard University Press).

McGUIRE, MARTIN (1968) 'The Arms Race: An Interaction Process', in BRUCE RUSSETT (ed.) *Economic Theories of International Politics* (Chicago: Markham).

McKINLAY, R. D. and COHAN, A. S. (1975) 'A Comparative Analysis of the Political and Economic Performance of Military and Civil Regimes', *Comparative Politics*, VIII, 1–30.

McKINLAY, R. D., and LITTLE, RICHARD (1986) *Global Problems and World Order* (London: Frances Pinter).

McKINLAY, R. D. and MUGHAN, A. (1984) *Aid and Arms to the Third World* (London: Frances Pinter).

McNEILL, WILLIAM H. (1982) *The Pursuit of Power* (Chicago: University of Chicago Press).

MANDELBAUM, MICHAEL (1981) *The Nuclear Revolution: International Politics before and after Hiroshima* (Cambridge: Cambridge University Press).

MANSINGH, SURJIT (1984) *India's Search for Power: Indira Gandhi's Foreign Policy 1966–1982* (New Delhi: Sage).

MARDER, A. J. (1961) *From the Dreadnought to Scapa Flow*, vol. 1 (Oxford: Oxford University Press).

MARTIN, LAURENCE (1980) 'The Determinants of Change: Deterrence and Technology', in *The Future of Strategic Deterrence: Part II*, Adelphi Paper 161 (London: IISS).

MARWAH, ONKAR (1977) 'India's Nuclear and Space Programme', *International Security*, II, 96–121.

MARWAH, ONKAR (1980) 'India's Military Power and Policy', in O. MARWAH and J. D. POLLACK (eds) *Military Power and Policy in Asian States* (Boulder: Westview Press).

MARWAH, ONKAR (1981) 'India and Pakistan: Nuclear Rivals', *International Organization*, XXXV, 165–79.

MARWAH, ONKAR and SCHULZ, ANN (1975) *Nuclear Proliferation and the Near Nuclear Countries* (Cambridge: Ballinger).

*Military Balance* (London: IISS, annually since 1958).

MOMOI, MAKATO (1981) 'Strategic Thinking in Japan in the 1970s and 1980s', in ROBERT O'NEILL and D. M. HORNER (eds) *New Directions in Strategic Thinking* (London: Allen & Unwin).

MORGETHAU, HANS J. (1948, 1978) *Politics Among Nations: The Struggle for Power and Peace*, 5th edn (New York: Knopf).

MOSLEY, HUGH G. (1985) *The Arms Race* (Lexington: Lexington Books).

MYRDAL, ALVA and BARNABY, FRANK *et al.* (1977) 'Disarmament and Development', *Development Dialogue*, I, 3–33.

NACHT, MICHAEL (1975) 'The Delicate Balance of Error', *Foreign Policy*, XIX, 163–77.

NEUMAN, STEPHANIE G. (1984) 'International Stratification and Third World Military Industries', *International Organization*, XXXVIII, 167–97.

NEUMAN, STEPHANIE G. and HARKAVY, ROBERT E. (1980) *Arms Transfers in the Modern World* (New York: Praeger).

NINCIC, MIROSLAV (1982) *The Arms Race: The Political Economy of Military Growth* (New York: Praeger).

NOEL-BAKER, PHILIP (1936) *The Private Manufacture of Armaments* (London: Gollancz).

NOEL-BAKER, PHILIP (1958) *The Arms Race: A Programme for World Disarmament* (London: John Calder).

NYE, JOSEPH S. (1986) 'Nuclear Winter and Policy Choices', *Survival*, XXVIII, 119–27.

OBERG, JAN (1975) 'Arms Trade with the Third World as an Aspect of Imperialism', *Journal of Peace Research*, XII, 213–34.

ORGANSKI, A. F. K. and KUGLER, J. (1977) 'The Costs of Major Wars: The Phoenix Factor', *American Political Science Review*, LXXI, 1347–66.

OSGOOD, ROBERT E. (1957) *Limited War: the Challenge to American Strategy* (Chicago: University of Chicago Press).

OSGOOD, ROBERT E. and TUCKER, ROBERT W. (1967) *Force, Order, and Justice* (Baltimore: Johns Hopkins Press).

PATTERSON, WALTER C. (1976) *Nuclear Power* (Harmondsworth: Penguin).

PAUKER, GUY J. *et al.* (1973) *In Search of Self-Reliance: US Security Assistance to the Third World Under the Nixon Doctrine*, Rand R-1092, ARPA, June.

PEARTON, MAURICE (1982) *The Knowledgeable State: Diplomacy, War and Technology Since 1830* (London: Burnett Books).

PIERRE, ANDREW J. (1982) *The Global Politics of Arms Sales* (Princeton: Princeton University Press).

PIERRE, ANDREW J. (ed.) (1986) *The Conventional Defense of Europe: New Technologies and New Strategies* (New York: Council on Foreign Relations).

POGANY, I. (1981) 'The Destruction of Osirak', *World Today*, 413–18.

PONEMAN, D. (1981) 'Nuclear Policies in Developing Countries', *International Affairs*, LVII 568–84.

POWELL, ROBERT (1985) 'The Theoretical Foundations of Strategic Nuclear Deterrence', *Political Science Quarterly*, C, 75–96.

PRINS, GWYN (ed.) (1984) *The Choice: Nuclear Weapons Versus Security* (London: Chatto & Windus).

QUESTER, GEORGE H. (1970) 'The NPT and the IAEA', *International Organization*, XXIV, 163–82.

QUESTER, GEORGE H. (1973) *The Politics of Nuclear Proliferation* (Baltimore: Johns Hopkins University Press).

QUESTER, GEORGE H. (1977) *Offense and Defense in the International System* (New York: John Wiley).

RAO, R. V. R. C. and IMAI, R. (1974) 'Proliferation and the Indian Test', *Survival*, XVI, 210–16.

RAPOPORT, ANATOL (1960) *Fights, Games and Debates* (Ann Arbor: University of Michigan Press).

RAPOPORT, ANATOL (1964a) 'Critique of Strategic Thinking', in ROGER FISHER (ed.) *International Conflict and Behavioural Science* (New York: Basic Books).

RAPOPORT, ANATOL (1964b) *Strategy and Conscience* (New York: Harper & Row).

RATHJENS, GEORGE W. (1973) 'The Dynamics of the Arms Race', in HERBERT YORK (ed.) *Arms Control* (San Francisco: Freeman).

RATTINGER, HANS (1975) 'Armaments, Detente and Bureaucracy: the Case of the Arms Race in Europe', *Journal of Conflict Resolution*, XIX, 571–95.

RATTINGER, HANS (1976) 'From War to War: Arms Races in the Middle East', *International Studies Quarterly*, XX, 501–31.

RAVENAL, E. C. (1982) 'Counterforce and Alliance: the Ultimate Connection', *International Security*, VI, 26–43.

REPORT OF THE INDEPENDENT COMMISSION ON DISARMAMENT AND SECURITY ISSUES (1982) *Common Security: A Programme for Disarmament* (London: Pan Books).

REPORT OF THE SECRETARY-GENERAL (1977) *Economic and Social Consequences of the Armaments Race*, United Nations General Assembly, A/32/88, 12 August.

REPORT OF THE SECRETARY-GENERAL (1985) *Study on the*

*Concepts of Security*, United Nations General Assembly, A/40/553, 26 August.

RICHARDSON, LEWIS F. (1960) *Arms and Insecurity* (Pittsburgh: Boxwood Press).

ROBERTS, ADAM (ed.) (1967) *The Strategy of Civilian Defence: Non-Violent Resistance to Aggression* (London: Faber & Faber).

ROBERTS, ADAM (1976/1986) *Nations in Arms* (London: Chatto & Windus; Basingstoke: Macmillan).

ROGERS, BERNARD W. (1982) 'The Atlantic Alliance: Prescriptions for a Difficult Decade', *Foreign Affairs*, LX, 1145–56.

ROPP, THEODORE (1981) 'Strategic Thinking Since 1945', in ROBERT O'NEILL and D. M. HORNER (eds) *New Directions in Strategic Thinking* (London: Allen & Unwin).

ROSECRANCE, RICHARD (1969) 'Bipolarity, Multipolarity, and the Future', in JAMES N. ROSENAU (ed.) *International Politics and Foreign Policy* (New York: Free Press).

ROSECRANCE, RICHARD (ed.) (1972) *The Future of the International Strategic System* (San Francisco: Chandler).

ROSECRANCE, RICHARD (1973) *International Relations: Peace or War?* (New York: McGraw-Hill).

ROSECRANCE, RICHARD (1975) *Strategic Deterrence Reconsidered*, Adelphi Paper 116 (London: IISS).

RUSSETT, BRUCE (1983a) 'Prosperity and Peace', *International Studies Quarterly*, XXVII, 1–7.

RUSSETT, BRUCE (1983b) *The Prisoners of Insecurity* (San Francisco: Freeman).

RUSSETT, BRUCE and STARR, HARVEY (1981) *World Politics: The Menu for Choice* (San Francisco: Freeman).

SAATY, THOMAS L. (1968) *Mathematical Models of Arms Control and Disarmament* (New York: John Wiley).

SAGAN, CARL (1983–4) 'Nuclear War and Climatic Catastrophe', *Foreign Affairs*, LXII, 257–92.

SAMPSON, ANTHONY (1977) *The Arms Bazaar* (Sevenoaks: Hodder & Stoughton).

SARKESIAN, S. C. (1978) 'A Political Perspective on Military Power in Developing Areas', in SHELDON W. SIMON (ed.) *The Military and Security in the Third World* (Boulder: Westview Press).

SATOH, YUKIO (1982) *The Evolution of Japanese Security Policy*, Adelphi Paper 178 (London: IISS).

SCHELLING, THOMAS (1960) *The Strategy of Conflict* (London: Oxford University Press).

SCHELLING, THOMAS (1963) 'War Without Pain and Other Models', *World Politics*, XV, 465–87.

SCHELLING, THOMAS (1966) *Arms and Influence* (New Haven: Yale University Press).

SCHIFF, BENHAMIN (1984) *International Nuclear Technology Transfer: Dilemmas of Dissemination and Control* (Totowa: Rowman & Allanheld).

SCHILLING, WARNER (1981) 'US Strategic Nuclear Concepts in the

1970s: The Search for Sufficiently Equivalent Countervailing Parity', in ROBERT O'NEILL and D. M. HORNER (eds) *New Directions in Strategic Thinking* (London: Allen & Unwin).

SCHLESINGER, JAMES R. (1985) 'Rhetoric and Realities in the Star Wars Debate', *International Security*, X, 3–12.

SCHUMPETER, JOSEPH (1951) 'The Sociology of Imperialism', in Paul Sweezy (ed.) *Imperialism and Social Classes* (Oxford: Blackwell).

SEGAL, GERALD (1983–4) 'Strategy and Ethnic Chic', *International Affairs*, LX, 15–30.

SEGAL, LEON V. (1979) 'The Logic of Deterrence in Theory and Practice', *International Organization*, XXXIII, 567–79.

SEN, GAUTAM (1984) *The Military Origins of Industrialisation and International Trade Rivalry* (London: Frances Pinter).

SEN GUPTA, BHABANI (1983) *Nuclear Weapons? Policy Options for India* (New Delhi: Sage).

SHAPLEY, DEBORAH (1978) 'Technology Creep and the Arms Race', *Science*, 201; 1102–5, 1192–6; 202: 289–92.

SHARP, GENE (1985) *Making Europe Unconquerable: The Potential of Civilian-based Deterrence and Defence* (London: Taylor & Francis).

SIMPSON, JOHN (1983) *The Independent Nuclear State: The US, Britain and the Military Atom* (London: Macmillan).

SINGER, J. DAVID (1961) 'The Level of Analysis Problem in International Relations', in KLAUSE KNORR and SIDNEY VERBA (eds) *The International System: Theoretical Essays* (Princeton: Princeton University Press).

SINGER, J. DAVID (1962) *Deterrence, Arms Control and Disarmament: Toward a Synthesis in National Security Policy* (Ohio State University Press).

SINGER, J. DAVID (1970) 'Tensions, Political Settlement and Disarmament', in JOHN GARNETT (ed.) *Theories of Peace and Security* (London: Macmillan).

STOCKHOLM INTERNATIONAL PEACE RESEARCH INSTITUTE *World Armaments and Disarmament Yearbook* (Stockholm: Almqvist & Wiksell, annually since 1969).

STOCKHOLM INTERNATIONAL PEACE RESEARCH INSTITUTE (1971) *The Arms Trade With the Third World* (Stockholm: Almqvist & Wiksell).

STOCKHOLM INTERNATIONAL PEACE RESEARCH INSTITUTE (1974) *Nuclear Proliferation Problems* (Stockholm: Almqvist & Wiksell).

STOCKHOLM INTERNATIONAL PEACE RESEARCH INSTITUTE (1978) *Arms Control: A Survey and Appraisal of Multilateral Agreements* (London: Taylor & Francis).

STOCKHOLM INTERNATIONAL PEACE RESEARCH INSTITUTE (1985) *Policies for Common Security* (London: Taylor & Francis).

SMITH, BRUCE L. R. (1966) *The RAND Corporation: Case Study of a Non-profit Advisory Corporation* (Boston: Harvard University Press).

SMITH, STEVE (1983) 'War and Human Nature', in IAN FORBES and STEVE SMITH (eds) *Politics and Human Nature* (London: Frances Pinter).

SMOKER, PAUL (1964) 'Fear in the Arms Race: A Mathematical Study', *Journal of Peace Research*, I, 55–63.

SNOW, DONALD M. (1979) 'Current Nuclear Deterrence Thinking', *International Studies Quarterly*, XXIII, 445–86.

SNYDER, GLENN (1971) 'Deterrence and Defence', in ROBERT J. ART and KENNETH N. WALTZ (eds) *The Use of Forces* (Boston: Little, Brown).

SNYDER, JACK L. (1978) 'Rationality at the Brink: The Role of Cognitive Processes in Failures of Deterrence', *World Politics*, XXX, 345–65.

STANLEY, JOHN and PEARTON, MAURICE (1972) *The International Trade in Arms* (London: Chatto & Windus).

STAUFFER, R. B. (1974) 'The Political Economy of a Coup', *Journal of Peace Research*, XI, 161–77.

STEINBERG, J. (1965) *Yesterday's Deterrent* (London: Macdonald).

STEINBRUNNER, JOHN (1976) 'Beyond Rational Deterrence: The Struggle for New Conceptions', *World Politics*, XXVIII, 223–45.

STEINER, BARRY H. (1973) 'Arms Races, Diplomacy, and Recurring Behaviour: Lessons from Two Cases', *Sage Professional Papers in International Studies*, no. 02-013 (Beverly Hills: Sage).

STORR, ANTHONY (1970) *Human Aggression* (Harmondsworth: Penguin).

*Strategic Survey* (London: IISS, annually).

SWEEZY, PAUL (1951) *Imperialism and Social Classes* (Oxford: Blackwell).

TAYLOR, A. J. P. (1979) *How Wars Begin* (London: Hamish Hamilton).

TAYLOR, TREVOR (1984) *European Defence Cooperation*, Chatham House Papers, no. 24, (London: Routledge & Kegan Paul).

THEE, MAREK (1986) *Military Technology, Military Strategy and the Arms Race* (London: Croom Helm).

THOMAS, RAJU, G. C. (1978) *The Defence of India* (New Delhi: Macmillan).

THOMPSON, E. P. and SMITH, DAN (1980) *Protest and Survive* (Harmondsworth: Penguin).

TREVERTON, G. (1980) 'China's Nuclear Forces and the Stability of Soviet-American Deterrence', in *The Future of Strategic Deterrence: Part I*, Adelphi Paper 160 (London: IISS).

TSIPIS, KOSTA (1975) 'The Arms Race as Posturing', in DAVID CARLTON and C. SHAERF (eds) *The Dynamics of the Arms Race* (London: Croom Helm).

TSIPIS, KOSTA (1985) *Understanding Nuclear Weapons* (London: Wildwood House).

TUCHMAN, BARBARA (1967) *The Proud Tower* (New York: Bantam).

TUCHMAN, BARBARA (1984) 'The Alternative to Arms Control', in ROMAN KOLKOWICZ and NIEL JOECK (eds) *Arms Control and International Security* (Boulder: Westview Press).

TUOMI, HELENA and VAYRYNEN, RAIMO (1982) *Transnational Corporations, Armaments and Development* (Aldershot: Gower).

VAN EVERA, STEPHEN (1984) 'The Cult of the Offensive and the Origins of the First World War', *International Security*, IX 58–107.

VAYRYNEN, RAIMO (1983a) 'Economic Fluctuations, Technological Innovations and the Arms Race in a Historical Perspective', *Cooperation and Conflict*, XVIII, 135–59.

VAYRYNEN, RAIMO (1983b) 'Economic Cycles, Power Transitions, Political Management, and Wars Between Major Powers', *International Studies Quarterly*, XXVII, 389–418.

VIKSNINS, G. J. (1979) 'Indo-Soviet Military Cooperation: a Review', *Asian Survey*, XIX, 230–44.

VOAS, JEANETTE (1986) 'The Arms Control Compliance Debate', *Survival*, XXVIII, 8–31.

WALLACE, MICHAEL (1979) 'Arms Races and Escalation: Some New Evidence', *Journal of Conflict Resolution*, XXIII, 3–16.

WALLACE, MICHAEL (1980) 'Some Persisting Findings', *Journal of Conflict Resolution*, XXIV, 289–92.

WALLACE, MICHAEL (1982) 'Armaments and Escalation', *International Studies Quarterly*, XXVI, 37–56.

WALLACE, WILLIAM (1984) 'European Defence Cooperation: the Reopening Debate', *Survival*, XXVI, 251–61.

WALTZ, KENNETH N. (1959) *Man, the State, and War* (New York: Columbia University Press).

WALTZ, KENNETH N. (1964) 'The Stability of the Bipolar World', *Daedalus*, XCIII, 881–909.

WALTZ, KENNETH N. (1979) *Theory of International Politics* (Reading, Mass.: Addison-Wesley).

WALTZ, KENNETH N. (1981) *The Spread of Nuclear Weapons: More May Be Better*, Adelphi Paper 171 (London: IISS).

WELTMAN, J. J. (1980) 'Nuclear Devolution and World Order', *World Politics*, XXXII, 169–93.

WHYNES, DAVID K. (1979) *The Economics of Third World Military Expenditure* (London: Macmillan).

WILLIAMS, PHIL (1976) *Crisis Management: Confrontation and Diplomacy in the Nuclear Age* (London: Martin Robertson).

WILLIAMS, PHIL (1983) 'Deterrence, Warfighting and American Nuclear Strategy', *ADIU Report*, V, 1–5.

WILMSHURST, MICHAEL J. (1982) *Nuclear Non-Proliferation: Can the Policies of the Eighties Prove More Successful Than Those of the Seventies?* (Ebenhausen: Stiftung Wissenschaft und Politik, SWP-AZ2322) September.

WINDASS, STAN (ed.) (1985) *Avoiding Nuclear War: Common Security as a Strategy for the Defence of the West* (London: Brassey's).

WINDSOR, PHILIP (1982) 'On the Logic of Security and Arms Control in the NATO Alliance', in LAWRENCE HAGAN (ed.) *The Crisis in Western Security* (London: Croom Helm).

WINTERS, FRANCIS X. (1986) 'Ethics and Deterrence', *Survival*, XXVIII, 338–49.

WINTRINGHAM, TOM and BLASHFORD-SNELL, J. N. (1973) *Weapons and Tactics* (Harmondsworth: Penguin).

WOHLSTETTER, ALBERT (1959) 'The Delicate Balance of Terror', *Foreign Affairs*, XXXVII, 211–34.

WOHLSTETTER, ALBERT (1974) 'Is There a Strategic Arms Race?' *Survival*, XVI, 277–92.

WOHLSTETTER, ALBERT *et al.* (1977) *Swords from Ploughshares* (Chicago: University of Chicago Press).

WOLPIN, M. D. (1972) *Military Aid and Counterrevolution in the Third World* (Lexington: D. C. Heath).

WOLPIN, M. D. (1978) 'Egalitarian Reformism in the Third World versus the Military: A Profile of Failure', *Journal of Peace Research*, XV, 89–108.

WOODWARD, E. L. (1935, 1964) *Great Britain and the German Navy* (London: Frank Cass).

WRIGHT, QUINCY (1942) *A Study of War* (Chicago: University of Chicago Press).

YAGER, JOSEPH A. (ed.) (1980) *Non-Proliferation and US Foreign Policy* (Washington: Brookings Institution).

YERGIN, DANIEL (1978) *Shattered Peace* (Boston: Houghton Mifflin).

YORK, HERBERT F. (1984) 'Beginning Nuclear Disarmament at the Bottom', in ROMAN KOLKOWICZ and NIEL JOECK (eds) *Arms Control and International Security* (Boulder: Westview Press).

ZIMMERMAN, WILLIAM (1969) *Soviet Perspectives on International Relations 1956–67* (Princeton: Princeton University Press).

ZURHELLEN, J. O. (1981) 'Arms Control: The Record of the 1970s and the Outlook for the 1980s', in ROBERT O'NEILL and D. M. HORNER (eds) *New Directions in Strategic Thinking* (London: Allen & Unwin).

# Index